THE MANAGEMENT OF URBAN PUBLIC TRANSPORT

The Management of Urban Public Transport

A marketing perspective

Peter J. HOVELL
Assistant Director of Business Studies
University of Liverpool
William H. JONES
Lecturer in Marketing
University of Aston in Birmingham
Alan J. MORAN
Senior Economic Analyst
with the Australian Government

SAXON HOUSE|LEXINGTON BOOKS

Published by
SAXON HOUSE, D. C. Heath Ltd.
Westmead, Farnborough, Hants., England.

Jointly with
LEXINGTON BOOKS, D. C. Heath & Co.
Lexington, Mass. USA

ISBN 0 347 01098 9

Printed in Great Britain
by Unwin Brothers Limited
The Gresham Press, Old Woking, Surrey
A member of the Staples Printing Group

Contents

List of tables

List of figures

ix

Acknowledgements

This work deals with several interrelated research programmes. Marketing research projects commissioned by the then Manchester City Transport Department and the Transport and Road Research Laboratory of the Department of the Environment provided an early stimulus. From October 1969 these were supplemented by a much wider programme of marketing experiments financed by the Greater Manchester Passenger Transport Executive and in September 1971 the Merseyside Passenger Transport Executive and British Rail made similar research facilities available on Merseyside to those in Greater Manchester. On completion of the Greater Manchester and Merseyside experiments in 1972 an investigation was commenced into the managerial dimension of public transport operation covering the UK Passenger Transport Executives and comparable organisations in North America and continental Western Europe. While all three authors have been closely involved in each phase of the research for this book, Dr Moran had prime responsibility for Part 1.

Clearly a project of this kind can only be completed with the help of a large number of people. We are indebted to the staff of those undertakings which participated in our several surveys, namely the Passenger Transport Executives for Greater Manchester, Merseyside, Tyneside and the West Midlands, London Transport Executive and British Rail in the UK, and the twenty-eight North American and continental Western European metropolitan transport organisations representing conurbations based on Atlanta, Chicago, Detroit, Miami, Montreal, New York, Pittsburg, and Toronto in North America, and Amsterdam, Basle, Brussels, Cologne, Copenhagen, Dublin, Geneva, Genoa, Hamburg, Hanover, Helsinki, Lisbon, Munich, Oslo, Paris, Rome, Rotterdam, Stockholm, Stuttgart and Vienna in Europe. Our gratitude is especially extended to P. Welding, K. Swallow, R. Hughes and R. Perkins at the Merseyside PTE; G. Gregg at British Rail; K. Holt, D. Lindsay and P. Evans at the Greater Manchester PTE; J. Ingleton and A. Brown at London Transport; and A. Finnamore at the Transport and Road Research Laboratory; all have provided invaluable assistance. We should also like to thank our colleague Professor A. M. Bourn for his continuous encouragement and interest in our work and for making many helpful comments after reading some of the draft chapters. Mrs Jean Taylor deserves a special vote of thanks for her hard and highly competent work in the typing and retyping, the checking and rechecking of the several drafts of the manuscript.

February 1975

Introduction

In charting the rise and decline of municipal transport in Great Britain Sleeman[1] points to four distinctive epochs in the industry's history. First he comments on the coincidence of municipalisation and electrification of tramways in the 1890's and 1900's: a period when town councils anxious to rehouse the poorer paid workers in slightly more salubrious surroundings sought better transport links. The Tramways Act of 1870 gave them the right to purchase any company-owned system in their area; a right which an increasing number of local authorities exercised as the economic advantages of the electric tram became apparent. Its capital and maintenance costs were lower than those of cable or underground conduit; its operating costs were considerably less than for horse or steam traction and in the high density traffic areas its bigger capacity and higher speed meant that more revenue per car-mile could be realised.

The second major phase identified by Sleeman was marked by the rapid growth of municipal tramways culminating in the 1920's. The number of trams rose from 7,000 in 1905 to a peak of 14,400 in 1927. In the third period identified, the motor bus supplanted the tram and the hybrid trolley-bus (the trolley-bus had itself started to replace the tram from about 1922). Advances in bus technology, giving increased carrying capacity, lower running costs and improved reliability, together with the bus's infinitely greater route flexibility, accounted for the ascendency of this mode in the 1930's and 1940's.

The Road Traffic Act of 1930 provided relief for the municipal tramways as they competed with the private bus operators. Under the Act motor bus companies needed to obtain road service licences for each route they ran and the area traffic commissioners responsible for administering the licensing system clearly gave protection to the existing tramways. Furthermore, local authorities who operated tramways were given general statutory powers to operate motor buses within their areas. The latter part of the 1930's and 1940's were prosperous years for municipal transport. The licensing system provided protection from other operators, especially for those local authorities who replaced their trams with buses. Large new housing estates built on the outskirts offered new markets for the operators. After the depression real incomes rose sharply. Motor car ownership, although growing, was largely confined to the wealthier people,

1

and thus the bulk of the public took to the buses for most of its journeys, except for those trips — mainly the shorter distance ones — which were completed on foot or by bicycle. The number of passengers carried by municipal undertakings continued to rise until it reached its 1950 peak.

The final epoch referred to by Sleeman relates to municipal transport's continuous decline from the beginning of the 1950's primarily due to the growth of car ownership and usage, which started to become noticeable as the supply of cars for the domestic market became more plentiful, and after the ending of petrol rationing in 1950. The Second World War and the aftermath period of reconstruction inevitably postponed the rapid rise of car ownership. It is probable that this postponement masked the real challenge which the car posed for public transport operators until the threat became so obvious that it could neither be ignored nor combated by the industry unaided. Between 1950 and 1960 total passenger numbers declined by 16·7 per cent and between 1960 and 1970 by 41·3 per cent.

In the United States, for most of the period reviewed, urban passenger transport was undertaken largely by limited liability companies operating under franchise. The rise and fall of the tram, trolley-bus and bus followed a similar pattern, although the car's impact was felt sooner and the operators have suffered more acutely from a declining market. On the continent of Europe the fortunes of urban public transport have also been adversely affected by rising levels of car ownership and usage, but, unlike the UK and US undertakings, municipalities have been less ready to jettison the tram: Amsterdam has a relatively wide and well patronised system serving its centre, Hamburg has a system which is steadily being converted into a modern rapid transit network. Many other cities have more or less successful tram networks, e.g. Basle, Berne, Antwerp, Bremen, Frankfurt, Stuttgart and Marseilles.

The inexorable increase in automobile ownership and utilisation over the last two decades has seriously threatened the viability of public transport in many large American and Western European cities. But as this work seeks to show, public transport must be a vital element if the social framework is to be maintained; particularly it is vital to the achievement of a harmonious balance between rural—recreational life and urban—work life. Without a public transport system the city has to become car-oriented, with consequent ill effects on social life; not only is a significant proportion of the population deprived of a means of transport but the city becomes a sprawling set of inter-connecting highways between spatially separated shopping, work and leisure activities. Once set in train, the seemingly relentless demand for better highway facilities, just in order to maintain unimpeded high speed mobility for the growing volume of car traffic, will

2

cause further urban boundary extension and population dispersion. Apart from the direct, but nevertheless enormous, cost of new road construction associated with a car-oriented policy, there are even greater social costs to bear: for example, those relating to traffic noise, pollution, accidents, policing, longer shopping, leisure and work journeys, the loss of agricultural and recreational land and of scenic amenity, the supply of a whole range of public services to communities living in relatively sparsely populated areas and the treatment of the many facets of social deprivation, especially prevalent in the decaying areas nearer the centre. Few major cities are likely to allow this process to continue unchecked indefinitely. Even Los Angeles, often quoted as the most car-oriented city in the world, seems ultimately to have rejected the consequent decline in the quality of social life and the environment. Clearly, if the process is not

Table Intro. 1
Peak hour capacities of alternative urban transport modes

Type of mode	Number of lanes or tracks	Person-trip capacity per peak hour (one way)	Typical speed (in mph)
Cars using:			
Urban freeways or motorways	8	9,000	32
Arterial roads	6	3,000	20
Subway/Underground/ Elevated fixed track	2	50,000	33
Buses using:			
Urban freeways or motorways (express)	2	8,000	22
Arterial roads (limited stop)	2	7,000	14
Trams using:			
Private right-of-way	2	34,000	25
Arterial roads	2	34,000	17

Source: Quinby[2]

3

contained soon enough many of the social and environmental effects may be irreversibly damaging.

Because the success of public transport, as will be shown, is so dependent on relatively high population, workplace and shopping densities, its future development has become part of the now fashionable environmental problem. Land as a scarce resource must be conserved and Table Intro. 1 illustrates how much more land intensive public transport-borne traffic can be.

These and other arguments have done much to influence official thinking, which now leans heavily towards revitalising public transport as part of any solution of the urban problem. In the UK the Government's attitude has been expressed as follows:

> One of the most precious achievements of modern civilisation is mobility. It enriches social life and widens experience. To build mobility into urban life without destroying the other elements of good living must be one of the major purposes of transport policy.
>
> The freedom to move easily about the city is something of great value. The nature of urban transport systems must be based on our ideas of the kind of cities we want.
>
> We have neither the physical space nor the economic resources to rebuild our cities in such a form that all journeys can be made by private car; and in any case we must provide for the large number of people — particularly many of the old, the young, the housewives, the poor — who will not have the use of cars.
>
> To provide an attractive and efficient system of public transport is therefore vital to deal with the immediate and pressing problems of our cities.[3]

This attitude forms the rationale of the 1968 Transport Act, which for the major conurbations has led to the creation of Passenger Transport Executives (PTEs) who, within the framework of local government land-use and traffic management policies, have responsibility for planning, integrating and operating existing and future modes of urban public transport for defined metropolitan areas. Once more government legislation has come to the assistance of urban public transport. However, this time, the organisational reforms, backed by the availability of large capital and, in some cases, operating grants, seem to be more radical in their design than earlier legislative attempts proved to be. Thus the PTEs may well herald a new epoch for the industry, aiming as they do to eliminate the wasteful and misplaced competition between public transport modes and to offer an effective and attractive alternative to the private car which financially weak public transport organisations, largely bereft of commercial and strategic planning resources, were unable to do in the past.

The PTEs have their parallel in other countries; many of the metropolises in North America and Western Europe, as we shall see later, have established public transport organisations with similar aims during the last decade. It is against the background of these reforms that this book has been written. The intention is to prescribe strategies and recommend organisational structures which will enable the managements of large passenger transport undertakings to exploit their market opportunities. To this end a diagnosis is made of metropolitan trends, travel patterns and mode preferences, and current managerial attitudes and practices, especially those prevailing in the English PTEs and comparable organisations in North America and continental Western Europe.

The authors have adopted the 'marketing concept'. In general terms, this seeks to ascertain market requirements by rigorously researching into consumer needs in order to develop and offer a package of satisfactions — the product — which meets these needs effectively, given the technology, expertise and objectives of the firm in the context of its competitive environment. This package of satisfactions forms a major constituent of the 'marketing-mix'[4] alongside sales and promotional elements which are essential if the target customer segments are to be made aware of the product's existence and are to be persuaded that it does in fact meet their needs.

Rather than just a fashionable management gimmick, the marketing concept has been developed as a total philosophy of management to meet real changes in the juxtapositioning of supply and demand, and particularly the increasing pace of environmental change. Kotler[5] summarises three stages in the growth of Western economies which reflect the different interfacings of producers and consumers:

> The first stage was characterised by a scarcity of goods and services and the central problem was to increase output. To this end, the major emphasis was placed on increasing productive efficiency. The business leaders of this era were engineers and innovators like Whitney and Carnegie and the firms were heavily oriented towards production.

> In the second stage the scarcity of goods was less pronounced and the real opportunities lay in the rationalisation of the industrial structure through mergers and financial consolidations. In this era, lawyers and financiers, men like Mellon and Morgan gained ascendency in

business enterprises through skilled financial consolidation.

The third and present stage of the economy is marked not by the scarcity of goods but by a scarcity of markets. The major problem of most firms is to find sufficient customers for their output . . . as a result each firm must examine customers' needs more closely to learn how it can improve the appeal of its present products and to discover which new products deserve to be born.

Thus market-related decision-making offers a bridge between selected customers and the supplier's productive, engineering and financial resources which harmonises the interests of the firm and the markets it serves. As a philosophy the marketing concept offers firms applying it two major advantages. First, it prevents the firm dedicating itself to one product and forces it to analyse more fully the business it is in. Thus public transport operators are not in the bus (or train or tram) industry, but in the business of fulfilling people's needs for mobility in the urban area. Hence their technological horizon must embrace present competitive products and include innovatory possibilities such as travellators and computer-controlled modules. Second, it stresses the need for more effective merchandising; the firm ceases to view its promotion as creating and servicing a demand in an amorphous market, but views itself in terms of supplying needs to particular segments and then engineers the product in its promotional milieu to meet these needs. This is the area of business operations which is most important in the short and medium terms and will be one treated in depth by the authors.

Thus the wider objectives for public transport management are twofold. Firstly, as part of the task of improving the urban environment, it must make its case on a political level which transcends free market economics. Secondly, within a competitive market economy, it must match itself to the needs of its customers, actual and potential. The first of these is extremely difficult to define since it involves subjective judgements about the quality of urban life. Nevertheless, public transport management must contribute towards the environmental decision-making processes, since planning for a more compact urban form and a viable and effective public transport network are mutually related. It has to convince public opinion and political bodies of the reciprocity of interests to be served by having concentrated work and to some extent residential locations, and it must also try to obtain preferential treatment in the use of road space. The second objective is the more conventional marketing task of satisfying the needs of the market. It is this aspect on which most of this study is concentrated, with the emphasis on a time horizon of the next two decades: it is unlikely that any dramatic technological break-through during this time will have ousted present modes of transport and management must concentrate on the more minor improvements of present technology and adapting its product (and promotional support) to market needs.

We do not claim that a managerial approach transformed by the acceptance of the marketing concept will produce immediate remedies for public transport's ills. Any thorough-going analysis of the urban travel market is bound to confirm the enormity of the operators' problems. These will not be easily alleviated, even by a balanced programme which seeks to foster a more sympathetic political environment, implement a whole series of product and service innovations aggressively promoted to selected demand segments and conduct imaginative publicity campaigns that illustrate the mutual interests of patronising a public transport system and maintaining essential urban functions. What we do claim is that though progress may be slow it is essential to pursue such an approach. Conversely, we criticise those managements who are content to maintain the operational *status quo* believing that benevolent external factors will be sufficient to resuscitate their ailing networks, e.g. the escalation of private motoring costs and the provision of more generous government subsidies and capital grants together with the imposition of far sterner controls on car use. Dramatic as recent petrol price increases have been they do not seem to have brought much relief to public transport. The logic of providing public transport with a much more favourable operating framework is strongly supported by the evidence available. However, the mood of the general public, and especially that of the motorist, is unlikely to match the convictions held by some politicians and most urban planners and operators about the social justification for measures involving large scale governmental subsidies and, in particular, car constraint. A rigorous examination of the needs of the urban traveller would indicate the extent to which a credibility or attitudinal gap exists in this respect; it would also provide insights for policy makers and operators who have to narrow that gap. A central theme of this book is that the case for sterner controls will be better understood and the restrictions themselves more acceptable if there are tangible signs of an improved public transport system being available. Furthermore, given the present operational framework these service improvements should be justifiable in themselves and lead to patronage gains.

Part I of this book aims to provide an environmental framework for analysing public transport management, and especially those functions having an interface with the urban travel market. More specifically, the purpose is: (i) to demonstrate the mutuality of interests between preserving the principal functions of central districts in large urban areas and promoting an effective system of public transport; and (ii) to identify the problems of operating a viable public transport network, emphasising the strength of its main competitor, the car. In chapter 1 a study is made of urban trends in population, workplace, shopping and leisure activities. All the major functions of cities are shown to be dispersing not only in terms of gross population but also in terms of their residential, work and shopping concentrations and the reasons for these dispersals are examined together with a discussion of the rationale for political intervention in the market forces stimulating dispersion. Chapter 2 links the dispersion of urban functions with the decline in public transport usage and studies the demand factors affecting the choice of transport mode and travellers' perceptions of public transport *vis-à-vis* its main competitors. The chapter concludes with a brief discussion on the future of urban transport within the context of developments likely to take place in its technological and political environments.

Part II shows how in five English PTEs and twenty-eight North American and continental Western European undertakings the functions of corporate planning, transport planning, service operations and marketing have reacted to their environmental pressures and how they might be expected to respond in the future. Our prime interest here is: (i) to identify the various types of market-related planning and strategy relevant to this industry and to trace the interrelationships between them; (ii) to describe their application by the organisations surveyed; (iii) to isolate some of the main problems impeding their successful application by examining the processes by which they have been introduced and developed; and (iv) to recommend better means for accommodating planning and marketing. However, in adopting these emphases we shall not dwell on the specific techniques and procedures which corporate and transport planners and marketeers might usefully employ at the tactical level since these tools are clearly enumerated for the practitioner in numerous readily available texts. Chapter 3 compares the nature of the industry's strategic, project and operational planning processes with those of large firms in the private sector and nationalised industries, and examines the planning approaches adopted and the tasks performed by the organisations surveyed. Marketing is the subject of chapter 4, which states the need for applying it to public transport organisations and identifies a precise role for this function. An analysis is made of marketing practices and the organisational acceptance of the function, the latter isolating a number of factors which have proved to be inimical to its successful adoption. Many of the observations made in chapters 3 and 4 are developed in chapter 5 which recommends how the corporate planning, transport planning, marketing and service operation functions can be better accommodated in an organisational sense so that their task performances can be improved.

Part III focuses on ways in which the industry can develop more competitive and profitable services by reviewing published findings of experiments already conducted and implementing controlled programmes of research. Chapter 6 reviews the growing body of published research findings from sources in the United Kingdom, Europe and America and chapter 7 summarises the results of some selective experiments involving the main elements of the marketing-mix piloted by us in the North West of England. As such, our own primary research represents an initial attempt at the kind of approach prescribed: we concentrate on short and medium term product modifications, but much of the methodology adopted will be transferable to the detailed planning — especially as it will impinge on the passenger — of longer run proposals for infrastructure developments, for example, urban 'rapid-transit' fixed-track systems scheduled for intro-duction in the 1980s. Finally, chapter 8 presents the strategic implications of the literature review and the primary research as the anchor-point of a strategy which must also include political and organisational considerations.

Notes

1 J.Sleeman, 'The rise and decline of municipal transport' *Scottish Journal of Political Economy*, vol. 9, 1962, pp. 46—64.

2 H. D. Quinby, 'Major urban corridor facilities: a new concept' *Scottish Quarterly*, April 1962.

3 *Public Transport and Traffic*, Cmnd. 3481, 1967.

4 The 'marketing-mix' is the term used to describe the selection and co-ordination of the many variables required to develop, offer, promote and make available a package of consumer satisfactions.

5 P. Kotler, *Marketing Management: Analysis, planning and control*, 1st ed., Prentice Hall, 1967, pp. 3 and 4.

PART 1

The Urban Environment and the Competitive Position of Public Transport

1 The Urban Environment of Public Transport

The modern conurbation is spreading over a progressively wider area and diminishing in its residential density. This chapter examines the centrifugal forces underlining these trends, analyses some of the main implications for town planning and public transport operations and provides a framework for studying public transport's market problems in more depth in the next chapter.

Industrial development is characterised by the rise of secondary and tertiary activities and the relative demise of primary ones. These secondary and tertiary functions are traditionally located in cities where transport and communications facilitate movements of materials, labour and finished products. During this last century an interesting reversal has occurred in the concentration of employment, a reversal which has only really started to have significant ramifications for cities over the past few decades. The reasons behind this change will be analysed in greater detail in the following pages, but the major reason is clearly bound up with the dramatic improvements in communications brought about first by the railway and later, and more especially, by the private car and commercial road vehicle. Meyer, Kain and Wohl[1] have made the most comprehensive study of these changes and their effects on public.transport in the US, while Kanwit and Eckartt[2] present even more refined and up-to-date evidence of the shifts in population, particularly over the past few decades.

Forces generating urban dispersal

Originating with the work of Christeller[3] in the 1930's, a body of theory has been developed to explain urban form and spatial characteristics. Christeller recognised a twofold function of a site: space and communications. These two primary attributes have led in turn to a theoretical framework for explaining the existence of the city and, especially, the central areas. Firstly, there is the 'ecological' concept which explains how the city centre is spatially closest to its catchment area and therefore represents the best compromise in terms of the minimisation of distance. Secondly, there is the notion of the 'central place' whereby the centre is seen to represent an area, the chief purpose of which is to facilitate face-to-face contact. The two aspects are complementary in explaining the functions which the centre performs. The first has a special relevance for distribution and the attraction of factors of production. The 'central place' function is more valid in maintaining a particular location for decision-making bodies once these have been established. Other writers have broadened the discussion. Alonso[4] noted: firstly, that any site offers both land and location: secondly, that central locations were more highly valued because route convergence tends to make them more accessible; and thirdly, land and location were to a great extent interchangeable. Poorer people in Western cultures substitute accessibility for incremental land inputs and tend to live near the city core. Middle class housing uses greater inputs of land, but is normally less central; although in London, for example, it is still considered desirable to live near the centre. The change in accessibility is the key element in the understanding of the centrifugal forces which are modifying the traditional urban setting and it is fruitful to examine these in detail, largely drawing on the works of Meyer, Kain and Wohl[1], Oi and Schuldiner[5] and Lansing and Hendricks.[6]

Employment dispersal

(a) *Technical developments in transport* Probably the most important single cause of the diffusion of urban employment — and all other activities — has been the technical development in transport. This has tended to make land use more homogeneous. In many industries, the ubiquity of the commercial vehicle has nullified the motivation for siting plants and depots at railheads and has reversed the traditional advantages of the congested city. With better transport the advantages of centrality are diminished, and the disadvantages of distance reduced.

(b) *Changes in manufacturing and wholesaling processes* Another factor which has reduced the attractiveness of central locations for industry is the increased use of automated processes in manufacturing. This calls for less intensive use of land, due to the need for single-storey assembly plants built with long highly automated production lines. Thus there is now less scope for offsetting the higher land prices in the centre by a greater concentration of production per square yard of factory space. The traditional nineteenth century factory usually comprised a multi-storey building with individual operatives each working on their own machine. The complexity of modern automated methods makes it far less easy to economise in land use to this extent since the productivity of the factory depends on a delicate and carefully controlled movement of the semi-finished products from process to process — this movement (except in specialised cases) is much more easily controlled if kept at one level. Moreover, single-storey factories are more flexible and permit easier modifications of the process.

Wholesaling, previously the archetypal central city service, like manufacturing, is dispersing. While the centre is the most convenient place from which to serve the entire catchment area, two circumstances now detract from this: increasing urban congestion and changing needs of wholesaling. Firstly, the effect of central city congestion on wholesaling will be more dramatic than for most other activities due to the key nature of the transport element involved. Secondly, the needs of wholesaling are becoming increasingly land extensive. Improvements in stock recordings and better handling of materials within the warehouses have brought greater productivity of warehousing labour. However, as in modern factories, land intensity is sacrificed and the incentive to move out to cheaper land on the periphery is that much greater.

(c) *Technical development in electronic communications* The advances made by the electronic communications industry have permitted greater centralisation of management control. The telephone, teleprinter, closed circuit television and the computer all allow management to direct and supervise with less personal contact.[7] While senior management may be grouped together in convenient city centre locations they can site their land-intensive functions in areas where lower rents are applicable. The extent to which such decentralisation between functions can take place will be largely governed by the nature of the production process. As Woodward[8] shows, small batch product manufacture requires close supervisory contact: continuous process plants, on the other hand, allow for an almost total spatial separation of non-production and production personnel. There are many examples of this improvement in communications, reducing the extent to which functions within firms must be in close proximity. The 'rag trade' has traditionally been situated together with its showrooms close to the great market centres, but in recent years production has been dispersed to cheaper and more accessible areas (i.e. for raw materials and distribution), with the sales function remaining in the metropolitan centre. Similarly, large scale processing industries like petrochemicals site their production units at points where bulk transport costs are minimised, which invariably means that the plant is normally not the location of the other three main functions — marketing, finance and research and development. In general this trend of manufacturing is well established, i.e. a movement towards increasingly large and automated factory units which need not be

15

close to sales and financial functions. Further, rationalisation of production is still releasing valuable central city sites, particularly in the longer established industries like brewing.

Increased personal affluence

Increased affluence is both a cause of the mounting congestion which detracts so much from central city sites and is also instrumental in creating a greater antipathy to these conditions. A more prosperous population demands easier mobility, better living space and shorter working hours, all of which help to promote urban dispersal and, as we will see in the next chapter, are detrimental to successful public transport operations.

(a)   *Car usage and urban dispersal* One of the more obvious symbols of increased affluence in Western countries over the last two decades has been the car. In the UK the percentage of households owning only one car in 1961 was 29: this had increased to 52 per cent by 1971. The number of two-car families is also increasing; only 2 per cent of households in the UK owned two or more cars in 1961; the proportion rose to 8 per cent by 1971. Lansing and Hendricks[6] showed in the US that although families with annual incomes over $5,000 (at constant 1957—59 US dollars) stabilised their car ownership levels at 82 per cent, after 1956 multi-car households increased their share. Table 1.1 shows the estimated numbers of American multi-car household families.

Table 1.1
Percentage of US families owning more than one car by income group

	Income group				
	$2,000—4,999	$5,000—7,999	$8,000—10,999	$11,000—13,999	Over $14,000
1950	1·4	3·8	9·0	17·6	21·0
1956	3·2	8·0	16·2	21·8	27·4
1960	3·2	10·0	17·6	27·6	38·0
1965	4·0	13·8	31·4	36·6	42·0
1974 (estimated)	6·6	23·1	42·8	56·7	—

Source: Lansing and Hendricks[6]

Clearly ownership of a car is, *per se,* a strong incentive to use it, especially, as will be shown in chapter 2, when it has also been perceived to enjoy a number of distinct product advantages. But what really needs emphasising here is that because the car's carrying capacity per unit of road space is obviously so much less economical than that of the bus or train, large scale use of the car for centrally-oriented work trips is the prime cause of the levels of road congestion now being experienced in the centres of major British cities.

With the dramatic increases in petrol costs in 1973 and 1974 many commentators expected car usage to decline and indeed, even apart from the effects of actions taken by oil importing governments, this was observed to happen for a short period. While it would be untrue to say that such major cost increases do not affect car use and the consequent trends of urban dispersal, it is now easy to see that this has represented only a slowing down of the rate of car usage. They cannot be regarded either as the salvation of public transport or as a change which will reverse the dispersal trends described above.

A possible solution to increased car usage, one which has been applied by many US town planners, is to provide extensive networks of urban motorways and multi-level car parks. Among the several drawbacks to such a policy is the way it encourages further expansion of city centres, thus reducing their value in the provision of face-to-face contact. Smeed[9] has calculated the size of the central area required for various degrees of car use. Calculations from his data suggest that for a city with a working population of 100,000 travelling by public transport the central business district can be confined to 0·363 square miles, as opposed to 0·423 square miles for a central area catering for the same number of workers but which had been purpose-designed for the car, i.e. where generous provision had been made for multi-level car parking lots and wide roads. However, the form of most UK city centres must be taken as given and largely comprises narrow roads (not to mention numerous historic buildings). Under these circumstances Smeed felt that the central area of a typical British town which attempted to ensure adequate car access and the necessary parking arrangements for 100,000 workers would need to be 0·554 square miles or 53 per cent greater than that of its 'public transport-fed' counterpart.

(b) *Increased demand for living space* Another aspect of increased affluence is the desire for more gracious living, one manifestation of which is the demand for more space per household. By reducing travelling time, and in effect distance, the car facilitates the 'trade-off' between distance and space. Table 1.2 shows the change in room occupation in England and

Wales. The trend is quite clearly towards more living space per person and this alone has vast implications for urban density. However, in terms of space this is only one facet of the total picture, since modern town planning designs give far more space per dwelling in terms of gardens, roads and parks.

Table 1.2
Population and its residential accommodation in England and Wales

	1921	1931	1951	1961	1966
Population ('000)	37,887	39,952	43,758	46,105	47,136
No. of rooms occupied ('000)	38,305	40,895	51,907	66,426	79,930
Average no. of persons per room	0·99	0·98	0·84	0·69	0·57

Source: England and Wales census data, HMSO

(c) *Television viewing* Television, which is now available in 91 per cent of UK households, permits a large amount of cultural and entertainment activity to be performed in the home. This greatly diminishes the need for one of the three prime functions of a central core — employment and shopping are the others. In Great Britain, cinema audiences have declined from 1,396 million in 1950 to 501 million in 1960 and 176 million in 1971. Along with dancing, eating out, gambling, spectator sports such as football, and the theatre, the cinema represents one of the key leisure activities of the centre. Not only has its demise been faster than that of these other pursuits, but the growth of out-of-town restaurant and discotheque patronage in Europe and the US has probably been greater than the growth for such establishments in city centres.

The dispersal of central shopping functions

Many factors, some of which have already been mentioned, conspire to undermine the attractions of the city centre shops relative to those in the suburbs.

Central city shopping centres receive a double blow from the car: firstly because it makes them less convenient due to congestion; and secondly, because it provides a suitable and commodious means by which the housewife can carry her goods and small children. Where the shopper was limited to public transport or to journeys on foot, a shopping hierarchy developed comprising central city shops and local parades of shops to serve the need for convenience and frequent purchase items. The car enables cross-town or out-of-town trips to be made — indeed it is often easier to drive many times the distance through suburban areas than it is to the town centre and it is much easier to park. This gives suburban supermarkets much greater catchment areas than hitherto, but other changes are also tending to favour non-central sites. Chief among these is the growth of domestic refrigeration (extending the effective storage capacity of key goods) and the increasing productivity of labour required for all activities. The refrigerator and especially the deep freeze means fewer trips and is complementary to the car's provision of a convenient receptacle in which to carry much greater quantities of goods. At the same time greater labour productivity means self-service stores offering attractive features, including free parking, and in effect substituting increments of land for more expensive increments of labour. Such land is only cheap enough outside the city centre. Labour costs account for only 5 per cent of total costs in hypermarkets compared to 12 per cent in conventional supermarkets and 15 per cent in central-sited department stores. With wage inflation virtually universally at a rate above that of other costs, the advantages of size will increase over time.

The dispersal trends in long term perspective

What we have seen so far is that accessibility, which once made the city centre the most attractive area for most urban functions, has been greatly impaired by congestion and, paradoxically, by road network improvements. The central area has become in many respects the least accessible part of the city. With the erosion of this advantage it becomes increasingly more attractive for many of those activities traditionally associated closest with it to move to more accessible locations where they benefit from easier transport and much cheaper land. The question arises as to whether the trends described are sufficiently definitive.

The effects of decreased city centre land rents

Clearly with increasing ease of communications, the trend is strongly in favour of lower priced sites beyond the centre and only a dramatic fall in land prices in central areas could nullify this. Such a fall is the corollary of a decline in demand but in the absence of a deep and general depression will ordinarily lag behind demand, falling at a slower rate and leaving surplus capacity in the short run. Because the supply of land in the centre is inelastic, a fall in demand will have a proportionally greater effect on prices and rents. Eventually the postulated fall in price might be expected to stimulate demand or at least moderate its future reduction. Lever[10] maintains that the out-movement will lead to a relative lowering of land prices and rents in the centre and that this is already happening in Manhattan. Allied to suburban congestion such property value reduction may even bring some sort of counter-trend in favour of the centre and the inner suburbs: with regard to the latter, the middle class takeover of a number of inner London boroughs offers an interesting but, perhaps, exaggerated example. However, it is doubtful whether land price and rent reductions in the central areas will ever have more than a mitigating effect in preventing urban sprawl. The trends are relative: relocation is occurring on the urban fringe but the centre still has advantages for particular functions, e.g. certain commercial tertiary services, expensive consumer durable and speciality shopping, which seem still to justify a premium rent. However, the absolute disadvantage of the centre, arising from congestion, will continue to be a handicap for grocery type shopping, wholesaling and manufacturing. This congestion could now only be eliminated by a dramatic modification in personal transport habits, i.e. the widespread use of public transport.

Other mitigating factors

Cameron and Johnson[11] after examining the dispersal out of Glasgow think the rate will be arrested because of the critical availability of skilled labour, the limitations of public transport and high density central city housing in that city. Their view would appear to be substantiated by Newman[12] who suggests that in the US dispersal has recently reached a plateau. Between 1954 and 1965, 63 per cent of all industrial buildings in 3,000 urban areas were built on the periphery, between 1960 and 1965 the corresponding figure was 62 per cent, thereby indicating that the drift from the cities has begun to decelerate. Of course, a deceleration can still represent a considerable net outflow, which the statistics in the next section demonstrate.

Some statistical evidence

Table 1.3 shows the percentage movements of the share of central city activities for twenty-four of the largest US Standard Metropolitan Statistical Areas (SMSAs). The figures show a pattern of dispersal across the whole range of activities measured — office employment, as will be shown for the UK, may run counter to the trend in certain instances but is something of an imponderable because it comprises many classifications of economic activity.

While they doubt whether these trends will be reversed, Kanwit and Eckartt (like Newman) expect the rate to decelerate because of urban renewal, downtown luxury apartments, growing suburban congestion and a reaction to the lengthening commuter trip.

The UK statistical sources are less comprehensive than those available for the US urban areas. Information is more elusive, but where available it tends to support the view of the Steering Group of the Buchanan Report which asserted that, 'though there are obvious differences between North America and Britain we think they are differences of degree only and not such as to invalidate a comparison'.[13]

(a) *Population* Table 1.4 summarises the position of five English provincial conurbations, showing them to have lost penetration of the overall population in three successive census periods.

The conurbations with cores in London, Glasgow, Birmingham, Liverpool, Manchester, Leeds and Newcastle-upon-Tyne are all in relative decline due to their peripheration and incursion into their surrounding regions. To take the core cities of each of these conurbations offers ample evidence of this. The percentages are given in Table 1.5 and relate the proportion of the central cities to their conurbations.

Even within the core cities the same trends can be seen; the peripheral areas have represented the only population growth and are only really part of the conurbations' sprawl.

(b) *Urban employment opportunities* Cameron and Evans[14] in an analysis of British conurbation centres distinguish between 'conurbation centre', 'rest of central city' and 'outer conurbation' and show how between the 1961 and 1966 censuses there has been a decline in the working population covered by the first two categories and how an increase in employment has been recorded in the third. Table 1.6 presents their findings. Cameron and Evans produce figures for the various service and manufacturing industries. Their analysis clearly indicates that for all the manufacturing industries and the distributive trades, in particular wholesaling, there were notable reductions in the numbers employed in the conurbation centres, while for such traditional central activities as professional/scientific

21

Table 1.3
Percentage of SMSA's total trade, jobs and population within central city

	1948	1963
Population	61	48
Employment	72	58
Wholesale trade	90	72
Retail trade	74	55
Manufacturing	67	53
Selected services	80	67

Source: taken from Kanwit and Eckartt [2]

Table 1.4
Population (in millions) and penetration of UK population of
English conurbations
(Percentage of total population of England and Wales in brackets)

	1931	1951	1961	1966	1971
Tyneside (Newcastle)	0·83(2·1)	0·84(1·9)	0·86(1·9)	0·83(1·8)	0·80(1·7)
East and West Riding (Leeds)	1·66(4·1)	1·69(3·9)	1·70(3·7)	1·71(3·6)	1·73(3·6)
North West (Liverpool and Manchester)	3·77(9·4)	3·81(8·7)	3·81(8·3)	3·74(8·0)	3·65(7·5)
West Midlands (Birmingham)	1·93(4·8)	2·26(5·1)	2·38(5·1)	2·37(5·0)	2·37(4·9)
Total	8·19(20·4)	8·60(19·6)	8·75(19·0)	8·65(18·4)	8·55(17·7)

Source: England and Wales census data, HMSO

Table 1.5
Penetration of English conurbation population by central city

	1931	1951	1961	1966	1971
Newcastle	34·6	34·9	31·6	29·9	27·5
Leeds	29·2	29·9	30·0	29·6	26·0
Liverpool	63·6	57·1	54·0	51·6	48·4
Manchester	31·5	29·0	27·2	24·9	22·6
Birmingham	51·8	49·8	46·1	44·8	42·6
London (% of S.E.)	—	—	49·0	46·1	43·1
Conurbations less London	41·5	39·7	37·7	35·9	33·1

Source: England and Wales census data, HMSO

Table 1.6
Percentage of employment in conurbation centre, rest of central city and outer conurbations, British conurbations 1961 and 1966

Conurbation	Conurbation centre			Rest of central city			Outer conurbation		
	1961	1966	Change	1961	1966	Change	1961	1966	Change
London South East	32·2	30·2	—2·0	24·4	23·7	—0·7	43·4	46·1	2·7
Lancashire	13·7	11·6	—2·1	21·3	21·0	—0·3	65·0	67·4	2·4
West Midlands Central	9·9	8·6	—1·3	43·7	42·7	—1·0	46·4	48·4	2·0
Clydeside	17·2	15·9	—1·3	45·0	43·5	—1·5	37·8	40·6	2·8
Merseyside	25·9	22·8	—3·1	40·1	40·5	0·4	34·0	36·7	2·7
Tyneside	20·3	19·1	—1·2	26·0	24·1	—1·9	53·7	56·8	3·1

Source: Cameron and Evans[14]

Table 1.7
Proportional changes in employment in the conurbation centres 1961—1966, percentage by industry

	Greater London	South East Lancashire	West Midlands	Central Clydeside	Merseyside	Tyneside
Service industries						
Wholesale distribution	—22·2	—39·1	12·6	—28·8	—25·1	—13·9
Retail distribution	— 6·2	— 4·7	—10·0	14·4	— 6·7	— 0·3
Transport and communication	—10·4	—18·2	— 5·1	—16·1	—17·2	2·3
Miscellaneous services	— 3·4	—12·3	— 2·3	— 4·0	— 2·2	— 3·0
Professional and scientific services	7·0	8·2	14·5	1·5	2·4	15·3
Insurance, banking and finance	3·4	— 0·1	5·8	— 1·6	— 6·3	2·4
Public administration	2·0	3·3	— 2·2	0·3	0·2	15·4
Total services	— 3·8	—13·0	— 2·2	— 5·8	— 9·9	— 2·0
Other industries						
Paper, printing and publishing	—13·6	—16·8	—29·9	— 8·8	—18·5	11·5
Construction	—11·5	—16·7	—22·7	—23·7	—10·4	— 5·6
Engineering	—26·5	—28·3	—19·3	—16·9	— 2·6	— 3·5
Leather and fur, clothing and footwear	—25·5	—41·0	—29·6	— 8·1	—30·7	—20·0
Other manufacturing and printing industries	—17·0	—23·2	—37·0	—26·4	—21·6	—19·0
Total manufacturing, etc.	—17·4	—25·1	—29·6	—13·0	—18·4	—13·3
All industries	— 7·7	—16·4	—10·2	— 9·2	—11·9	— 2·1

Source: Cameron and Evans[14]

services, insurance, banking and finance, and public administration. job opportunities in most cases increased. Table 1.7 gives a breakdown of this.

The growth in office employment has been rapid since 1951. Cowan[15] found that between 1951 and 1961 office employment accounted for 70 per cent of the increase in job opportunities. According to Wright[16] it was probably only after 1967 that the UK provincial office growth really started to boom. He has estimated the planned increase in central city floor space between 1965 and 1981 to be: Manchester 26·7 per cent; Birmingham 17·9 per cent; Liverpool 9·7 per cent; Leeds 36·8 per cent; Newcastle 27·8 per cent and Cardiff 32·5 per cent.

(c) *Shopping trends* The National Economic Development Office's report

Table 1.8
Percentage penetration of the centres of 24 US conurbations — retail sales by type of goods

	1948	1954	1958
Convenience	11·9	7·9	5·9
Shopping goods	62·4	42·6	39·7
Other	19·0	11·0	9·5

Source: Meyer, Kain and Wohl[1]

on 'The future pattern of shopping,'[17] estimates that in the UK by 1980 some 400 supermarkets each with over 100,000 square feet of floorspace, will sell more than 10 per cent of food and a large proportion of non-food purchases. Such facilities can only be established away from town centres where car parking can be included cheaply. Already a 90,000 square feet store exists outside Nottingham and the French hypermarket firm, Carrefour, has built a 100,000 square feet store in Shropshire. These are small by French standards where the 115 hypermarkets have an average floorspace of 140,000 square feet. Future developments will naturally depend upon the policies of the central and local government authorities, and as yet firm policies regarding hypermarket planning permission have not been established in the UK.

The forces for retail dispersal are less compelling when considering shopping goods, such as expensive consumer durables, where shoppers want to make direct comparisons between different retail outlets in close proximity to one another. These, it is generally thought, will largely remain by force of inertia in their traditional central place locations. However, the US statistics given in Table 1.8 show that even shopping goods are dispersing from the centre, albeit at a reduced rate to convenience goods. A contributory factor in this respect has been the growth of discount stores, selling a wide range of consumer durables, which are able to support their extremely competitive prices by locating on cheaper out-of-town sites as well as keeping display and service costs to a minimum.

Schiller[18] produces some UK evidence of the move away from major centres by specialist retail outlets, e.g. those stocking costly items of apparel, which are often cited as having the greatest affinity for central place location. After comparing two nearby centres, Slough (with a population of 93,000 in 1969) and Beaconsfield (with a population of 12,000 in 1969), he found that the former — a predominantly working class town — had only four such outlets to the latter's — an upper middle class area — twenty-seven. This illustrates how such specialist shops can locate near to large bodies of their customers, which being car borne anyway, may find cross-town trips easier than ones to the centre.

The case for governmental intervention

The foregoing shows an unmistakable trend towards greater urban dispersal. Whether this will eventually result in a form of urban development without a recognisable physical centre is a subject of controversy. The example of the US demonstrates, and the trends in the UK support the notion, that unless we choose to take positive steps to avoid it, metropolitan areas will in future be less densely populated and will have more dispersed work and shopping trip-patterns. The issue is whether or not governmental intervention is justified.

While market forces may be the best way of optimising resource utilisation of many goods it is highly questionable that they are sufficient to justify leaving them to determine the fabric of urban form. *Laissez-faire* or market economics are dependent for maximising efficiency on a number of conditions being met, the most important of which is that individual personal gains are broadly in accordance with those of society. The potential conflict of personal and public satisfactions has resulted in the development of welfare economics as a separate branch of economics. Governments have increasingly taken the view that to maximise the national wealth, they can only permit a somewhat constricted play of market forces. In allowing free choice of household location, apart from any wider issues of environment, the net result may be to curtail real preference. This paradox results from the decisions of the people electing to move out of a city affecting the welfare of those people wishing or being forced to remain. Society as a whole must determine its scale of preferences, and by fiat and incentive shape the favoured system.

The conflict between the public good and private benefit has called for a comparatively new range of evaluatory criteria to be devised for public authority decisions — cost/benefit analysis. But the difficulty when not relying on market forces is to know what values to allocate to those social costs and benefits which often prove less tangible. Typical of these are values to be allocated to time where a faster means of public transport is to be developed or where a policy restricting the use of cars is being considered. In such cases values have to be allocated to time not only for the actual passengers directly concerned but for users of other modes, who might be affected by the change. For London's Victoria Line 40 per cent of the benefits were estimated to accrue to people using other means of travel. However, as Tipping[19] points out, 'there is rather more at stake than just knocking a few minutes off the average length of journey'. Time is only one attribute to be considered, others such as pollution are coming increasingly to the fore.

The less tangible factors must be evaluated and although cost/benefit analysis as yet provides a somewhat imperfect methodology for attempting this, consciously or unconsciously, quantifications have to be made.

Methodological difficulties aside, not everyone accepts the case for governmental intervention. Shipman[20] cogently argues in favour of a *laissez-faire* policy. His arguments are twofold. Firstly, even though there may be some imperfections and inequities in the way the price mechanism is applied, in general private motorists exhibit more realism in their payment for road space than do public transport passengers. Hence public transport should not be supported by the community since it is manifestly not in the real interest of that community. Secondly, the evidence of all studies on the drift to the suburbs is that the overwhelming majority, except for select groups at a particular life-stage (e.g. young unmarrieds and newly-weds), want to live away from the city centre. By the same token retailers and industrialists find it more profitable to relocate and we should not disregard people's preferences by maintaining an out-dated method of social organisation. Shipman concedes that public transport subsidisation may be valid when it is activated by political decisons to aid the poor, and other deprived groups. However, the tenet of his argument is that the *laissez-faire* policy will broadly offer the best solution to society. This will mean that public transport will be increasingly replaced by the car for the journey-to-work and the work place would change its location. Off-peak public transport use will continue to decline as shopping diversifies and multiple car ownership per household grows; fare increases will be required. These factors in turn will lead to a further dispersal of employment until residential, commercial and employment locations are sufficiently dispersed to allow the journey-to-work to be made by the car. He argues that it is possible that the social waste of, say, empty offices in central areas may in fact be offset by residences and work places being closer together.

Nobody has written a scholarly reply to the argument against continued high density work locations in the centre. However, some rejoinder, in the context of public transport, is necessary since its future, given its present technology, is dependent on high density centre-oriented radial routes.

27

Broadly speaking there are four principal arguments which can support the notion of maintaining the nature of the city much as it already exists:

1 the social costs of abandoning capital development,
2 the need for a central location to act as a focus of skills,
3 the difficulties for under-privileged and those sections of the community without a car, and
4 the need to preserve rural areas.

The social costs of abandoning capital development

It is sometimes difficult to justify the retention of the urban *status quo* without appearing as a conservative opponent to change. The same sort of problem faces national government in its decision *vis-à-vis* declining areas and industries. Most governments have opted to offer some buttress to regions which face a decline due to a shift in demand for their basic products. The rationale is that once an industrial location has been established it generates utility over and above that comprising the sum of the parts of the capital investment made, which if abandoned represents a loss to the nation. Therefore, an individual firm taking the decision to relocate from its existing traditional base does so after quantifying its own costs and benefits, e.g. those relating to labour, raw materials, plant flexibility and proximity to markets, but normally it would take no account of the social costs involved.

In much the same way the case is argued for preserving the city centre even though firms and populations prefer to relocate in the suburbs. Obviously the case is less trenchant than that for maintaining regional centres, since the abandonment of a once flourishing region due to its industrial demise represents a far more serious loss in terms of social capital: in a regional centre the existing housing stock is more likely to become redundant; in a declining city centre it should retain some utility because of the adjoining employment opportunities. A study of industrial relocation in Boston[21] found that many workers retained their peripherally relocated jobs and commuted from the core and although they personally suffered a net loss in time and/or expense, housing and other social wealth continued to be used. Moreover, some inflow of jobs such as public and private office work might replace some of the lost demand for housing. Even so, the less intensive use of social capital in the centre (comprising, for example, power grids, roads, offices and other buildings, and sewers) will represent a net loss to society, a factor which those such as Shipman fail to take into account. The real problem, of course, is one of measurement and obviously some estimates must be made before a political decision broadly to maintain the current urban form can be taken.

The need for a focal centre

Although individual firms acting in isolation may benefit economically from moving out of the centre, this may not hold for an entire industry. For example, the concentration of financial intermediaries may bring considerable economies to the business community at large because of the advantages of inter-personal contact. If one or a few organisations move out, the industry can absorb the dis-economies thus created and the dispersed firms may gain in rental and labour cost. However, for the entire industry to move to peripheral locations may strain the communications system and bring a net reduction in efficiency. A similar argument might be used in respect of population sprawl. Individual households located outside the urban nexus impose basic service costs far above the average.

Preservation of public transport facilities for underprivileged groups

Only where routes with high traffic densities are possible can public transport be effectively operated. To offer attractive headways and a frequent service, public transport must have a volume market. In order to operate on lines which conform to traditional concepts of profitability, it requires at least a certain level of non-peak traffic so that the system's overheads can be spread over a longer period and a greater number of passengers. For work journeys alone, and even without the necessity of profitable operations, the dispersed locations of the labour force of each employer means that public transport must serve several employment catchments and residential locations simultaneously if it is to be effective. Given the present technology this is impracticable.

But by almost any criterion upwards of 25 per cent of the working population will not have access to a car even in the next three or four decades. In order to provide economic public transport facilities, which allow for a reasonable choice of jobs and main shopping opportunities for this and other groups without the use of cars (such as the old, the young and many housewives), extra passengers must be attracted. Work and shopping locations must be concentrated on similar lines to those of today. Without such concentrations the current operational economics and the public's strong preference for the car will certainly not allow for a break-even, high frequency public transport system. To reduce frequency levels of public transport is to reduce its overall effectiveness and therefore, in turn, its demand.

One aspect of this, the effects of 'transit deprivation' in stimulating social disturbances, has been widely researched since it was considered to be one of the contributory factors towards the Los Angeles Watts riots in 1967. In the US the decay of public transport brings an urgent problem for those who cannot afford a car or cannot use one for other reasons. In Britain, given better public transport facilities and, as yet, far more compact cities, the curtailment of services is unlikely to have the same drastic consequences as it has had in the US. However, 'transit deprivation' — itself the result of the twin effects of industrial relocation on the periphery and of car use for the journey to work by the more affluent workers — should not be ignored.

Of itself, such an outcome, as many would argue, justifies a public transport subsidy on humanitarian grounds. However, the argument in favour of subsidisation may also be supported because society at large will function with sharply reduced efficiency should the underprivileged segments be further denied a satisfactory system of transport. For example, firms which have located 'inconveniently', some distance from the centre, may find it increasingly difficult to attract essential types of workers with consequent inflationary effects. High sunken costs reduce firms' abilities to switch their locations and, therefore, they may be forced to raise wages and inflate other labour costs. While some categories of workers like London's office cleaners, decreasingly housed within walking distance of their work place, have benefited from a scarcity resulting from this and other factors by large increases in their wages, not all groups have fared as well.

The preservation of the urban—rural balance

Environmentally 11 per cent of the area of the UK comprises urban development and the remainder is virtually all rural. The urban area increased by 44,000 acres per year for 1960—65, and is projected at 15·4 per cent of the total 40 million acres by the year 2,000. By American standards, where a collossal 1 million acres per year are being transferred to urban use, the UK rate of sprawl is quite low and in fact it is now only two-thirds the rate reached in the 1930's. However, there are three main reasons why these figures should not be treated with complaisance and why they understate the magnitude of the progressive reduction in our recreational environment. Firstly, there has been a marked tendency recently in favour of low density housing which may mean the projections understate the trend. The UK households are far less land-extensive than those in the US, but as we have posited already increased affluence may create a demand for more residential land space. Already new towns are adopting far lower targets for the number of households per acre — Harlow had 42, Cumbernauld has 27, Milton Keynes is proposed to have only 8, which compares to the standard of 6 households per acre fairly general in US suburbia. Unless closely controlled the replacement of the compact housing stock built sixty or more years ago by much more liberal plots in suburban housing estates may yet make nonsense of the present forecasts. Secondly, the development itself is far from evenly spread. The ecological balance in the South East and North West is particularly acute. Thirdly, the nature of rural land is changing. In an article in *The Sunday Times*[22] it was shown that between 1949 and 1967 the predominantly rural county of Dorset lost 9,300 out of 44,000 acres of open country. The land was ploughed and its recreational value lost.

Thus the cultural role of the city should be considered alongside that of the countryside. In the UK the Green Belt policy has attempted to achieve an urban-rural balance. While offering a reputed — and in some cases real — enrichment of the environment the policy has unwittingly been instrumental in extending the boundaries of conurbations and large cities. Green Belt erosion by urban development has often followed a 'leap-frogging' process. Other plans might be considered more imaginative in their attempt to maintain a felicitous environment. Starting in 1948, the Copenhagen 'Finger' plan rechannelled growth along specific corridors which could support a viable public transport system but which left green wedges between them. Stockholm and Moscow have followed similar patterns, and the recent plans for both New York and Washington propose the same radial corridor approach. In addition to facilitating high density public transport, such a star-shaped urban structure offers a rural area much closer to the main residential areas than is possible with a concentric Green Belt, but of course rigorous control is needed to prevent the green wedges becoming the means for an augmentation of urban activities.

The problems facing large UK cities are not as grave as those facing many of the US metropolises. Admittedly some of the symptoms of social breakdown associated with American city ghettoes are beginning to appear in Britain and as we have seen the extension of municipal boundaries has been rapid. This said, it should be recognised that most UK suburbs are of a different character from their US counterparts; they are closer to the city centres and in comparison have well established and superior public transport links. Furthermore, British town and country planning institutions have taken root and, despite their innumerable frailties, are working to preserve existing focal city locations and achieve some kind of urban-rural accommodation.

However, there is little room for complacency. The UK motorist seems to have a fond and growing attachment for the car as a means of transport and if the ratio of motor tax payments to road expenditure (see table 1.9) is indicative of the price he is willing to pay for its use he is not easily deterred.[23] Similarly, it would appear that his predilection for this mode has not been undermined by the escalating fuel costs he has had to bear during 1973 and 1974. But his disposition to pay must not be seen as a sign of his acquiescence. On the contrary, his demand for better road facilities,

Table 1.9

Motor taxation and road expenditure in the UK — £ millions

	Taxation				Total road expenditure
	Fuel tax	Licence duty	Purchase tax	Total	
1970	1,144	419	234	1,797	610
1971	1,263	421	267	1,951	738
1972	1,296	473	300	2,069	761

Source: *Basic Road Statistics, 1972,* British Road Federation

including the provision of urban motorways, has been so forcibly expressed that many politicians have felt unable to ignore it. The lessons to be derived from car-oriented US 'megalopolises' such as Los Angeles are unambiguous and we would conclude it is unacceptable to argue that because it is easier to make judgements of what people want by observing their behaviour in the market place than it is to evaluate the wider costs and benefits, then the market measure should be used.

Notes

[1] J. R. Meyer, J. F. Kain and M. Wohl, *The Urban Transportation Problem,* Harvard University Press, 1965.

[2] E. L. Kanwit and A. F. Eckartt, 'Transportation implications of employment trends in central cities and suburbs' *Highway Research Record No. 187,* pp. 1—14.

[3] W. Christeller, *Central Places in Southern Germany,* Prentice Hall, 1966.

[4] W. Alonso, 'A theory of the urban land market' *Papers and Proceedings of the Regional Science Association,* vol. 6 (6th annual meeting).

[5] W. Y. Oi and P. Schuldiner, *An Analysis of Urban Travel Demand,* Northwestern University, Chicago 1962.

[6] J. B. Lansing and G. Hendricks, *Automobile Ownership and Residential Density,* Survey Research Centre, University of Michigan, 1965.

[7] Meyer, Kain and Wohl[1] speculate that this will induce a minor counter trend in that it will cause top management to be grouped together but in *selected* convenient city locations.

[8] J. Woodward, *Industrial Organisation, Theory and Practice,* OUP, 1965.

[9] R. J. Smeed, 'The road space required for traffic in towns' *Town Planning Review,* no. XXXIII, January 1963, pp. 279—92.

[10] W. F. Lever, 'The intra-urban movement of manufacturing firms: a Markov approach', privately circulated paper, *University of Glasgow,* 1971.

[11] G. C. Cameron and K. M. Johnson, 'Comprehensive urban renewal and industrial relocation in the Glasgow area' in S. C. Orr and J. B. Cullingworth (eds) *Regional Economic Studies,* Allen and Unwin, 1969, pp. 242—71.

[12] Article by D. K. Newman in *United States Bureau of Labour Statistics,* Division of Economic Studies, 1966.

[13] *Traffic in Towns,* HMSO, 1963, para.10.

[14] G. C. Cameron and A. W. Evans, 'The British conurbation centres' *Regional Studies,* vol. 7, 1973, pp.47—55.

[15] P. Cowan, *Developing Patterns of Urbanization,* Oliver and Boyd, 1970, see especially p. 200.

[16] M. Wright, 'Provincial office development' *Urban Studies,* vol. 4, 1967, pp. 218—57.

[17] NEDO, *Distributive Trades, EDC,* 'The future pattern of shopping', HMSO, London 1971.

[18] R. K. Schiller, 'Location trends of specialist services' *Regional Studies,* vol. 5, 1971, pp. 1—10.

[19] D. G. Tipping, 'Time savings in transport studies' *Economic Journal,* December 1968, pp. 843—54.

[20] W. D. Shipman, 'Rail passenger subsidies and benefit — cost considerations' *Journal of Transport Economics and Policy,* January 1971, pp. 4—37.

[21] E. J. Burt, 'Plant relocation and the core city worker' *US Department of Housing and Urban Development,* Washington 1967.

22 'Dorset Downs in danger' *The Sunday Times*, 16 May 1971.

23 However, if the social costs of congestions are added, plus hospital/accident and 'policing' costs, it can be argued that motorists pay far less than the full social cost attached to their travel.

2 The Demand for Urban Transport

The previous chapter forms a natural introduction to the market place problems of public transport in the major cities and conurbations. We now examine the problems in greater detail, and in particular attempt to account for the factors affecting the demand for urban travel and modal choice so that an evaluation of public transport may be made *vis-à-vis* its competing modes.

The market decline of public transport

Statistical evidence of the decline in demand for public transport

Table 2.1 shows the extent of the decline in the number of urban public transport journeys made in the US and UK since 1950. The average decline in the US for the period 1950—71 was 4·2 per cent per annum. It was between 1950 and 1960 that the rate of decrease was most marked; a time when the proportion of families owning one or more cars rose sharply (see Table 2.2). In the UK average decline per annum was 3·6 per cent for the period 1950—71, but as the proportion of British families acquiring one or more cars increased markedly during the 1960's so the rate of decline in public transport has accelerated. This is also shown in Table 2.2.

The volume of traffic on urban roads provides additional evidence for the relationship between car ownership and usage for urban travel needs. For the UK this is indicated by table 2.3, which shows that between 1966 and 1971 car and taxi traffic grew by 30 per cent, whereas buses and coaches recorded a decrease in volume of 10 per cent.

Apart from considerations already mentioned, the effect of governmental intervention and the policies which public transport undertakings might implement, modal choice will be influenced by urban population, size and density as well as urban age and form. In 1962 Schnore[1] found when examining 13 US cities that each of these variables helped to explain public transport's share of the total journey-to-work trips made. The correlations were as follows (a) city size: 0·568; (b) city density: 0·672, and (c) city age: 0·752. Obviously, the higher the population and its density the more able

Table 2.1

Passenger journeys by urban public transport, 1950—71, US and UK
(in millions)

	1950	1955	1960	1965	1966	1967	1968	1969	1970	1971
US total journeys:	17,246	11,529	9,395	8,253	8,083	8,172	8,019	7,803	7,332	6,847
Electric (a)	6,168	3,077	2,313	2,134	2,035	2,201	2,181	2,229	2,116	2,000
Trolley	1,658	1,202	657	305	286	248	228	199	182	148
Bus	9,420	7,250	6,425	5,814	5,764	5,723	5,610	5,375	5,034	4,699
UK journeys in main urban areas (b)(c):	10,943	n.a.	8,289	6,970	6,589	6,324	6,077	5,823	5,344	5,032
Electric trams (d)	1,743	769	157	15	14	13	12	12	10	10
Trolley	1,972	1,598	990	285	188	106	68	50	34	15
Bus	7,228	n.a.	7,142	6,670	6,387	6,205	5,997	5,761	5,300	5,007

(a)   Includes surface railways (trains) and 'subways' and elevated railways.
(b)   Passenger journeys by London Transport central buses, local authority undertakings and passenger transport authorities.
(c)   Very slightly inflated by the inclusion of all London Transport's bus services, i.e. not just those operated in the urban areas of the capital.
(d)   Note should be taken that unlike the US figures the passengers carried by London Transport's tube system are excluded.

Sources: US — *Statistical Abstract of the US, 1972*, US Department of Commerce
UK — *Passenger Transport in Great Britain, 1970* and the *Annual Abstract of Statistics, 1972*, both HMSO publications

Table 2.2

Percentage of households owning one or more cars, 1950—71, US and UK

	1950	1955	1960	1965	1968	1969	1970	1971
US	59	70	77	79	79	79	82	83
UK	—	—	30	41	49	51	52	52

Sources: US — *Statistical Abstract of the US, 1972*, US Department of Commerce
UK — *Highway Statistics, 1971, HMSO*.

Table 2.3
Traffic on urban roads in Great Britain by class of vehicle
(index 1966 = 100)

	1966	1968	1969	1970	1971
Cars and taxis	100	110	114	124	130
Motor cycles	100	75	66	61	59
Buses and coaches	100	94	94	89	90
All goods vehicles	100	95	95	98	99
(a) light vans	100	93	94	100	102
(b) others	100	96	96	96	95
All motor vehicles	100	105	108	116	120
Pedal cycles	100	78	72	68	66

Source: *Highway Statistics, 1971,* HMSO

are operations to justify high frequency and closely enmeshed services, leading to a stimulation of demand. Cities which have been created largely during the motor age have, to an increasingly greater extent, been purpose-built for the car. European cities in general are older than those in North America and tend to be far more densely populated, and although the automobile age is bringing a fall in this density, their public transport systems have an advantage over US ones at a comparable stage of car ownership.

Factors impairing the efficiency of public transport operation

In chapter 1 we described the main forces adversely affecting the centres of major cities; many of these also serve to exacerbate the difficulties faced by public transport operators and thus further increase the relative attractiveness of the car. The relationships involved here will now be briefly discussed.

(a) *Dispersed trip patterns* The continued dispersion of residential and work place locations from high density areas means that public transport is less able to serve the diffuse trip patterns resulting, simply because it requires high volume route corridors to gain profitable load factors and operate at attractive levels of frequency.

Only in very special circumstances might a redistribution of residential and employment locations permit profitable public transport operation. One such case may be where a new satellite area — say, a large trading and housing estate — becomes an important centre in its own right, thus providing the means for a considerable two-way flow of work traffic (e.g. white-collar workers commuting to the centre and industrial workers travelling in the opposite direction).

(b) *Increased off-peak demand difficulties* Reductions in working hours have impacted on operational costs and fares. For example, the reduction of the working week from six to five days meant that overheads had to be spread over $16\frac{2}{3}$ per cent fewer journey-to-work trips. Present indications are that a four and a half day working week may well be close to hand, while a four day week may come during the 1980's. The trend towards longer holidays is expected to continue and by 1981 a minimum four weeks' annual holiday should be universal; further, for the UK, membership of the EEC is likely to increase public holidays.

Perhaps of greater importance is the reduction of mid-day work trips. Partly in response to longer commuting distances and partly due to the social preference for a more compact working day — especially as the length of that day is reduced — there are indications that mid-day peak traffic has declined as workers eat lunch at or near their work places. This type of traffic operation can be carried out at a relatively low marginal cost.

Television, a factor in generating urban dispersal because it allows more leisure activities to take place in the home, brings about a reduction in demand for low marginal cost off-peak services.

Similarly, the number of social visits may have decreased as a result of the increase in private telephone installations — in 1955, 21 per cent of UK households rented telephones, in 1970 the figure was 35 per cent (for the Greater London area it was as high as 51 per cent).

More significant is the accelerating trend in the acquisition by families of the second and third car: in 1961 2 per cent of UK households had two or more cars, by 1970 the figure was 8 per cent. Ownership of the first car has brought about the decline of male public transport passengers: the second will affect more drastically female and young riders, and this will exacerbate the operators' problems by greatly reducing the volume of off-peak business which can most economically be handled, especially the shopping traffic. However, work done by Tyson[2] in Oldham suggests that because of the rather unrefined and inequitable methods adopted for allocating overheads, operators are not sufficiently aware of the low costs of providing many of the off-peak services and there may be a danger of them

38

over-reacting to demand decreases for these when cutting back on routes and frequency and resorting to fare increases.

(c) *Congestion, service levels and the car* The difficulties created by the changes referred to are compounded by what Bennett and McCorquodale[3] refer to as the 'chicken and egg' problem, the escalation effect brought about by more cars on the roads causing congestion leading to a deterioration of bus services, thus providing a greater incentive to use cars in 'choice' situations; this in turn results in service levels being further impaired and so on. Spiralling congestion while it affects all forms of traffic, tends to impinge far less on the motorist whose greater control over departure times, route selection and general manoeuvrability and speed merely emphasises the car's relative efficiency.

(d) *Labour costs and service levels* A comparable 'chicken and egg' situation arises from the industry's high labour constituent of total costs. Typically with two-man bus operation, platform labour costs are some 70 per cent of the total; with one-man bus operation it has been estimated that these can be reduced to, perhaps, 54 per cent (savings which have still to be realised by most operators). A pincer phenomenon occurs on the industry's profit margins — especially in an inflationary economy. On the one hand, the secular decline in traffic reduces labour productivity and, on the other hand, wage demands have a more marked effect than in industries where labour inputs form a lesser share of total costs. In the face of such constraints the pressure to prune operational costs has been considerable; yet the cost-cutting solutions of having fewer routes, less frequent schedules and one-man bus operation need to be adopted judiciously if they are not to rebound adversely. Evidence from the US demonstration projects and UK operating statistics suggest that in certain cases elasticity of demand with respect to frequency may be greater than unity, and a service reduction, therefore, may lead to a disproportionately high fall off in volume. Similarly, one-man bus operation, though reducing labour costs, imposes other drawbacks such as increased boarding times and slower journeys, capable of provoking highly antagonistic passenger reactions.

However, even where operators have sought to maintain and, perhaps, improve upon existing service levels, an inability to recruit and retain an adequate labour force has in some cases caused a noticeable deterioration of standards with consequent adverse effects on public relations. These conditions were most discernible throughout 1972 and 1973, especially in areas where employment opportunities were highest and where living costs had escalated most. The chairman of the London Transport Executive, Sir

Richard Way, has drawn attention to how, for example, governmental restraints on public service wage and tariff increases, expanding job opportunities outside the industry which offer better pay and working conditions (e.g. standard hours), and the inflationary costs of housing (especially in the vicinity of the main bus garages and train depots of inner London) have conspired to bring about acute staff shortages, resulting in a deterioration and cancellations of some quite basic services.[4]

Public transport and its competitors

Urban public transport, despite its own decline, must be viewed within the context of a growing market. Increasing population, income, and car ownership levels all ensure that the number of trips is growing in total and per capita. The differential trip rates between car and non-car owning households show that the car is exploiting a latent demand potential untapped by public transport. Further, the market is growing because of the changing character of the trips made as trip lengths increase through residential and employment dispersal. Any attempts to redress public transport's fast declining market share must commence with an analysis of demand and the factors influencing choice between modes.

The nature of consumer needs for urban travel

People travel to satisfy certain economic and social needs. These include the need to communicate with others; to be in physical proximity to others (e.g. to work as a team); to provide a personal service; or for a change of environment. Within this general market, one may hypothesise, following Kemp[5] and Thomson,[6] that the demand for public transport is dependent upon two factors: (i) the desire to make a particular trip at all, and (ii) the desire to do so by public transport.

With respect to the desire to make a trip at all, an essential characteristic of the urban transport market is that demand is derived and the costs of making a trip are weighed against the benefits deriving from the purpose of the trip. Oi and Schuldiner[7] broadly categorise journeys as 'production' or 'consumption' oriented. For the former, e.g. journeys-to-work and those made in connection with work during business hours, the costs attached to the trips are likely to be insignificant in relation to the rewards and, therefore, demand will not be very sensitive to changes in travel costs. 'Consumption' oriented trips such as those made for leisure, social, or recreational purposes, in classical economic terms, are 'optional' rather than 'necessary' and demand, therefore, will be more sensitive to the costs of the trips. Shopping travel tends to be a hybrid 'production' — 'consumption' oriented activity and the sensitivity of demand will fall between that for the two categories discussed.

The strength of the desire to make a particular trip by public transport is also related indirectly to trip purpose, the choice between modes being determined by the costs attached to them, including non-money costs such as time. Demand for the various trip purposes concentrates at certain times of the day, and this affects the relative costs, particularly the time costs of competing modes. For example, because of excessive demand and resulting congestion during peak travel hours, the time costs attached to car use are much greater than at off-peak times; on the other hand, the time costs connected with rail use are nothing like so affected, because of the latter mode's relative unsusceptibility to congestion.

The need to make a trip at all and to do so by public transport, is also determined by the available choice of origins and destinations for any particular trip. A large conurbation may demonstrate a highly varied pattern of trip making for all the common trip purposes. For example, journeys can be made from outside the metropolitan area to core, and reverse; from the outer suburbs to core, and reverse; from the inner suburbs to core, and reverse; and *between* and *within* neighbourhoods involving cross-town trips.

The vast majority of trips are home based and in the short term there is little flexibility in changing this as the origin of many journeys. Although in the longer term, of course, the consumer may be triggered to change residential location because of changes in the costs of making various journeys. There is probably also little flexibility in the short term for changing the destination of 'production' oriented trips, such as the journey-to-work, although once again, in the longer term, new employment may be sought because of travel cost changes.

By comparison, however, for 'consumption' oriented journeys there is considerably greater flexibility, and a change of destination may be made with relative ease and little consideration. For example, rising bus fares may encourage housewives to shop locally rather than in the city centre, or teenagers to visit suburban rather than central cinemas or discotheques. Therefore, where flexibility exists as in these cases, if the cost of the journey to destination 'i' is increased for a particular mode, there is the possibility that, rather than ceasing to make the journey at all or switching modes, an alternative destination 'j' may be chosen. This has been the case in recent years for many car-borne shopping trips, in particular where the increasing parking costs and congestion time 'costs' associated with city-centre shopping have not led to the abandonment of such trips or to a transfer to a public transport mode, but rather to a switch in favour of car-based journeys to suburban and even out of town shopping centres. This further reinforces the greater sensitivity of demand which we hypothesise to exist for trips of this nature.

Demand factors affecting modal choice

So far we have considered the broad nature of urban travel demand but not the entire range of specific factors determining modal choice. In the analysis, reference has been made to both time and money costs as determining modal choice. The nature of the factors comprising these costs, their relative importance and interrelationship, is only imperfectly understood. The transport economist, particularly in predictive analysis, distinguishes these two major elements, time and money costs, and much effort has been expended in attempts to quantitatively value time savings. Quantification is necessary, for example, for transportation modelling purposes where a common unit of analysis is required in order to allocate trips to particular modes in a statistical model. Units of time are therefore given a money value and may be combined with the cost or fare incurred by the traveller when making a particular trip to give its total cost. This single quantity is commonly referred to as the 'generalised cost' and trips are assigned to particular modes on the assumption of preference for the one with the lowest generalised cost.

However, there is little doubt of the inadequacy of generalised cost, as it is now computerised, as an explanation of modal choice. Stopher[8] for example, has shown by statistical analysis that time and money cost factors explain modal choice in only 44—64 per cent of cases for 'choice' riders (i.e. those with access to both car and public transport modes). This is inevitable because generalised cost takes no account of convenience, comfort, promotion, nor of the behavioural circumstances which undoubtedly affect many decisions. Further, as is demonstrated below, the valuation of time savings is itself a contentious process.

The transport manager must extend his analysis beyond the assumption of a simple two-element consumer decision-making process when determining the most competitive mix of service and promotional attributes in comparison with other modes. While the importance of cost and time elements must not be underrated, it is contended that modal choice decisions result from an evaluation of the following elements, which we define as the marketing-mix for public transport:

1 Service attributes: (a) Price
                        (b) In-vehicle time
                        (c) Mesh density (i.e. route density affecting access time to and from the mode)
                        (d) Frequency
                        (e) Reliability
                        (f) Comfort

2 Promotion

While mesh density, frequency and reliability undeniably affect total journey time and might therefore be subsumed under time in another model, they are treated here, and in chapters 6 and 7, as independent elements. There are a number of reasons for this. They are undoubtedly, as we shall show, perceived to be separate and discrete service aspects by the consumer and one may assume, *a priori*, that changes in different elements will bestow varying levels of utility upon him. Further, they extend beyond the time dimension; for example, high frequency lowers the traveller's need for journey planning and detailed knowledge of timetables, while low reliability increases the risk attached to using a particular mode. Finally, these items represent the range of discrete variables available to the operator for manipulation. In determining the most competitive service levels it is these variables he must consider and inevitably 'trade-offs', as for example, between frequency and mesh density, will be involved.

1 *Service attributes*

(a) *Price* In general, the importance of travel varies with the good for which it is jointly demanded. The cost will be relatively unimportant in trip purposes where journey costs are a very small proportion of total costs, or represent a small price to pay for the resultant reward. For most 'production' oriented journeys, especially the journey-to-work, lower journey costs are unlikely to stimulate more travelling since the rewards are normally vastly greater than these costs; however, price differentials may possibly by instrumental in modal choice. In particular, they might affect long term decisions such as whether to purchase a car.

Shopping trips are often more sensitively balanced because of the respective pulls of city centre and local shopping locations. For leisure trips, the price sensitivity of the consumer can be widely different according to the nature of the trip; for example, one would anticipate a difference in sensitivity between, on the one hand, a visit to an expensive night club and, on the other, an irregular social call.

(b) *In-vehicle time* We have suggested that quantification of the consumers' valuation of time savings would aid managerial decision making and that considerable effort has been expended by transport economists in this area but that such work is complex and only partially solved.

When comparisons are made between a range of cost-time mixes offered by the different modes available — the principal issue is the way time savings can be used for alternative purposes. As Sharp and Jennings[9] point out, savings of small time quantities have very different values from longer periods saved. To save ten minutes might permit some constructive and valuable leisure or work activity, whereas one minute saved might be worthless. However, there will be occasions when even a minute's saving may be vital either to the completion of a task or the opportunity of commencing one.[10] Attempts to overcome these difficulties have been made by estimating an average value for given uses and users but the subject is highly controversial. For example, the Department of the Environment values working time saved at the average wage rate plus associated costs, the assumption being made that the average wage equals the marginal value product. Given market imperfections, particularly in relation to the utilisation of time savings, the approach is somewhat crude. The majority of empirical research work has concentrated on deriving values of non-working time, especially with regard to commuting, from statistical analyses of observed 'trade-offs' of travel time savings against cost. In general the findings support the *a priori* notion that work time saved, as compared with non-work periods gained, attracts a higher value. Furthermore, there appears to be support for the intuitive hypothesis that better paid people are willing to pay a greater money price in return for time savings. Beesley's study at the Greater London Council Offices[11] showed that the mean value of transport time of clerical officers was approximately 16p per hour. Stopher,[12] using a sample of the academic staff of University College, London, in an attempt to predict car usage for car owners, derived a value of time of 62½p per hour. A subsequent survey undertaken by Stopher[12] at County Hall, London, analysed the value of time of car owners in different income categories. The results are reproduced in Table 2.4.

For incomes over £3,000 (1966 levels) the relationship does not appear to hold which might reflect the highest income group's affinity to in-vehicle leisure or work activities (e.g. reading reports) and a dislike of driving the longer distances which would normally be required of wealthier commuters who probably live some distance from their work place. However, in Stopher's case the sample size and statistical significance of the results for this class were relatively low.

Table 2.4

Value of time by income category among London local government office staff

Income (£)	Value of time (New pence per hour)	Correlation co-efficient	Value of time as a proportion of the wage rate	Sample size
Under 1,000	11·25	0·77	0·32	415
1,000—1,499	16·25	0·80	0·26	514
1,500—1,999	20·00	0·77	0·23	321
2,000—2,999	27·50	0·66	0·21	214
3,000 and over	5·00	0·49	—	73

Source: Stopher[12]

Although one must bear in mind the shortcomings of existing valuation techniques, social cost-benefit analyses demonstrate that time savings are often a significantly high proportion of the total benefits; for example in the Victoria Line study over 50 per cent of the benefits accrued from time savings both to travellers on the system, but more importantly, to those remaining on the less congested roadway system.[13] Similarly, in most transportation models the accepted time valuations suggest that time costs far outweigh money costs as a determinant of modal choice.

(c) *Mesh density* Most of the studies referred to in the discussion of time estimate values which apply to total journey time, and do not disaggregate particular values for walking, waiting, and in-vehicle time, which one would expect to be different according to the disutility attached to each activity. Studies by Quarmby[14] and the Institut d'Amenagement et d'Urbanisme de la Region Parisienne[15] support this hypothesis and suggest that time savings for walking and waiting time are valued at 2—2½ times the rate for in-vehicle time. One would, therefore, expect access time to have a relatively high weighting as a determinant of modal choice and mesh density to be an important characteristic of the transport system. (This finding also has implications for the importance of reliability and frequency, see below.) There is every reason for supposing that modes which provide a direct door-to-door service will be clearly favoured.

(d) *Frequency* This is another important determinant of modal choice.

The more frequent a service the greater the probability that public transport schedules and desired arrival times will harmonise so that total journey time is likely to be less for frequent services. Highly frequent services are therefore more 'convenient' while they also reduce the need for expensive route schedule information. Finally, they lower the consumer's dependence on reliability and particularly his susceptibility to considerable inconvenience resulting from missed journeys caused by breakdowns or labour shortage.

(e) *Reliability* Reliability comprises punctuality of vehicle arrival at the embarkation point; punctuality of vehicle arrival at the destination; avoidance of periodic breakdowns of the vehicle; and avoidance of periodic and unpredictable breakdowns of the total transport system.

Control over (or having complete confidence in stated) departure and arrival times can be an essential attribute in urban travel. Workers with rigid starting times are likely to place a premium value on trip punctuality, but the priority is likely to be lower for the journey home. For shoppers this feature is, perhaps, of less importance because shops are open much of the day and lost time can usually be made up. Leisure trips exhibit different characteristics with respect to punctuality; for those designed to culminate in a fixed rendezvous time this aspect will, of course, be significant. In summary, given the high disutility attached to waiting time, whether it be at the embarkation point or in the vehicle, one would expect reliability to be an important determinant of modal choice.

(f) *Comfort* Comfort is an amalgam of a large number of elements. For example, in-vehicle comfort might be expressed in terms of (i) the noise, visual and balance disturbance arising from a particular mode's different states of motion, (ii) ventilation — e.g. temperature, humidity and air composition, (iii) illumination levels, (iv) body fatigue caused by the inclination, position and number of seats available and the materials used to construct these, (v) the amount of privacy afforded, (vi) the capacity of, and access to, space for packages accompanying travellers, and (vii) the visual and textural aesthetics, e.g. decor and lay out design. In addition, where the trip cannot be completed by one door-to-door mode, there are the various aspects of comfort or discomfort associated with waiting at, or walking to and from, points of interchange. Such combinations are understandably difficult to quantify owing to the interrelationships involved and not least because psychological factors tend to play a large part in deciding acceptable standards of comfort. Tolerance levels will differ widely among individuals, age and socio-economic groups and cultures, and will be further linked to trip length and purpose. For example, it can be expected that more elderly, and especially infirm, passengers will focus on the problems of getting into and out of vehicles and be generally more concerned with the physical ease of riding. The more affluent will tend to place a relatively higher premium on the provision of a range of convenience 'extras'. Most travellers undertaking longer trips will obviously appreciate more space, better air conditioning and other facets of comfort designed to reduce body and mental fatigue, while those en route for, say, the theatre may require different standards of many dimensions from housewives on shopping excursions.

2   *Promotion*

Modal choice will be further determined by consumers' perceptions of the characteristics of competing modes; this choice is made not on what is 'objectively' true about alternative modes, but on the basis of what is perceived to be true. The various media used to promote the product attributes will have a bearing on these perceptions. Promotion comprises a number of diverse elements, including advertising, public relations and control of the corporate image, but common to each element are two basic concepts, information and persuasion. The former may be expected to be particularly important for complex services, particularly where they involve interrelated systems as for the public modes. With regard to the second, it has already been stated that the competitive characteristics of the alternative modes may be expected to vary according to trip purpose and origin and destination configurations. In a competitive environment one would anticipate that the advantage of the various modes *vis-à-vis* these factors would be persuasively presented by the respective organisations.

Competitive travel modes

Alternative urban transport modes can be identified easily as (a) those involving human motive power, such as walking and cycling; (b) various public transport media, buses and fixed track vehicles; and (c) the private car — under this heading would be included the car driver, car passenger, motorcycle and scooter rider, commercial vehicle user and taxi passenger (although the taxi cab concept can be applied with modification to public transport).

Walking and cycling can be largely discounted. The former is becoming a fast declining mode because of the greater journey distances created by 'urban sprawl'; the latter, apart from some short distance, local neighbourhood trips is adversely affected due to its technological obsolescence, and the density of motor traffic, especially in inner and central districts, makes it an increasingly less safe means of travel.

Thus, the range of effective competition is largely confined to private automobile and public transport modes and, as has been demonstrated, the car is steadily eclipsing public transport in most of its markets. Public transport is only holding its share in certain cities where, because of acute city centre congestion and severe parking restrictions, the car is not as effective an alternative for most commuters, e.g. as in New York, Chicago, London and Geneva.

In general the market for urban transport falls along the following spectrum:

| The pole of the captive car user | _____ | The pole of the captive public transport user. |

People without access to cars represent one end of the spectrum; at the opposite are those travellers who need their cars for work — e.g. travelling sales representatives, service engineers and the like — and these clearly cannot be attracted to public transport usage. Others have to a varying degree a choice of their transport mode. The automobile offers one or all of the following advantages to such riders:

(a) The journey time is faster by private car for the vast majority of journeys. The only exceptions are journeys of less than ¼ mile, where walking may be faster (cycling may be a quicker mode for distances up to ¾ mile), and for longer distance commuting journeys to the central area where rail might be faster, given that their home and work locations are in close proximity to the rail system. In recent years bus speeds have declined both absolutely and relatively. The relative decline is effectively demonstrated by Smeed and Wardrop,[16] who show that journeys by car are as much as two and a half times faster than by bus and that average car speeds have increased 22 per cent between 1963 and 1972 relative to bus. The car's advantage stems from the greater control the motorist has over speed and route selection and, of course, he is not subject to the delays involved in having to pick up and disembark passengers. The widening gap between bus and car is further explained by the greater relative benefit given to the car by the traffic management schemes of the 1960's; for example, the introduction of one way systems, which often meant circuitous routes for public road transport which led them away from their optimum pick-up and set-down points. The advent of one-man bus operation has also meant much longer stop times.

(b) Depending on the availability of parking space, door-to-door transport is more likely when the journey is made by car. Parking is increasingly difficult in central areas, but by the same token dispersal of employment and shopping locations usually means ample parking facilities for those not travelling to the city core.

(c) The car invariably affords far greater flexibility of timing in leaving home and more particularly in leaving work, or in completing shopping and social visits. The great advantage of flexibility is where the parameters of time are relatively unestablished and it will be especially prized by the housewife whose curriculum is, more than the commuter's, one for individual choice and without rigorous routine.

(d) For most modes of private transport, the journey itself is likely to be more comfortable in terms of, say, seating and ventilation. The car also offers convenient storage capacity, particularly useful for journeys involving shopping.

(e) Finally, travelling by car is considered by many drivers to be positively enjoyable; the actual sensation of driving is thought to be pleasurable. It is often argued that there are very strong emotional drives associated with car ownership and use not simply because of the possible utilitarian benefits to be gained, but also because of a host of associations so frequently coupled with the product in conversations and in the popular literature. These have clearly been fostered by aggressive promotion of the motor car by manufacturers. This factor, and the relatively weak promotional mix adopted by transport operators will be explored more fully in chapters 4 and 6. Unfortunately there appears to be a paucity of research-based published material available to support or deny the existence of these associations, although one motivational study conducted in America has confirmed that the motor car satisfies a gamut of intangible needs only tenuously linked to transport requirements. It highlighted the role of the car as a social symbol and as a means of expressing individual personality or self image. However, one wonders, against a background of increasing car ownership levels and use constraints, whether these factors are still, or will remain, as potent as the 1957 study indicated.

By way of offsetting these advantages, public transport has usually been seen to offer very little, especially as its services are at present marketed. For some it can reduce the physical strain which might be associated with driving in congested areas and allow travelling time to be used more remuneratively. It relieves the traveller, especially the city centre commuter and shopper of parking problems and where they are at their most extreme it may offer, occasionally, a faster service, e.g. for longer journeys into city centres catered for by rail or by special express bus services. While public transport has difficulty in catering for diverse types of demand because of its relative inflexibility and unreliability it can be advantageous for organised group travel. However, a new competitive advantage to public transport seems to be emerging as a result of the dramatic increases in petrol costs since 1973.

Evidence exists[18] which indicates that for a very large proportion of motorists petrol costs constitute the major part of the perceived expenses of making a trip. Prior to the energy crisis it could be concluded from a comparison of car fuel costs and public transport fares that the latter were decidedly dearer for most journeys. Extensive though the post-1973 petrol price increases have been, and as much as they will undoubtedly have caused motorists to reflect on the considerably changed pattern of cost differentials between travel modes, they do not seem to have influenced a significant number of car users to switch to public transport. During 1974 UK petrol consumption demonstrated remarkable resilience. Even taking into account the period of the oil embargo when consumption was reduced by an estimated 10 per cent, total 1974 demand was only reduced by an estimated 5 per cent; however, this must be measured against the 5—6 per cent increase in petrol sales which has been common in recent years.

Several explanations can be posited for this relative buoyancy of demand. Firstly, approximately 40—50 per cent of motorists are able to treat motoring as a business expense. Many companies involved have thus been in a position to pass the extra costs on to the consumer in the form of higher prices for products and services, although some firms faced with an increasing 'price-cost squeeze' may in the circumstances have reappraised their executive car policies and travelling expense procedures and reduced employee entitlement accordingly. Secondly, rapid though the escalation in petrol prices has been, it is probably true to say that each increase has been less than motorists were conditioned to expect from numerous media predictions, e.g. British motorists were repeatedly warned that they might have to pay as much as £1 per gallon by Christmas 1974 when in fact the average cost had risen to 72p by this time. Where petrol cost rises have fallen short of the rates anticipated, and where these have been viewed against the background of rising wage levels, their impact on modal choice will have been somewhat muted. Thirdly, the more cost conscious motorists have been able to adopt several ploys to mitigate the effects of petrol price increases, for example, (i) by travelling at reduced speeds; (ii) by selecting more rational itineraries; (iii) by making fewer trips and in particular by reducing the number of 'consumption' oriented ones; (iv) by travelling to nearer destinations where a choice is available (e.g. with regard to shopping); and (v) by joining car-pool arrangements for the journey-to-work. In the longer term, higher motoring costs can also be offset by the purchase of replacement models offering more economical petrol consumption performances. Car manufacturers claim to have already discerned a sales trend towards models which are much more economic in their use of fuel.[19] In the case of one-car households the decision to acquire a second vehicle can also be deferred or even abandoned.

For traditional public transport users the effects of much dearer petrol will certainly have reinforced the attitudes of riders favourable to public transport and probably weakened the perceptions of those normally hostile, and possibly also reduced the desire of captive travellers to acquire a car of their own. As might be expected, a few urban public transport operators feel confident that they will be able to announce a small increase in the number of passengers carried in 1974 against 1973 returns and most undertakings are predicting that the rate of passenger recession will fall.

Thus, while dearer petrol has had some effect on modal choice, the influence of the 1973 and 1974 increases is only marginal, emphasising the importance of the non-cost benefits attached to car use. This is not to say that subsequent petrol cost increases of a very substantial order would not begin to exert a greater influence, and clearly the impact of the price variable in this respect should not be dismissed because of the experience to date.[20] However, indications suggest that for 1975 at least the differential between petrol costs and public transport fares should not be affected by, for example, fuel cost increases of the magnitude experienced in the previous year. In fact relative price changes could be to the advantage of the motorist, given the very high probability that extensive fare rises will have to be introduced during 1975 in order to combat mounting operational deficits, which will inevitably be exacerbated in a highly labour intensive industry by additional wage demand pressures.

The evidence afforded by surveys of consumers' perceptions of public and private modes and of actual modal-choice adopted provides substantial confirmation of the relative strength of the car as a mode of transport and in particular underlines the significance of the non-cost attributes.

A major attitudinal study has been carried out by the University of Maryland[21] and covered travellers' perceptions in Baltimore and Philadelphia. The study was concerned to determine the perceived importance of mode attributes and the level of relative satisfaction with them for car and typical public transport users for (a) work trips and (b) 'non-work' journeys. Using a sample of 471 household respondents made up of car and public transport users, the researchers, firstly, developed a hierarchy of key trip attributes for both types of journey and, secondly, measured the respective adequacy of the automobile and public transport modes in meeting these. In order to establish both the relative importance of the key attributes and the modal scores of satisfaction to be assigned to each, self-completion questionnaires containing seven point Likert scales and factor analysis were employed as part of the methodology of data collection and analysis. The findings have been summarised in Tables 2.5 and 2.6.

Table 2.5

Comparative importance of transport attributes and the effectiveness of the car and public transport — work journey

Key attributes	Mean importance[a]	Standard deviation	Net mean advantage of automobile satisfaction[b]
1 Arrive at intended time	6·40	0·96	+1·05
2 Speed:	(6·01)		
(a) fast as possible	6·13	1·28	+1·41
(b) arrive in shortest time	5·88	1·57	+1·00
3 Comfort prior to trip, e.g. protection from weather while waiting	5·97	1·54	+1·98
4 Mesh density:	(5·79)		
(a) avoid walking further than one 'block'	5·48	1·90	+0·67
(b) avoid changing vehicle	6·10	1·39	+0·86
5 Frequency — avoid waiting more than 5 minutes	5·83	1·61	+2·09
6 Cost	5·28	1·78	+1·14
7 Comfort — on vehicle:	(5·25)		
(a) uncrowded vehicle	5·10	1·72	+1·89
(b) clean vehicle	5·59	1·42	+1·01
(c) comfortable	5·62	1·41	+1·14
(d) package/baggage space	4·70	2·01	+1·74

Source: University of Maryland[21]

  [a]Scores are based on a 7 point scale, e.g. 1 = not at all important; 4 = of average importance; and 7 = of greatest importance.

  [b]The advantage of the automobile refers to the mean rating of satisfactions received by this mode less those received by public transport.

Table 2.6
Comparative importance of transport attributes and the effectiveness of the car and public transport — non-work journey

Key attributes	Mean importance	Standard deviation	Net mean advantage of automobile satisfaction
1 Comfort prior to trip: e.g. protection from weather while waiting	6·01	1·45	+2·31
2 Mesh density:	(5·79)		
(a) avoid walking further than one 'block'	5·58	1·72	+1·69
(b) avoid changing vehicle	5·99	1·41	+1·34
3 Arrive at intended time	5·67	1·47	+1·25
4 Frequency — avoid waiting more than 5 minutes	5·40	1·69	+2·30
5 Cost	5·24	1·81	+1·37
6 Comfort — on vehicle	(5·14)		
(a) uncrowded vehicle	4·01	1·45	+1·98
(b) clean vehicle	5·58	1·34	+1·08
(c) comfortable	5·65	1·30	+1·25
(d) package/baggage space	5·33	1·65	+1·82
7 Speed	(5·02)		
(a) fast as possible	5·23	1·61	+1·52
(b) arrive in shortest time	4·82	1·78	+1·05

Source: University of Maryland[21]

For the work trip, the major priority is clearly punctuality. Speed is also a high priority and for those using public transport, the importance of shelters is very much underlined as are the closely interrelated attributes of frequency, interchange and the distance between and from the pick-up and disembarkation points. With regard to frequency, unfortunately the figures fail to differentiate the opinions of those public transport users living near to the arterial routes (particularly those living closer to the centre and having this as their work destination) and those living in the more sparsely populated suburbs. The former, one would expect, take little note of timetables and rely on catching the first public service vehicle to arrive and are therefore more likely to value increased frequency; the latter are probably more conditioned to catch the same service every day and hence greater frequency would not be valued so highly. Comfort on vehicle was also considered important, but the wide standard deviations recorded probably reflect a polarisation of those making only short trips, and therefore able to tolerate lower levels of comfort, and those spending rather more time on the vehicle. Significantly, cost was allocated a relatively low priority.

Non-work trips were amalgamated; this is unfortunate since the different types involved — shopping, leisure, social — should emphasise contrasting trip attributes. The set of higher standard deviations is indicative of the more varied journey purpose as compared with the work trip profile. General 'comfort' and related factors are relatively much more important, in particular 'shelters', 'avoid changing vehicle', 'uncrowded vehicle' and 'frequency'. Punctuality is less vital, speed is almost irrelevant and cost again is not ranked high among the priorities.

The car was regarded as more advantageous with regard to all attributes for both trip purposes. In the work trip the differential was perceived to be greatest for travel time, susceptibility to weather and self-esteem. The car-bus differential was less marked, however, for mesh density, thus suggesting a concentration of work places in the centre which were relatively well served by radial public transport services. The differentials were even greater for non-work journeys which are explicable in terms of the more scattered destinations such trip purposes will have and the more random times at which such trips would be made. Also it probably reflects the greater average distance of intra-city trips in the US and the even lower levels of off-peak transport services available in that country as compared with those provided in the UK.

Thus the Philadelphia and Baltimore findings, useful as they are, should not be applied without a certain amount of qualification to the UK scene; it must be borne in mind that the US has far higher levels of car ownership and as indicated is less well endowed with public transport facilities. Nevertheless, useful hypotheses emerge from the Maryland study and some of the findings can probably be transferred directly to specific UK areas, for example, those containing higher socio-economic groups poorly served by public services.

In spite of lacking the same detailed analysis of trip facets, Wilson's research[22] carried out in Coventry and London is in many ways more useful as management information, even though the analysis was confined to the work journey. Wilson divided his respondents into non-car owners using public transport, car users not travelling by public transport and car owners using public transport. He also distinguished between work journeys made to central and peripheral locations. As such, twelve segments are considered and for work trips there is therefore a better breakdown than that offered by the Maryland study. Tables 2.7, 2.8 and

2.9 emphasise his salient findings.

A most interesting aspect of Wilson's studies is that they allow a comparison to be made between two highly polarised cities: Coventry, as one of the principal centres of the car industry, is highly car-oriented, while London has a public transport system more developed and better utilised than in any of the other conurbations.

Table 2.7

Comparison of inconvenience factors cited by public transport users in London and Coventry surveys: percentages

Inconvenience factors	Coventry core trips (sample 1637)	London core trips (sample 838)	Coventry non-core trips (sample 2237)	London non-core trips (sample 1203)
1 Comfort on bus/train/ tube:	(29·0)	(35·7)	(13·2)	(17·4)
(a) Not certain of seat	19·6	27·9	8·8	11·8
(b) Having to go upstairs (bus)	1·7	6·6	0·9	3·5
(c) Smoking allowed on top (bus)	7·7	1·2	3·5	2·1
2 Frequency:	(27·6)	(16·9)	(18·2)	(37·4)
(a) Too long to wait	26·0	15·3	16·0	35·3
(b) Bus/train/tube arrives at inconvenient time	1·6	1·6	2·2	2·1
3 Mesh density:	(26·0)	(19·4)	(50·0)	(18·1)
(a) Bus/train/tube stop too far away	24·1	12·8	27·0	10·3
(b) Have to transfer	1·9	6·6	23·0	7·3
4 Comfort off bus — no shelter	(16·6)	(4·0)	(13·2)	(15·4)
5 Others	0·8	23·5	6·8	11·7

Note: London figures do not differentiate between car and non-car users. Coventry figures relate only to non-car users.

Source: Derived from Wilson[22]

It will be noticed that the main inconveniences quoted by public transport users are the lack of comfort, the infrequency of service and the inaccessibility of the network. For the centre-oriented journeys in both Coventry and London the lack of on-vehicle comfort was roundly criticised,

Table 2.8

Comparative reasons for use of car in London and Coventry: percentages

Inconvenience factors	Coventry core (sample 923)	London core (sample 97)	Coventry non-core (sample 2704)	London non-core (sample 353)
1 Captive car users	(20·8)	(24·8)	(5·3)	(7·4)
2 Semi-captive car users:	(13·0)	(18·5)	(9·2)	(13·1)
(a) Use car after work	11·6	4·1	8·6	12·5
(b) Drive firm's car to work	1·4	14·4	0·6	0·6
3 Journey by bus/train/ tube too long	(23·9)	(8·3)	(31·1)	(27·4)
4 Frequency — wait too long	(20·4)	(9·3)	(14·8)	(19·7)
5 Mesh density:	(19·5)	(6·2)	(37·9)	(16·5)
(a) No public transport service	9·0	0·0	14·9	0·6
(b) Bus/train/tube stop too far away	8·1	3·1	14·3	9·4
(c) Have to transfer	2·4	3·1	8·8	6·5
6 Comfort on bus/train/ tube	(2·4)	(11·6)	(1·6)	(3·7)
7 Others	—	21·6	—	12·2

Source: Derived from Wilson[22]

primarily because of insufficient seating capacity during peak travel periods; this was seen as being particularly acute on the London underground system. Infrequency of service was the area most emphasised by riders making outer London work journeys and was also an important priority for trips to Coventry's core, and a not inconsequential priority for journeys made to and within Coventry's suburbs. The mesh density of Coventry's public transport system was seen as being in need of urgent improvement; understandably this caused much less inconvenience to London's commuters.

Wilson's analysis (see table 2.8) demonstrates how many more car-owners used public transport for central journeys in both Coventry and London, but how this was much more marked for London. The superiority of most facets of London's public transport system, especially for centre-oriented journeys, over Coventry's is further indicated by the large proportion of the 'other reasons' given by car commuters bound for

Table 2.9
Comparative reasons for car owners not using their cars in London and
Coventry: percentages

Inconvenience factors	Coventry core (sample 351)	London core (sample 1078)	Coventry non-core (sample 748)	London non-core (sample 1203)
1 Car not available:	(37·8)	(8·5)	(30·1)	(38·8)
(a) Being serviced	15·6	0·7	14·3	21·1
(b) Being used by wife/husband, etc., for work	18·8	1·7	6·9	8·1
(c) Being used by wife for shopping	3·4	6·1	8·9	9·6
2 Roads too congested	(35·0)	(28·1)	(27·4)	(27·4)
3 Journey takes too long by car	(15·0)	(25·8)	(20·2)	(17·7)
4 Came to work by 'car pool'	(9·4)	(0·1)	(17·9)	(0)
5 No suitable parking at work	(2·7)	(30·1)	(3·0)	(16·1)

Source: Derived from Wilson [22]

London's centre, representing uncoded and possibly highly idiosyncratic
responses. Once more frequency and mesh density failings were
underlined by the Coventry respondents.

The patronage benefits to be gained from a highly developed public
transport system together with the quite severe constraints on car use and
parking in central London was further reinforced by the fact that only 8·5
per cent of the car owners travelling by public modes to the centre of
London were without access to their cars (e.g. because they were being
serviced or being used by wives when questioned in 1966). The
corresponding percentage is considerably higher for each of the other three
groups.

Neither the Maryland nor the Wilson studies attempt to differentiate
perceptions of the market as determined by socio-economic and
demographic characteristics of demand (although the car may be perceived
in part as a proxy variable for the former). However, a study commissioned
by General Motors, US,[23] did analyse their findings in terms of income and
age. For the elderly (i.e. over sixty), attention was heavily focused on the

physical problem of getting on and off vehicles, and emphasis was placed on getting a seat, avoiding transfers, and the lowering, if possible, of fares. A significantly lower emphasis than for the total population was placed on time. Low income groups (i.e. less than $5,000 at 1971 income levels) placed a higher importance on minimising waiting time, the existence of shelters, and longer hours of service, while the young (under twenty) were characterised by much lower concern with the physical ease of riding than was the case for the elderly. For this group, convenience factors (e.g. 'adjustable air, light and sound' and 'coffee, newspapers, etc. on board') are relatively more important. The social consciousness of the young is also less primed, for they are much less concerned about 'riding in privacy' and 'avoiding unpleasant individuals' than were any of the other groups.

The future of urban public transport

The trends examined at the beginning of this chapter seem to portend an inexorable penetration of most trip-purpose segments by the car with a consequent further deterioration in public transport's fortunes and service levels. Before making such a prognosis, however, it is necessary to look at the technological and political developments which can be expected to shape the industry's future.

The technological environment

(a) *Some limitations on innovation* Changes which appear feasible and innovatory in public transport modes on closer examination would seem to be unobtainable in the near future for technical reasons and because of their exorbitant cost. Innovations such as extensive usage of moving pavements or individual, automatically guided city modules might only have very distant applications as major solutions. While others may look more proximate, many of them have less relevance to the real problem, at least in the UK. For example, the introduction of 'dial-a-bus' (which provides a personalised point-to-point service by responding to individual travel requests and is organised through a dispatching centre) might well demonstrate a consumer-oriented management stance and may even generate some traffic; but its application will be limited because it presupposes extensive telephone ownership and, unrealistically, a reluctance to use the car for off-peak trips when roads are far less congested.

(b) *'Rapid transit'* For many conurbations the most innovatory introductions during the next decade are likely to involve modernisation of part of the suburban fixed-track facilities. By using mainly conventional metropolitan rail concepts, such as those incorporated in London's tube network, these facilities will probably be extended so that additional corridors are served and fast and comfortable 'rapid transit' services operate into the very heart of the city.

(c) *Bus improvements* However, for the foreseeable future buses will remain the mainstay of public transport operations; and even in those cities such as Chicago, Munich and Hamburg which already have established rapid transit systems, the bus has an important interchange/feeder role to play — and, of course, it will maintain its traditional function in corridors where rapid transit is not to be developed.

It is in these respects that a more marketing-oriented approach, which has been woefully lacking in the industry, should spawn some helpful service improvements. We have in mind a faster and more widespread diffusion of such developments as: (a) 'express buses', which, if they are to do justice to their name, will require a combination of bus-only lanes, special feeder gates at traffic lights and the use of special roads on which cars and lorries are banned completely; (b) vastly improved on and off-vehicle comfort amenities for passengers; (c) two-way radio which will facilitate control of buses and could be used to prevent 'bunching'; (d) bus-rail interchange; and (e) more sophisticated and practicable fare collection and change dispensing systems which will allow full advantage to be taken of the cost savings realised by one-man operation without the attendant deterioration in journey times as is now the case. These together with a willingness to experiment with other elements of the marketing-mix, e.g. pricing and promotion, should, *when* allied to a favourable political environment, give the industry a much needed boost.

The political environment

(a) *The role of central government* There has been a growing awareness in government circles of the economic, social and environmental implications for urban life of complete car-orientation. Certainly, in the UK successive Conservative and Labour governments have during recent years shown themselves reluctant to submit urban public transport to the logical consequences of its unsuccessful competition with the car. Through a number of policy statements, published from 1967 to the present time,[24] the objective has been stated as limiting the use of private cars in urban areas, especially for peak work journeys to the centres of large cities and to make public transport a more attractive alternative. The essential elements of the Government's strategy has been: (a) to establish the organisational framework for urban transport planning to be undertaken and to provide a range of infrastructure and operating grants and subsidies to be made available (together with a considerable amount of technical advice); (b) within these organisational and financial parameters to place the responsibility on local authorities for determining their transport needs; and (c) to encourage local authorities to make comprehensive statements of their transport plans in the context of the wider aspects of land-use planning.

Under the 1972 Local Government Act, county councils are required to submit to the Department of the Environment transport plans encompassing policies and programmes of expenditure for the county as a whole and for large urban areas within them. Assuming these are demmed to be sufficiently comprehensive and integrated with other forms of county planning, and the transport choices made are based on an *adequate* level of evaluation of a *suitable* range of options, then it should be possible for county councils to receive a number of specific central government grants for developing local transport systems.

In the areas now governed by the new Metropolitan County Councils more formalised and professional administrative machinery was created by the 1968 Transport Act, which, anticipating the local government reforms implemented in 1974, established in 1969 four Passenger Transport Executives (PTEs) for the conurbations of Greater Manchester, Merseyside, Tyneside and the West Midlands. Subsequently, additional PTEs were created in 1973 and 1974, namely Greater Glasgow, West Yorkshire and South Yorkshire. The PTEs, which are our prime concern when studying the UK scene, have as their overriding duty to provide a properly integrated system of public transport, capable of attracting passengers from private modes through improved efficiency and convenience. In the planning and execution of this task allowance must be made for the effective implementation of the metropolitan council's town planning and traffic and parking policies. As an interim measure (i.e. until the metropolitan county councils were inaugurated in April 1974), Passenger Transport Authorities (PTAs) were set up to represent the interests of the constituent councils and to act as final arbiters in policy determination. To facilitate an integrated approach to transport operation, the PTEs were given at the outset complete control of the various independent municipal bus undertakings operating in the selected conurbations, were granted full licensing powers over any private operators and were charged with negotiating agreements with British Rail and the newly formed National Bus Company (NBC) over the range and quality of the services both are to supply *within* the metropolitan areas. The principle of ministerial control does not differ in essence from that described for the county councils' policy statements, and transport plans have to be submitted to the Minister according to an agreed timetable and he can prevent the implementation of programmes requiring central government financial backing if they are regarded to be incompatible with the broad criteria mentioned; however, he cannot ensure that 'optimum' decisions are taken in limiting the use of the car.

(b) *Local government attitudes* Individual local authorities are in something of a dilemma in the attitude they have towards the car. On the one hand, they fully recognise the dangers of its fecundity, while on the other, acknowledging that to discriminate too strongly and suddenly against it will effectively induce optional travellers to stay away from the centre and, perhaps, ultimately force necessity users to foresake the traditional central areas.

Quarmby[14] estimated that of the 69 per cent of the motorists who commuted to work in Leeds (in 1966) only 17 per cent would switch to buses given free travel. (Experiments reported in chapter 6 suggest that even this prediction is an optimistic one.) More effective, he argued, would be to increase car parking costs by 15p per day which he felt would induce 28 per cent to change to a public mode (conditioned more recently by inflated cost levels, together with increases in real incomes it is, of course, highly improbable that an extra 15p parking charge recommended in 1966 would act today as a deterrent).

While the number of car restrictions adopted by local authorities may seem prolific, the planners' hostility is being tempered in some cases by the expectation that stronger measures may well be self-defeating. Nottingham should provide an interesting test case for this hypothesis for they have recently introduced the most audacious package of restrictions, including the prohibition of on and off-street parking in a considerable section of the central area and an array of traffic management controls which provide for a large number of pedestrian and bus-only streets as well as extensive stretches of reserved public transport lanes and exclusive right-turns for buses at strategic junctions. As the scheme has not yet run its full course it would be premature to comment on its effectiveness and acceptability to the citizens of Nottingham.

The majority of the councillors elected by the first metropolitan county and district elections in 1973 appear strongly committed to advancing the twin interests of urban conservation and public transport; for example some urban motorway plans have been ritualistically torn up, and no doubt such policy changes will facilitate the task of designing and operating a revitalised bus and rail system. However, benevolent as the present political climate may seem for public transport, operators should not overlook how wide the gap can become between declared political intention and policy enactment: governmental administrative machines, driven as they sometimes are partly by the force of their own momentum, are not the best instruments for handling, at speed, sudden reversals of policy. Nor should the power of the motoring lobby by underestimated; its channels of expression are likely to be numerous and articulate.

Of all the environments the political one could be public transport's most unpredictable. Management can, however, reduce some of the turbulence by (i) formulating more attractive and efficient services rather than solely relying on the imposition of punitive constraints on the motorist to achieve its operational objectives, and (ii) adopting promotional strategies designed to foster more favourable attitudes towards public transport and explain the role it can play in improving urban life. In its dealings with political bodies it should arm itself with detailed and irrefutable information on its markets — which will be essential anyhow for designing its strategy and new service offerings — so as to reduce the element of political controversy to the minimum. These are matters on which the remaining chapters concentrate.

Notes

[1] L. E. Schnore, 'Use of public transport in urban areas' *Traffic Quarterly.* October 1962, pp. 488—99.

[2] W. J. Tyson, 'A study of peak cost and pricing in road passenger transport', privately circulated paper, Department of Economics, University of Manchester, September 1970.

[3] R. F. Bennett and D. McCorquodale, 'Public transport's role in urban areas' *Traffic Engineering and Control,* April 1968, pp. 596—601; also, R. F. Bennett, 'Road transport in a rapid transit system' *Institute of Transport Journal,* March 1968, pp.333—44.

[4] *London Transport Executive's Annual Report for 1972,* published 26 April 1973, and Sir Richard Way, 'London's transport crisis: getting what we pay for' *The Times,* 25 September 1973.

[5] M. A. Kemp, 'Some evidence of transit demand elasticities', working paper, Urban Institute, November 1971, pp. 327—77.

6 J. M. Thomson, 'An evaluation of two proposals for traffic restraint in Central London' *Journal of the Royal Statistical Society*, series A, vol. 130, pt.3, 1967, pp. 327—77.

7 W. Y. Oi and P. Schuldiner, *An Analysis of Urban Travel Demands*, Northwestern University, Chicago 1962.

8 P. R. Stopher, 'A probability model of travel mode choice for the work journey' *Highway Research Record No. 283*, pp. 57—65.

9 C. Sharp and A. Jennings, *The Value of Small Quantities of Time*, University of Leicester, 1971.

10 In this kind of circumstance it would suggest that journey time might be a key attribute in the decision to take an impulse trip. By and large, it is in terms of inter-city and, especially, international travel that significant time savings become possible and most highly valued.

11 M. E. Beesley, 'Value of time spent travelling: some new evidence' *Economica*, May 1965, pp. 174—85.

12 P. R. Stopher, 'Report on the journey to work survey, 1966' *GLC, Department of Highways and Transportation Research Memorandum 48.*

13 C. D. Foster and M. E. Beesley 'Estimating the social benefit of constructing an underground railway in London' *Journal of the Royal Statistical Society*, vol. 126, 1963, pp. 46—58.

14 D. A Quarmby, 'Choice of travel mode for the journey to work: some findings' *Journal of Transport Economics and Policy*, vol. I, no. 3, September 1967, pp. 273—314.

15 *Choix du Moyen de Transports par les Usagers*, Institut d'Amenagement et d'Urbanisme de la Region Parisienne, October 1963.

16 R. J. Smeed and J. G. Wardrop, 'An exploratory comparison of the advantages of cars and buses for urban areas' *Journal of the Institute of Transport*, vol. 9, 1964.

17 J. W. Newman, *Motivational Research and Marketing Management*, Harvard University Press, 1957, chapter VII ('Automobiles — what they mean to Americans').

18 See P. M. Williams, 'Low fares and the urban transport problem' *Urban Studies*, vol. 6, no. 1, February 1969, pp. 83—92, and M. Hillman, I. Henderson and A. Whalley, 'Personal mobility and transport policy' *PEP Broadsheet 542*, June 1973.

19 The *Financial Times*, 28 January 1975.

20 The extent to which motorists might be prepared to pay petrol prices very much higher than those of 1974 is indicated by a survey conducted by *The Sunday Observer* (13 October 1974) which analysed questionnaire replies from over 2,000 of its readers. When asked at what price they would finally stop purchasing petrol the figure most commonly quoted was an

astonishingly high £1.70 per gallon. However, long before the forecourt price level rises by over 2½ times in real terms the majority of motorists can naturally be expected to take steps to reduce their petrol consumption.

[21] E. T. Paine, A. N. Nash, S. J. Hille and G. A. Brunner, *Consumer Conceived Attributes of Transportation*, Department of Business Administration, University of Maryland, 1967.

[22] F. R. Wilson, *Journey to Work*, Maclaren and Sons, London 1967.

[23] T. F. Golob, E. T. Canty and R. L. Gustafson, 'An analysis of consumer preferences for a public transportation system' *Transportation Research*, vol. 6, no. 1, March 1972, pp. 81—102.

[24] See *Public Transport and Traffic*, Cmnd. 3481, December 1967, and *Urban Transport Planning*, Cmnd. 5366, July 1973.

PART II

The Managerial Response of Urban Public Transport

3   Planning in Urban Public Transport Organisations

Urban public transport as a 'product' has remained relatively inflexible in the face of the changing elements of demand. While we would not wish to minimise in any way the potency of the other contributory factors described in the previous chapters, we feel that the strategic planning and marketing processes from which the 'product' emerges have also contributed to the industry's long term decline.

In chapters 3, 4 and 5 we evaluate these processes as they have been adopted by the London Transport Executive (LTE) and the new metropolitan Passenger Transport Executives (PTEs) which were formed by the Transport Act of 1968 largely to remedy the strategic deficiencies of the highly fragmented public transport undertakings operating within the selected conurbations of Greater Manchester, Merseyside, Tyneside and West Midlands. The focus will be on the strategy formulation and implementation, undertaken by the corporate and transport planning and, in particular, the marketing functions, designed to handle the demands and uncertainties of the various environments — customer, competitive and political — reviewed in chapters 1 and 2.

Where the available data permits comparisons will be made between the five English executives and some of their foreign counterparts serving twenty-eight selected metropolitan areas in North America and continental Europe.[1] Such comparisons will be contained in an appendix at the end of this chapter.

The interrelationships between planning and marketing

Although in this chapter our primary concern is with corporate planning, it is important at the outset to understand the close interrelationship between this and marketing in order to show how successful corporate planning is a necessary requirement to foster the development of efficient marketing activities. Denning's definition of the corporate planning process provides a useful starting point in this respect. According to him it is:

A formal, systematic, managerial process, organised by responsibility, time and information, to ensure that *operational* planning, *project* planning and *strategic* planning are carried out regularly to enable top management to direct and control the future of the enterprise.[2]

The differentiation between planning types is important for they have different, but compatible purposes and require separate information inputs and planning techniques and the interdependencies between each must be carefully structured. The organisational means for achieving harmony in this respect are examined in chapter 5.

The determination of corporate strategy is the source of all other planning. Its main purposes are to compose a long term market-technology scenario outlining where the organisation's present and forward interests are thought to lie, and to prescribe performance objectives to be achieved. Those which are of a quantitative nature should be so formulated that they can be translated to the various management functions enabling them to undertake their contributions to operational and project planning, and be meaningful throughout the corporate hierarchy. The danger is that if they are not sufficiently precise they will exist only to be ignored.

Operational planning, having a somewhat shorter term, but consistent, horizon, and demanding a greater depth of approach, is concerned with integrating the future development of the existing range of each function's operations. It embraces such activities as formulating sets of functional objectives, resource allocation, scheduling and budgeting.

Project planning relates to specific commitments outside the actual scope of the present operations but which arise out of the corporate strategy and operational planning processes, or even those suggested by the short term exigencies of the present operations. As such, the time scales involved will be determined by the nature of the projects being considered, developed or tested: public transport examples may include designs for the major elements of an integrated bus-rail system based on rapid transit concepts, new vehicles or the development of existing ones, fare collection systems, experimentation with various components of the marketing-mix, i.e. journey time, frequency, regularity, interchange, price, comfort, promotion, etc.; and trials with a range of traffic management schemes. Marketing, as the function dealing with the customer and competitive environments, makes an important contribution to all three forms of planning, the precise nature of which is explained in chapter 4.

The need for corporate planning

The recent attempt to formalise, systematise and integrate these planning areas is the central aspect of corporate planning as a new departure in many enterprises, particularly with respect to the strategic element.

The factors which have been found in empirical studies to be associated with the existence of corporate planning indicate the advantages to be achieved.[3] For example, Denning found that corporate planning existed to a greater degree in firms whose environments are competitive and demonstrate high rates of technological change, in firms which are highly capital intensive, and in firms where growth is either above or below average. Further positive relationships have been found between the incidence of planning and company size and the complexity of its organisational structure.

The general benefits accruing from the existence of this function are several. Obviously a firm should demonstrate an improved ability to cope with change, because critical factors affecting performance are established, future problems are anticipated and thus reliance on intuitive reaction to events is reduced. Greater degrees of innovative thought and creativity should result from the need to search for alternatives and formalising the exercise should lead to a better appreciation of the likely outcome of particular courses of action and of the consequences of decisions. Finally, such planning should improve motivation of individual personnel, lead to an increased sense of identity with the corporation and reduce the risks of individual departments going their own way.

The case for planning in the PTEs is clear. Growth has been negative for a considerable time, predating their formation by some twenty years; and the inability of their predecessors to cope with the secular adverse environmental forces underlines the need for a major strategic rethink. Similarly, the 1968 Transport Act created organisations of some size and complexity involving the merger of many municipal bus undertakings and obliging them, once merged, to integrate their operations with the complementary services supplied by British Rail and the simultaneously created National Bus Company. The task of establishing a cohesive corporate unit from a number of independent units is obviously a complex matter requiring formal considerations. Anticipated levels of central government finance are also considerable, between £200 million and £300 million in most conurbations.[4] It is expected that such sums would not be allocated without proof of fully reasoned and detailed proposals for their expenditure.

The Government itself has encouraged the development of forecasting procedures to cope with these problems. In 1965 local authorities in the major conurbations were asked to undertake land-use transportation studies so that the mixes of land use and private and public transport usage could be planned in a co-ordinated and reasoned way.[5] Strategic plans are, therefore, essential to deal with long product development times where major infrastructure changes are almost inevitably necessary, and the methodologies developed in these studies have obviously greatly assisted the adoption of long term planning by the subsequently created executives.

In recognition of all these necessitating factors, the 1968 Transport Act included a statutory requirement for each executive to complete its first major transport plan within two years of its inception and, as will be shown, this requirement has dominated PTEs' planning activities over this period, and longer in most cases, since the time period has had to be extended.

Constraints on public transport strategy formulation with private sector and nationalised industry comparisons

The formulation of corporate strategic objectives by the PTEs is severely affected because they have a considerably greater number of controls constraining their present and possible future operations than do the vast majority of commercial companies in the private sector. The large body of management theory fails to prescribe objective formulation in a meaningful way in these circumstances. Before discussing in detail the corporate objectives that PTEs might and do establish, a brief analysis of both commercial and nationalised organisations will indicate more clearly the limited discretion available to the PTEs and the unique problems they face.

Strategic constraints and freedoms of commercial companies

Commercial companies enjoy considerable freedom compared with public industry and municipal undertakings.

(a) *Product-market scope* Private sector organisations may adopt whatever product-market posture they feel offers the best opportunities in relation to their broad corporate aims. Hence approximately one-quarter of the turnover of Tube Investments Limited comes from activities with which it was not directly concerned six years ago (i.e. merchanting and automotive exhaust systems). Such movement is facilitated by the relative freedom to develop new products in line with identified market gaps or opportunities, or often by acquisition and mergers with companies already established or with potential in such areas.[*] Although companies have to fulfil legal obligations and while most firms seek to promote their corporate images by observing what society generally perceives — and what governmental

70

regulatory agencies such as the Monopolies Commission from time to time 'pronounces' — to be good business ethics, the only real major constraints on the posture adopted by private enterprises are those provided by competition, resources and technological expertise.

Furthermore, private companies are not limited to a defined geographical market and indeed cover a spectrum in geographic scale from local or regional to multinational. This freedom provides not only unlimited potential opportunities for expansion into promising new geographical areas but withdrawal from those where saturation or other factors make it unprofitable to continue trading there.

(b) *The exercise of managerial discretion* The degree to which owners of private sector companies exercise control over the management is normally limited to negative feedback, such as, for example, when the executive directors fail to achieve rates of earnings and growth per share in line with shareholders' expectations. Feedback would in practice involve the selling of shares, especially if an attractive takeover bid is made;[7] only at worst would it entail a decisive vote of no confidence in the board at annual or extra-ordinary general meetings leading to its dismissal. The divorce of ownership and control effectively both frees management for the day-to-day running of the business and gives it relative freedom to take long range strategic decisions with the knowledge that in the overwhelming majority of cases they will not be set aside by any nominally higher authority. To a limited extent, some companies in the private sector may find their strategic freedom circumscribed by the 1975 Industry Bill (when this becomes law). Firms in which the Government acquires a share or who otherwise receive financial aid from the state are more likely to feel constrained, but others may also feel adversely affected by the provisions for disclosure, consultation and planning agreements.

Traditionally, the Government does not interfere with the prices set by private industry or with other elements of the marketing-mix, save in highly exceptional circumstances, as when the Monopolies Commission investigated the seemingly high advertising cost/price ratios in the detergent industry in 1966 and its scrutiny in 1972 of Kellogg's cereal prices after allegations of excessive profits had been made. Admittedly, more widespread government controls of a non-selective kind have recently been instituted as part of a wider package to combat inflation, but these may only be relatively short term measures arising out of the exigencies of near 'hyper-' inflationary conditions, and on the grounds that permanent price controls are both 'impracticable and objectionable' they could well be phased out.[9]

(c) *The setting of objectives* The objectives which are involved in this relatively unfettered environment often relate in qualitative terms to some development of, or departure from, the existing product-market scope. These objectives gain quantitative expression in terms of, say, target rates of return on investment. Thus despite the acceptance of other objectives such as, in particular, growth and survival, and perhaps social responsibility, a hierarchy exists which is undoubtedly headed by profitability.

Against this relatively unconstrained background private sector enterprises do not usually have much difficulty in establishing project and operational planning objectives. For example, when evaluating the feasibility of a particular project a specified rate of return can be used as an important criterion, although as O'Meara[10] has argued, additional indices are required to assess some of the intangible elements associated with the proposal. Similar financial targets can provide the marketing function with one measure of its market share penetration plans. For other departments alternative standards for testing the efficacy of plans may be necessary, for example, labour turnover and absenteeism rates and productivity levels for the personnel and production departments.

Strategic constraints/freedoms of nationalised industries

The situation is very different, of course, in the nationalised industries. Apart from the fact that public corporations are invariably denied the diversification opportunities[11] open to their counterparts in the private sector, many of the planning problems have arisen from the obligation to discharge quite divergent objectives. As Beacham[12] commented (on the NCB in 1950) '"Efficiency", the "public interest" and "balancing one's budget" are difficult horses to run in triple harness.' While acknowledging that more clarity of purpose now prevails, Long,[13] writing in relation to BR in 1969, remarked how the conflict between the 'profit motive' and 'public service' had led to 'soggy' objectives which had been difficult to translate into operational terms.

The nature of governmental control in many ways exacerbates the difficulties in the planning process.

(a) *Public service and the profit motive* On the one hand nationalised industries have to accept a range of social obligations which include having to: adopt quite stringent safeguards designed to prevent the abuse of monopoly power; make adequate and efficient supplies and provide special services, and often unremunerative ones; consult consumer councils; and from time to time employ specified factors of production, especially indigenous ones. On the other hand, they are expected to 'break even' financially, which since 1961[14] has been interpreted to mean at least covering operating costs over, say, a five-year period, meeting the costs of interest and depreciation and making reserves available to enable assets to be replaced at current prices to fund future capital development.

After many faltering steps during two decades of public enterprise experience the Government, in a 1967 White Paper,[15] recognised explicitly that where significant social and wider economic costs have to be borne and these are in conflict with a public corporation's commercial interests a subsidy payment or appropriate adjustment to the board's financial objectives would have to be made. The general problem, however, and one which has yet to be resolved satisfactorily, is establishing a practical formula that relates the amount of the subsidy to the net social benefits involved, the extent to which the nationalised industry concerned is deflected from its financial goal and maintaining, or preferably improving, the cost efficiency of that industry.[16]

(b) *External scrutiny* Pryke[17] posits the view that the nationalised industries have been scrutinised more than any other part of the economy. Parliament's Select Committee on Nationalised Industries (SC/NI), special *ad hoc* committees and the Prices and Incomes Board (1967—71) have all made far-reaching and searching enquiries. While the flow of reports has brought about improvements in administrative techniques and practices both within the corporations and the Government departments supervising them, they have probably had some adverse effects on planning continuity.

In addition, and most importantly, there is constant ministerial control. This was intended to be confined to laying down broad policy guidelines and overall supervision and not to be concerned with the implementation of policies. Practice, so the SC/NI on Ministerial Control says ' . . . has revealed an almost reversed situation . . . Apparently Ministers have given insufficient guidance . . . "in regard to either sector policies or economic obligations . . ." but have been ". . . closely involved in many aspects of management, particularly the control of investment".'

Certainly the nationalised industries are ready to hand to act as instruments of a Government's economic policy, often influenced by short term (political) exigencies. Because price rises in the public sector attract the maximum amount of hostile publicity — for Government and nationalised industries alike — it has always been customary for proposed tariff rises to be subjected to critical governmental examination and often the full rate of increase sought has been disallowed. This control, together with other limitations on profit generation, has meant that the investment funds of public enterprises have had to be largely topped-up from Government sources, but not before capital expenditure plans have been thoroughly vetted by the ministries concerned and the Treasury. Refined discounted cash flow techniques may be applied, as Pryke suggests, but the Government's need to inflate or deflate the economy, often for electoral reasons, has also been a weighty consideration. Then there are the more fundamental changes in Government policy relating to public enterprise generally or to particular nationalised industries which a new administration may adopt once it has established itself in office.

What emerges is that against the extended time scale which most public corporations require to implement major strategies, they are presented with a very short period during which stability for planning can be assumed. This is not to say that the nationalised industries' role is a passive one. Some board chairmen have been known to press successive ministers, quite forcibly, not to make too many sudden policy changes which might undermine plans already being implemented. Similarly, they argue for financial targets and rates of growth (or decline) when developing new long term strategies that provide for a certain amount of flexibility and allow them to proceed systematically with their operational and project planning.

Understandably, their credibility will be linked to performance achievement and for several of the public corporations the financial record is a poor one. British Rail is a well publicised example, but nonetheless relevant in the PTE context. In 1963 on the abolition of its predecessor — the British Transport Commission — £1,192 million of capital debt was written off. The 1968 Transport Act, widely acclaimed as an imaginative approach to a perennial problem and a practical attempt to apply the social benefit principles of the 1967 White Paper, was intended to offer a new deal to British Rail, setting it on its feet and eliminating deficit financing for all times. Under the Act a further £628 million of accumulated debt was waived and approximately £60 million per year of social grants were made available for unprofitable passenger services (raised to £68·2 million in 1972). British Rail made a loss of £26·2 million in 1972 compared with £15·4 million in 1971 and a surplus of £9·2 million in 1970. In 1972 the deficit occurred notwithstanding the receipt of government subventions of £68·2 million for unprofitable services, £27 million partly to compensate for fare constraint and £32 million to meet a cash shortfall. In addition, British Rail has received a new generous range of infrastructure grants. Whether the problem lies with the management or outside the railways, there is clearly mounting pressure for revised obligations to be placed on the board.

The strategic constraints/freedoms of the PTEs

Into this somewhat confused and largely financially unsuccessful environment the first four Passenger Transport Executives were born in 1969, also having been spawned by the Transport Act of 1968.

In many ways the situation of the PTEs resembles that of the nationalised industries. Their operations must be conducted within a clearly delineated product-market scope, comply with social and commercial criteria, and remain strongly accountable to external authorities able to exercise close examination. On the other hand, the differences — largely of degree — need emphasising. Obviously, the PTEs are very much more restricted as to where and how they should operate. In relation to the scale of their activities the social obligations are possibly more intrusive; as we have seen this is because of the valuable contributions which a well-patronised public transport system can make towards improving the quality of urban life. The nature of external control exercised is more diffuse, probably more ambiguous and conceivably more turbulent. Owing to the way urban transport affects the every-day life of large numbers, and primarily because of the high rates of central and local government grants required to maintain a reasonably sized public network, the scrutiny of these, and other bodies such as the local press, can be more relentless.

(a) *The purpose of the PTEs* The prime purpose and the broad obligations of the PTEs are specified by the Act as follows:

> In the case of each designated Area it shall be the general duty . . . of the Executives so to exercise and perform their functions under this Part of this Act and section 24(2) thereof with respect to the provision of passenger transport services as to secure or promote the provision of a properly integrated and efficient system of public passenger transport to meet the needs of that Area with due regard to the town planning and traffic and parking policies of the councils of constituent areas and the economy and safety of operation . . . and . . . to ensure as far as is practicable that the cumulative net balance of the consolidated revenue account of the Executives and any subsidiaries of theirs do not show a deficit at the end of any accounting period.[19]

(b) *External relations of the PTEs* Since inception the PTEs have been dependent on the Department of the Environment (DOE) for expert assistance and, above all, funds for capital expenditure; until 1974 they were accountable to Passenger Transport Authorities (PTAs) in the sphere of policy decision taking, and during the same period relied on the co-operation of the constituent local councils, who were responsible for traffic management and highways; they also have to seek the 'administrative' approval of the Traffic Commissioners when implementing fare increases, route changes and new services.[20] On 1 April 1974, under the reorganisation of local government, the role played by the PTAs was transferred to the appropriate committee of the newly constituted Metropolitan County Councils.

The framework for much of the negotiation between a PTE and the DOE has been the long range land use/transportation plan for the area, one regarded as acceptable in broad principle by both the local councils concerned and the Department, and which emerged from a study of a range of options. The study in each case was instigated by ministerial 'suggestion' and was financed by a specific Government grant.

The main instrument for influencing the policy of a PTE was the provision of investment grants, which principally, but not exclusively, related to the development of infrastructure. The prescribed heads under which grants were allocated were:

Major rail projects, busway construction, railway and rolling stock, resignalling schemes, improved systems of train control, automatic fare collection and capital expenditure on buses receive up to 75 per cent infrastructure grant. New buses receive 50 per cent and . . . (rail) . . . station improvements, including interchanges, and ferries in urban areas may receive up to 50 per cent grant, bus stations, up to 25 per cent.[21]

In some cases grant approval was almost automatic, e.g. for new buses, but in other instances, e.g. a grant for a new rapid transit system, involved considerable negotiation. Some of the evidence given to the House of Commons' Expenditure Committee on Urban Public Transport Planning [21] was critical of this grant system: in the case of new buses it was felt that it had induced wasteful replacement; many of the academic witnesses argued that because the infrastructure grants had biased expenditure toward capital-intensive solutions it might have cultivated the feeling that these were automatically superior. As we shall see below, this grant system has been considerably modified subsequent to the reorganisation of local government.

Since inauguration, and until 1 April 1974, each PTE was accountable to a PTA made up of, in the main, influential aldermen and councillors who represented those local authorities whose combined geographical area of responsibility corresponded to that of the PTEs. The PTAs' controlling and policy-watching brief had been prescribed by the Act. The rationale for creating the PTA structure was to bridge the gap between the time the PTEs were established in 1969 and the creation of the Metropolitan County Councils in 1974; the latter assuming the first tier local government powers — including those for highways, traffic management, parking and passenger transport. The PTE had to consult and seek the PTA's approval on the following matters: all major estimates of expenditure to be incurred; any major reorganisation of services; any extension of services involving substantial outlay on capital account; agreements with BR and the NBC; and fare changes. Also the PTA has appointed Executive members and directly controlled the precepting of subsidies out of local rates and, therefore, the pricing policy of the Executive. The level of precept, if any, was determined by it but had also been subject, ultimately, to veto by the Minister.

Obviously, a number of these items were open to some interpretation and the level of detail into which a particular PTA probed depended to a large degree upon the attitude and ability of the chairman. If the resignation of the West Midlands PTA chairman in early 1972 [22] over the issue of the division of powers is discounted, the PTE—PTA relationships seemed to have been reasonably harmonious, although the Greater Manchester PTE suggested in its transport plan [23] a slight difference of opinion over the rate precepting policy which had been adopted. Generally it is suspected that most PTAs had been largely willing to be led given their temporary nature and the diffuse allegiances of its members.

One wonders, however, how much more vigilant the PTAs' successors will be after the Metropolitan County Councils get into their stride. From 1 April 1974, under the provisions of the Local Government Act, 1972, S. 202, the functions performed by the PTAs and by the several constituent local councils in respect of traffic management and highways have been fused. Also from that date any major anomalies between a PTE's operational boundaries and those of a metropolitan county have been adjusted. Thus a PTE has now become accountable to a council able to take an overview of land use and transportation.

That the Metropolitan Councils should be in a postition to adopt such a perspective was probably an important factor which prompted the DOE to propose its revised grant system. The DOE's aim has been to move away from the method of giving specific grants on a piecemeal basis to one which involves a transport supplementary grant. The key to the new approach is for the Metropolitan (and other) Counties to submit annually integrated 'transport policies and programmes' (TPPs), embracing all aspects of

77

private and public transport, roads, traffic management and parking. According to a proposal issued by the DOE the TPPs:

> would relate to and be informed by the medium term transport plans covering a period of 10—15 years ahead emerging from studies, many of which are already being pursued throughout the country. TPPs would, however, go on to translate the policies into costed programmes for action, firmly for the first year, with some confidence up to 5 years and more tenuously up to 10 years ahead . . . A fresh TPP would be submitted each year, rolling the expenditure programme forward a year.[24]

The broad (and somewhat ill-defined) criteria by which the DOE proposes to assess a local authority's package would relate to the adequacy of the methodology employed, the balance of costs and resources available and the extent to which the national as well as regional considerations have been taken into account.

In a paper, J. B. Cooper [25] of Liverpool Corporation was quick to point out how he saw the new grant scheme as forming '. . . an integral part of a local authority's corporate planning process . . .', one which gave it the opportunity to take the lead. In some respects the position may become analogous to that which has existed in London, where the GLC, since 1970, has been responsible for the activities of the London Transport Executive and has a large body of planners formulating plans relating to strategic issues (i.e. its Department of Highway and Transportation Planning) and thus it can counter the LTE's policy ideas with its own research information, and even take the offensive as far as strategic planning is concerned. Its interest in these broader issues is indicated by the publication of documents such as the two Green Papers on Transport.[26] The atmosphere seems to be one of relatively tough bargaining with the LTE defending its right to formulate transport strategy and handle its own day-to-day affairs.

With the gradual dissemination of ideas on the urban problem, public transport has been gaining importance as a political issue, and this helps to explain why the GLC has been taking a far more positive interest in transport planning. In the 1973 GLC and new Metropolitan County Council elections, car-use constraint and free or heavily subsidised fares were given prominent places in the Labour Party's manifestoes. If these pledges are enacted in full by the Labour Party-controlled council, in the light of the probable consequences party political policies on urban transport are bound to become polarised. For example, Tyson[27] has estimated that for Greater Manchester, if completely free public transport were made available, the rate poundage would have to be doubled. This would surely evoke hostility, not least from rate-paying motorists. More recent proposals to levy a fixed charge on all those using private cars in central districts — a notion favoured by the GLC traffic planners who suggest a £1 a day levy — are likely to arouse even more inimical feelings among motorists and, given many of the inflexibilities and inequities attached to such schemes, are bound to sharpen political party differences.

It is important that the PTEs should contribute major strategic inputs towards a total planning process, both during the transitional period when the new grant and planning system is launched and in the long term. As it is the transitional.phase may extend over an inordinate period of time according to the scepticism expressed by the Expenditure Committee's report. [21]

Given the political turbulence that could be experienced the more the mechanics of transport planning is allowed to pass into the hands of local government officials servicing relevant committees, the more difficult it will be for the PTEs to absorb some of the possible major switches in policy direction. Within a three-year election cycle such charges might seriously undermine the Executives' ability to develop and implement consistent strategies during the time period required to make even modest adjustments to existing land-use patterns and the public transport infrastructure.

It is our impression that the PTEs who will be able to exercise a reasonable measure of planning and managerial independence will be those who, since 1969, have established a strong corporate identity, formulated good long range planning techniques, and introduced some commercial acumen (e.g. tight cost control and energetic marketing) into organisations which traditionally have been too bound up in just running buses.

Planning undertaken in PTEs

Our research indicates that in all cases the bulk of managerial planning effort has been directed to the publication of a transport plan intended to prescribe a detailed infrastructure network in accordance with the demands of the Act (Section 18.2). Despite this, and notwithstanding an additional requirement that they should publish policy documents within twelve months of inauguration (Section 18.1), few of the Executives have explicitly defined their primary objectives beyond restating those broadly decreed for them. There is, therefore, a danger of evolving transport systems in a vacuum without the proper means for evaluation or control. What seems to be missing in this respect is a real appreciation of the philosophy of planning. Certainly in four of the five organisations studied, planning is largely regarded as a technical exercise, one which is based on a sequential relationship between land use and transportation study forecasts and transport plans. The former have been accepted as oracular statements: little attempt has been made to question whether the studies themselves have been founded on too few options, distinguished between the 'mobile' (or car-borne) and 'immobile' sections of the community, demonstrated the strong commitment prevalent in the 1960's towards urban motorway development or taken into account the consequences of car-use constraint and improvements in the public transport system. The impression gained is that in most cases the PTEs have not seized the initiative and stated with sufficient cogency what, in their opinion, the future pattern of public transport *ought* to be. Furthermore, there is only sketchy evidence that systematic and permanent machinery exists for conducting corporate strategic planning — as opposed to the narrower aspect of transport or network planning — both for the long term and for the future development of the entire range of existing functions and resources.

Strategic objective formulation in the PTEs

No PTE seems to have established objectives which are capable of being translated into practical project and operational planning terms, with the possible exception of Tyneside whose goal is to maintain 'the existing modal split until the end of the decade', but makes no attempt to justify the retention of the *status quo*. West Midlands and Greater Manchester have nothing specific to say on the subject, although in the case of the latter this in no way reflects a reluctance to make policy statements and engage in formal planning. London Transport expresses its objective as the maximisation of passenger mileage within the given financial constraint. Merseyside seeks 'to stabilise the number of passenger miles by public transport while at the same time attempting to increase total earnings'. A problem with objectives employing mileage as the prime unit is that the information systems available only permit crude estimates to be made.

It would seem considerably more sensible, therefore, to link strategic objectives to existing land use/transportation studies which, in view of the implicit criticisms made earlier, would need to be broader in their scope and, naturally, brought up to date. The unit of measure then becomes the modal split which could be applied to each major corridor and main segment of demand. Modal split is superior to passenger mileage as a criterion in exactly the same way that market share, all things being equal, is superior to ex-factory sales. Given the revised land use/transportation data the strategic implications of a range of modal splits for each segment can be assessed so that the most appropriate ones can be selected. For example, each would suggest: (a) the social benefits/costs accruing to the area as a whole; (b) the nature of the public transport structure required; (c) the degree of bus-rail integration and, in broad terms, the service network quality necessary; and (d) the internal and external financial consequences.

Such an approach, besides requiring the development of sophisticated planning techniques, might also involve persuading many prominent officials at central and local government levels to depart from committed positions, especially if these can be shown to exhibit an undue bias in favour of private motorists and are likely to lead to a dispersal of major urban functions with costly consequences in social, economic and environmental terms. While PTEs must be politically responsive, we feel they should spell out the ramifications of having to pursue policies which they regard as ill-advised, even if in the very last resort this involves a public debate. Nevertheless, it is difficult to dismiss without some considerable sympathy the comment of one PTE director:

> When I came . . . (here) . . . local politicians, officials, the business community and the press felt they had over-debated the . . . (land use/transportation study) . . . report. They all knew it had deficiencies and they were certainly not in a mood for us or any other body going back to the drawing board. Public transport and the problems of congestion were getting visibly worse, action was demanded and any plan that we could produce in about two years simply couldn't fail to make an impact for the better.

Long term transport planning

It is in the more technical sphere of transport planning that most effort has been made by the PTEs, although the emphasis found and progress made seem to be related to the Executive's attitude towards planning generally, the resources provided and the availability of the land use/transportation study for each area.

In the conurbations other than London the problems, methodologies and solutions of the studies — all of which have been completed — are remarkably similar. A natural commitment exists to the present periphery-core land use relationship and means are therefore sought to accommodate high density flows, at least for the journey-to-work to the centre. Some limitation in the rate of car use is proposed as is a measure of modernisation and extension of the public transport system; but a sizeable proportion of many study budgets was obviously pre-empted for new highway construction, e.g. the Tyne-Wear study assigned £109 million out of a suggested investement ceiling of £250 million, the South East Lancashire North East Cheshire (SELNEC) study (relating to what is now Greater Manchester) earmarked £50 million, and about £70 million was thus committed by the West Midlands study.[4]

Of the three PTE transport plans which have emerged, the West Midlands'[28] seems to be completely dependent on what the new Metropolitan County Council's interpretation of the area's land use/transportation and other studies would be; Merseyside[29] acknowledges the conclusions of its area's study (MALTS) with very little modification, while Greater Manchester[23] has accepted the principles of the SELNEC study (SALTS) but challenged some of its assumptions as well as arguing for a network more heavily oriented to public transport. Tyneside postponed drawing up its strategic plan and instead concentrated all its planning activities on submitting detailed plans for a rapid transit metropolitan railway — the North Tyne Loop — which it is estimated will form the backbone of its proposed future system at a cost of about £65 million, of which £50 million in grants has been earmarked from central government funds. Important as the Loop may prove to be in meeting the conurbation's future travel needs, it has nevertheless been conceived ahead of a through-going strategic plan being established and thus it may narrow down the range of options which can be considered, but in terms of the demonstration effect involved, the Tyneside PTE's efforts might well capture the public's imagination. A fortuitous side effect of this is that, by being single-minded in its determination to establish a rapid transit system, this PTE was able to submit its application for substantial government grants-in-aid at a time when far less stringent controls were being exercised. London's long term infrastructure planning has been awaiting the outcome of the Greater London Development Plan Enquiry but with a relatively refined tube and railway network is less in need of the radical reorientation which is required in the provinces.

It is interesting to compare the three plans. To a considerable extent the documents perform the same functions. They describe the land use/transportation planning framework inherited at inception; outline the procedures for updating this framework; state the infrastructure plan

82

adopted and the progress being made towards implementation; and, finally, suggest liaison procedures with central and local government.

However, despite these similarities, important differences are apparent. In the first place the West Midlands' plan is in a class of its own: it is completely passive, contains hardly one proposal that is not included in the area's study, and apart from a few speculative comments restricts its time scale to five years. In comparison with Greater Manchester's plan, Merseyside's is a descriptive document. The planning horizon is 1990. The immediate priorities contained in the plan are already being acted upon, including the building of the terminal loop and exchange central link and the establishment of a series of demonstration projects to test the interchange concept which is at the heart of the long term plan. Its stress is on adaptive planning. The MALTS study has been updated in very broad terms to 1976 with the possibility of a second five-year plan following that. The emphasis would be argued to be correct by the management concerned, at least until the feasibility has been affirmed by the demonstration project results. The Greater Manchester plan is a much more assertive document; its style is more flamboyant. Commencing with a synopsis entitled 'Lifeline 2000', it proceeds to place public transport in a travel market which will enjoy rising demand with increasing discretionary income and car ownership. Existing operations are reviewed and then forecasts presented, including the SALTS' forecasts and the PTE's opinions on these. Future plans are then placed in a strategic framework, and medium and long term plans enunciated for both·bus and rail, including the consideration of the phasing and financing of these.

Criticism of the SALTS study, while not directed at the fundamentals, covers four important assumptions made: (1) bus speeds and frequencies could be maintained at 1966 levels; (2) public transport fares could be held at 1966 levels at constant money values; (3) improvements to public transport can be carried out before significant losses of patronage occur; and (4) the increase in energy supplies necessary to accommodate the increase in private car travel can be found.

Each of these is refuted in turn and the case for public transport is explained by an evaluation of the competing modes in the existing and likely future environment. The medium term plan arising from this establishes priorities to be achieved on a five year base to 1977. The long term plan covers the period 1977—84.

One of the major emphases of the medium term five-year plan is for large scale provision of bus priority schemes and this reflects in part road congestion problems that are worse during the peak periods than in most other conurbations outside London. It also reflects a very basic approach where the bus is rightly perceived (in terms either of passenger mileage or numbers) to be the mainstay of the public transport system, so that while short term measures testing the feasibility of an integrated road-rail system are essential, effort must be made equally in less glamorous and more traditional directions. In the longer term the horizon is extended beyond the SALTS year, 1984, to the end of the century, to accommodate the long gestation required to build the necessary infrastructure. It is made clear that for the long term it is not a plan but a number of options that must be considered. The options outlined offer an alternative selection of rapid transit routes.

Of the three plans, this one looks further ahead, it is much more adventurous — and more professionally presented — and expresses an independent line on several issues. For example, it not only criticises the precept/fares policy pursued by the PTA but argues for higher levels of operating subsidy, on the sound welfare economic principle that non-users, in particular motorists, benefit from an improved public transport system in ways not currently reflected by the costs borne by these non-users (see Tyson[27]).

PTE project planning

Given the degree of uncertainty which must be attached to systems projected for completion in twenty-five to thirty years, and given the novelty and the hypothetical nature of certain of the product characteristics to be adopted, major short and medium term plans are being formulated in the PTEs to test these concepts and reduce the uncertainty attached to the long term strategy. Where such projects are of national importance they qualify for a central Government grant, earning demonstration project status. Such plans are, therefore, an important bridge between strategic and operational planning procedures, testing in microcosm the larger process which must evolve smoothly over the strategic time period. Essentially these plans test market alternative mixes in specific areas or corridors. For example, on Merseyside sixteen experiments are being conducted, aimed at identifying the willingness of the public to accept mode transfers as part of their journeys, the circumstances most likely to encourage transfers, the costs of operating the combined services and the overall economies of integration compared with services existing at present. In the Manchester conurbation a similar project is being planned to test the viability of purpose-built bus-train interchanges combined with a high frequency rail service. As such the Executive view the project as a 'test bench' for ideas before incorporation into the proposed Piccadilly-Victoria rapid transit network. Not only do such projects test concepts, they provide valuable, but as yet largely unrealised, opportunities for all categories of planning and marketing staff to work closely together in a manner which will be essential to the success of the long term strategy.

Operational planning and planning mechanisms

As defined earlier, there is little systematic and comprehensive operational planning undertaken in the PTEs, i.e. the strategic development of the present scope of the organisation's existing activities over some short to medium time period. What planning does take place invariably relates to budgetary control (in which the standards are established on a twelve monthly basis) and the short time-scale scheduling and manning of routes and services. However, only rarely are these two exercises, one financial and the other logistical, augmented by core corporate planning activities.

Admittedly, it is claimed in two of the UK survey organisations that 'corporate planning' posts exist. One of these is London Transport where the individual concerned controls a small unit operating within the finance function and is responsible for the *ad hoc* financial assessment of proposed projects. The other post is with the Greater Manchester PTE where the officer involved serves on a 'Corporate Planning Committee' consisting of three Executive members. However, little tangible proof of comprehensive planning seems to have emerged and the interrelationship between this committee and those engaged in transport planning seems obscure.

It would seem inconceivable when surveying the total planning process in the PTEs that the present highly fragmented perspective can continue indefinitely. If for no better reason the emphasis now being devoted to transport planning will force the issue in this respect. The infrastructure and network consequences of long and medium term transport planning will themselves start to predetermine 'operational' planning, as defined earlier. By allowing 'project' planning, and this is what most transport planning seems to be in the PTEs, to initiate and dominate the entire process of which marketing is a part, the 'strategic' element is virtually excluded. Most urban public transport systems in large cities, if they are to become competitive, require to be updated, and large scale investment allied to professionally conducted transport planning is demanded. However, more is required than technical planning expertise. For maximum effectiveness to be achieved, transport planning must be rooted in a thorough-going long term strategic land use plan designed to solve both the urban problem and the enormous difficulties of public transport operation, and during all its phases it should be guided by the marketing concept.

APPENDIX

Some planning comparisons between the five English PTEs and their foreign counterparts serving 28 selected metropolitan areas in North America and Continental Europe

The character of any organisation reflects its antecedents and the nature of its various environments. Thus it can be expected that the UK PTE-type structure will in some ways be unique. However, as was stated in chapters 1 and 2, most of the large public transport organisations serving the travel needs of North American or Western European metropolises face market problems whose differences seem to be more of degree than principle. Consequently many of the essential features of the PTE system described — the nature of its ownership, external relationships, prime aim and objectives and strategic decision-making processes — should equally apply to major urban public transport organisations in North America and Western Europe.

From Table 3.1 it is clearly evident that the majority of the survey organisations are completely owned by a public authority; and as Table 3.2 indicates, most of them are responsible to one governmental agency, such as an elected state, regional or municipal assembly with ultimate powers for traffic management and highway and land use planning for the areas coinciding with the operators' networks.

A major role assigned to the PTEs by the 1968 Transport Act is to plan and implement the integration of existing and future modes of urban public transport within defined metropolitan areas. As Table 3.3 suggests there are several international examples where a similar role is exercised or is in the process of being assumed. Admittedly the way it has been conferred differs: in some cases it owes its origin to state legislation or a municipal ordinance, and in others it has evolved by, say, a dominant operator, through a series of commercial acquisitions, taking over the remaining public transport franchises. Whatever the source there is an unmistakable trend towards greater planned integration of public transport modes in most North American and Western European cities.

In a small number of metropolises complete integration has been achieved, for example, Stockholm, Oslo and Rome, and the Executives concerned own all the public transport modes, namely the buses, fixed track systems, suburban railways, etc. Apart from the PTEs the operators serving the conurbations based on Chicago, New York, Pittsburg, Montreal, Toronto, Helsinki, Copenhagen, Amsterdam, Munich and Hamburg anticipate that they will become unified planning and

86

Table 3.1
The nature of ownership of the transit organisations*serving selected North American and West European conurbations — with PTE comparisons

	PTEs including LTE (total = 5)	North America (total = 8)	Western European (total = 20)
Completely owned by a public authority	5	6	15
Between 50% and 100% owned by a public authority	—	1	5
Less than 50% owned by a public authority	—	1	—
Entirely owned by stockholders	—	—	—

* Transit = urban public transport
Source: The operators

Table 3.2
Selected PTE, North American and West European transit organisations responsible to a government agency having powers for traffic management, highways and land use planning

	PTEs including LTE)	North America	Western Europe
Number in this category	5	6	14
Total number of organisations	5	8	20

Source: The operators

Table 3.3
Amount of responsibility vested in survey transit organisations for planning and implementing the integration of all transit modes

	PTEs including LTE (total = 5)	North America (total = 8)	Western Europe (total = 20)
Complete integration possible — overall executive planning and operational responsibility vested in transit organisations	—	—	3
Substantial integration relies on *formal* liaison between independent controllers of each transit mode	5	5	13
Limited integration possible — relies on *informal* liaison between independent controllers of each transit mode	—	3	4
Operators who anticipate assuming unitary responsibility for transit planning and operations within next five years	5	3	5

Source: The operators

operational Executives within the next five years. Some of these, notably Pittsburg, Munich and Hamburg, while having partially integrated systems of metropolitan public transport, have achieved a higher degree of integration than any of the PTEs.

Another important facet of the UK systems is that while the Executives are charged with having to formulate detailed long term strategic plans as well as commercial policy, relating to the existing networks (e.g. current objectives, tariffs, etc.), they must also be politically responsive to elected authorities who, in practice at least, have set broad planning guidelines to follow and approve the final plans. As Table 3.4 demonstrates, the pattern which emerges in this respect for the North American and Western European operators is similar to the one applicable to the PTEs.

When comparisons are made between the types of strategic objectives chosen and the basic considerations guiding the tariff policies of the PTEs with those relating to the majority of their North American and Western European counterparts, some points of similarity once more become apparent. Tables 3.5 and 3.6 underline these.

Table 3.4
The measure of control exercised by elected authorities over (a) the long term strategic objectives and (b) the current commercial policies of selected PTE, North American and West European transit organisations

	PTEs including LTE (total = 5)		North America (total = 8)		Western Europe (total = 20)	
	(a)	(b)	(a)	(b)	(a)	(b)
Decision-making processes fully controlled by an elected public organisation	—	—	1	1	5	8
Decision-making processes shared between transit organisations and authorities	5	5	6	4	13	8
Transit organisation has virtually complete autonomy	—	—	1	3	2	4

Source: The operators

Table 3.5
Principal strategic objectives of selected PTEs, North American and West European metropolitan transit organisations

	PTEs including LTE (total = 5)	North America (total = 8)	Western Europe (total = 20)
Improving profitability	4	1	6
Increasing passenger revenue	—	2	4
Maintaining/increasing passenger numbers	5	8	16
Maintaining/increasing passenger miles/km. covered	2	3	9
Attracting more passengers according to a specified modal-split target	1	—	14

Note: More than one objective stated by each organisation
Source: The operators

Table 3.6
Basic considerations guiding the pricing policy of select transit organisations

	PTEs including LTE (total = 5)	North America (total = 8)	Western Europe (total = 20)
Fares related directly to:			
(a) full cost	—	1	2
(b) direct/variable costs	—	1	3
Fares held at existing or some specified level by:			
(i) *mainly* cost reduction scheme	—	—	2
(ii) *mainly* public subsidies	5	6	13
Free or *largely* subsidised fares for:			
(a) all routes at all times	—	—	—
(b) specified routes at all times	—	—	—
(c) specified trip purposes (e.g. peak)	—	1	3
(d) specified types of passengers (e.g. aged)	5	2	14

Note: More than one consideration stated
Source: The operators

Table 3.7
Capital grants allowable from central and/or local government by selected PTEs, North American and West European transit organisations

	PTEs including LTE (total = 5)				North America (total = 8)				Western Europe (total = 20)			
	100%	≤50%	> 50%	Nil	100%	≤50%	> 50%	Nil	100%	≤50%	> 50%	Nil
Additional land and buildings	—	5	—	—	4	3	—	1	11	5	—	4
New fixed track infrastructure	—	5	—	—	4	3	—	1	9	8	—	3
new transit vehicles	—	5	—	—	4	3	—	1	9	2	2	7

Source: The operators

Increasing or, more realistically, maintaining the numbers of passengers carried and extending or, more practically, preserving the existing network are given high priorities by most of the operators as far as strategic objectives pursued are concerned. However, Table 3.5 does highlight a notable difference in this area: a far higher proportion of Western European organisations, as compared to the PTEs and North American undertakings, claim as a goal to attract more passengers to public transport in line with a specified modal-split target. If this does represent a pivotal objective on the part of the operators concerned then this would suggest that a more logical approach to corporate and transportation planning is being adopted. In this respect it should be borne in mind that the information on North American and Western European organisations was obtained by using self-completion questionnaires, and that relating to the five English PTEs surveyed resulted from extended personal interviews, and thus this conclusion must be regarded as somewhat speculative. Table 3.6 suggests that most of the operators are guided to a large extent when formulating their tariff policies by the desire to hold their fares at the existing or some specified level and primarily attempt to achieve this end through operating subsidies received. Table 3.7 indicates that the English, North American and Western European metropolitan public transport operators rely heavily on governmental or local authority subventions for financing new capital projects. If anything the grants-in-aid obtained by most of the North American and Western European organisations are more generous than those received by the PTEs in the past. However, higher levels of capital subsidy can result in less decision-making autonomy, which for some of the European operaters seems to be the case—see Table 3.4.

Notes

[1] Thirty-two major public transport organisations serving metropolitan areas in North America and contintental Western Europe were approached and twenty-eight of these agreed to complete and return questionnaire forms sent to them. The participants represented conurbations based on Montreal, Chicago, Pittsburg, New York, Detroit, Toronto, Atlanta and Miami in North America; and Oslo, Amsterdam, Copenhagen, Helsinki, Rome, Lisbon, Dublin, Geneva, Cologne, Basle, Genoa, Stuttgart, Brussels, Vienna, Paris, Rotterdam, Munich, Hamburg, Hanover and Stockholm in Europe.

[2] B. W. Denning, *Corporate Planning: Selected Concepts,* McGraw-Hill, 1972, p. 2.

[3] See B. W. Denning and M. E. Lehr, 'The extent and nature of corporate long range planning in the United Kingdom — I' *Journal of Management Studies,* May 1971, pp. 145-61. See also B. W. Denning and M. E. Lehr, 'The extent and nature of corporate long range planning in the United Kingdom — II' *Journal of Management Studies,* February 1972, pp. 1—18.

[4] The Department of the Environment has indicated by way of a 'guideline for design' the following grant allocations: Greater Manchester, £250 million for 1968—84; Tyne/Wear, £245 million for 1966—84; Merseyside, between £225 million and £275 million for 1966—91; and West Midlands, £200 million to 1981. See the Expenditure Committee's Second Report on *Urban Transport Planning,* HMSO, 14 December 1972.

[5] See the recommendations in the report of the Planning Advisory Group to the Ministry of Housing and Local Government, 1965. Also *The Future of Development Plans,* HMSO, 1965. Previously the only formal strategic planning conducted in this context by the local authorities were co-ordinated highway proposals based on projections of past incremental trends of traffic.

[6] *Transport Act, 1968,* HMSO, 1970, pt.II, ch.73, s.18, p. 33.

[7] See R. Marris, *The Economics of Managerial Capitalism,* Macmillan, 1964, and A. Singh and G. Whittington *Growth, Profitability and Valuation,* 1969.

[8] *Industry Bill 1975 (Bill 73),* HMSO, January 1975.

[9] See the ninth report of the all-party House of Commons Committee on *'Public Expenditure, Inflation and the Balance of Payments',* HMSO, August 1974.

[10] J. T. O'Meara, Jr, 'Selecting profitable products', in E. C. Bursk and J. F. Chapman (eds.) *New Decision-Making Tools for Managers,* Mentor, 1965.

[11] The industries' parameters are defined by Acts of Parliament. Each corporation is not free to diversify, with minor exceptions, into other distinct technologies which it feels offer better returns on investment. Some geographic flexibility is possible: NCB and BSC are able, and have been encouraged to develop foreign markets; BR and naturally the State airlines extend or contract their networks abroad. However, a proposal to withdraw from a traditional domestic market may well be rejected on social grounds.

[12] A. Beacham, 'The position of the coal industry in Great Britain' *Economic Journal*, March 1950, pp. 9—18.

[13] R. A. Long, 'Planning in British Railways' *Long Range Planning*, December 1969, pp. 72—7.

[14] See *Financial and Economic Obligations of the Nationalised Industries*, Cmnd.1337, HMSO, 1961.

[15] Cmnd.3437, HMSO, 1967.

[16] One would expect the Government to use social-cost benefit analyses to test whether an activity which, in itself, does not accord with traditional accounting criteria should be subsidised. A. Prest and R. Turvey — 'Cost-benefit analysis' *Economic Journal*, vol.75, 1965, pp. 683—735 — have highlighted some of the limitations of the methodology. In terms of compensating the supplier for providing service the economist would advocate the opportunity cost principle being employed. However, assigning a figure to the most remunerative option available poses a number of not inconsequential problems, e.g. (i) choosing a profitable alternative, (ii) calculating the net savings which would accrue if the activity were not performed and (iii) estimating a hypothetical net profit from the potential reinvestment, which would also include assessing the consequences of reallocating the overheads. Nevertheless, the principle seems superior to that of using incremental costs entailed since this would not only ignore the opportunity cost element but would not provide an incentive to make the supply more efficiently.

[17] R. Pryke, *'Public Enterprise in Practice'*, McGibbon and Kee, 1971.

[18] The Select Committee on Nationalised Industries report on *Ministerial Control of the Nationalised Industries*, HMSO, 1968.

[19] Op.cit., s.10, p. 15 and s.11, p. 21.

[20] Area traffic commissioners, who were originally appointed as a result of the 1930 Road Traffic Act to defend the 'public interest' and act as arbiter between private and municipal operators competing for licences, are grouped into eleven semi-independent tribunals for the whole of the country. Each is chaired by a permanent official of the DOE. The role of the traffic commissioners could become largely redundant in an area served by a PTE, since under s.19 of the Transport Act of 1968, the Minister has the

right to appoint a date from which no person other than the executive shall provide a bus service without the PTE's agreement.

[21] The second report from the Expenditure Committee on *Urban Transport Planning*, vol.1. HMSO, 1972, pp.xxxix.

[22] *Motor Transport*, 3 March 1972.

[23] *Public Transport Plan for the Future*, issued by Greater Manchester PTE, January 1973, p. 99.

[24] J. C. Collier, 'Transport policies and programmes associated with transport grant', a paper read to a seminar organised by the Planning and Transport Research and Computation Company Ltd., 25-29 June 1973 at the University of Sussex.

[25] J. B. Cooper, 'Transport policies and programmes — a local authority view', a paper read at the University of Sussex seminar.

[26] The Green Paper on *The Future of London Transport*, Greater London Council, 1970, and The Green Paper on *Traffic and the Environment*, Greater London Council, 1972.

[27] W. J. Tyson, 'Financing of public transport' *Local Government Finance*, July 1972, pp. 273—6.

[28] *A Passenger Transport Development Plan for the West Midlands*, prepared by the West Midlands PTE, 29 November 1972, p. 88.

[29] *A Transport Plan for Merseyside*, jointly prepared by the Merseyside PTA and PTE, March 1972, p. 158.

4 Marketing in Urban Public Transport Organisations

The nature of marketing

In any commercial enterprise marketing is intended to achieve certain corporate objectives, such as target levels of sales and profitability, by (i) identifying and defining the needs of selected customer groups, (ii) translating these requirements into product and service specifications, and (iii) through the formulation and implementation of demand-influencing policies, delivering the resulting products and services to the organisation's various market segments. Thus a company's marketing programme needs to be based upon information about its actual and potential markets — the number, type and location of customers involved, the economic, social competitive, legal and technical factors which impinge upon and influence their purchasing behaviour and offer-response patterns. Market presentations of policies concerned with the product or service offering, its promotion and availability, represent ultimate expressions of a process which essentially involves adapting the firm to its environment in such a way that its objectives are met.

The marketing-oriented firm is to be contrasted with the production-oriented company: the latter first produces goods and services and subsequently attempts to sell them at a profit; the former moves back a stage and systematically seeks out those customer needs which it feels it can best fulfil. In the production-oriented company, the accent is on making a desired profit through minimising expenses in the productive processes; there is also a tendency to believe that price and aggressive promotional tactics will create custom, although for this kind of firm operational viability normally depends on there being an excess of demand over supply. A marketing-oriented company, on the other hand, while sharing the same financial goal focuses on market need and acknowledges that consumers are influenced by a constellation of factors. The underlying premise for the marketing concept is that a customer's wants are developed from his overall circumstances and are not 'created' by the firm.

It is these circumstances which require to be thoroughly analysed and their changes predicted. They provide the rationale for establishing a marketing function designed to evaluate the efficacy of existing products

95

and services and to direct and focus the search for, and creation of, new product and market opportunities so that corporate objectives and resources, and the needs of selected customers are linked. Apart from the opportunity to formulate new product and service ideas in terms of improved performance attributes and design aesthetics, marketing management will be expected to seize other opportunities, for example, those leading to greater efficiency. The challenge exists continually to deliver goods at lower prices and with better timing, and by providing greater convenience as to their spatial availability. Other opportunities might well include the creation of some competitive advantage by bestowing through the application of, say, promotional skills, marks of distinction on the company and its product range, thus carving out a market niche or a series of selective segments for which the company will seek to be a dominant source of supply. These and other openings will be sought within the context of the constraints impacting on the firm; the more obvious ones being market size and growth trends, competitive strategies, corporate capacity as to the quality, amount and range of resources available, and the special legal and political restrictions prevailing.

The need to apply marketing to public transport

There can be few industries whose traditional markets have been so affected by external events during the last twenty or so years and, perhaps, even fewer whose marketing responses to such changes have been so indigent as those of the urban public transport operators.

Attention has already been drawn to the dilemma facing civic planners having an overall responsibility for combating those adverse effects arising out of, and partly contributing to, 'metropolitan sprawl'. Many of them recognise that passenger transport's outstanding strength is the economy with which it employs scarce resources, not only fuel but particularly land. Yet some, but clearly not all of them also acknowledge that to impose swingeing controls over the use of private vehicles in central areas in order to facilitate the efficient operation of public transport would almost certainly, in the present circumstances, be counter-productive, in as much as the remaining attractions of city centres (e.g. shopping, entertainment and cultural ones) might seem suddenly and dramatically to diminish for those strongly attached to private car usage — especially if adequate suburban substitutes exist.

However, community attitudes are not immutable. This is a point which requires emphasising, in particular as the methodology of the land-use and transportation studies has been severely strictured for not allowing predictions to be made about the number of motorists who will be deterred from using their normal mode under certain restrictions or how many will be induced to use public transport facilities if these are substantially improved or if new ones are introduced.[1] While the public's attitudes towards urban transport are generally unfavourable they are probably capable of being changed towards a more favourable set. Research conducted by the Opinion Research Centre in 1971 for the London Transport Executive strongly suggests a reliable, regular and comfortable service is demanded on buses and railways and while reaction is generally hostile towards a better service being obtained by imposing physical constraints on competitive forms of transport such as the private car, resistance to further discriminatory measures against motorists would come from only 57 per cent of motorists and 26 per cent of passenger transport users. Furthermore, it was found that public support for established bus priority schemes was favourable and there was some willingness to consider forms of subsidisation to assist the operators.

Although London Transport, and perhaps other metropolitan transport executives, might draw considerable comfort from these figures and feel more inclined to press the politicians to implement without further delay ' . . . some fairly drastic measures to reduce the amount of *(private)* traffic on roads . . .' [2]care should be taken in interpreting such attitudinal data literally. It should be understood that the respondents in question were mainly faced with hypothetical situations which in different ways must surely have caused some doubt to be cast on the value of their predictions. For example, up to the present time there are still relatively few bus priority schemes — in 1971 there were even fewer — and many of these bestow obvious advantages, e.g. as does the one for Oxford Street, London. These advantages might well have been uppermost in the minds of those polled for opinions on bus priority schemes in general. Compared with the degree to which many planners and operators would wish to curb private traffic in central city areas, motorists as yet remain largely unfettered. Consequently, while car users may be prepared to accept some small measure of additional constraint, it certainly does not follow that they would agree to the panoply of controls which many planners would like to see imposed here and now. Not surprisingly, as several social psychologists point out, statements of belief can be poor predictors of behaviour.[3]

On the other hand, when faced with the reality of a particular set of regulations the public might, under certain conditions, find their attitudes changing, even if they had anticipated reacting in a hostile manner in advance of their legal enforcement. Pedestrianisation proposals frequently invoke considerable antagonism from shop owners because they fear these will drastically reduce custom; actual experience to date has invariably proved otherwise — admittedly the schemes implemented have been confined to a few prominent shopping areas. Insko and Schopler, among others, have found that where behaviour is 'forcibly' changed this may lead to the adoption of attitudes consistent with the conduct prescribed.[5] The process of bringing about a more harmonious balance between attitudes held and the new form of conduct to be pursued can be accelerated if: (i) credible information justifying the action to be taken, e.g. the introduction of the regulations, is effectively promoted and continues to be after the enforcement has commenced; and (ii) the new activities to be adopted are not seen to impinge too unfavourably, or better still are perceived to offer tangible benefits.

Such behavioural insights which characterise the marketing approach should influence the thinking of urban transport planners and operators. We would suggest that just prior to and after the introduction of each series of traffic restrictions a strong case is made out for their need, one which underlines the beneficial consequences. While the measures should make a noticeable impact on reducing congestion and provide advantages for the public transport system, they must not be viewed by motorists as being too severe, otherwise they might bring about a sharp fall in patronage for essential city centre facilities. Similarly, if the restrictions are regarded as being unwarranted and too politically doctrinaire in their form, motorists and others adversely affected may, through influential lobbies, press for their repeal. Thus urban planners and transport operators should prepare themselves for a period of public persuasion and phased implementation of restraints. It is one of our main contentions that success at each stage is more likely to be assured if the general public first has evidence of some meaningful and imaginative improvement in basic service levels. Naturally, the availability of an up-dated network involving, say, a rapid transit system will doubtless have the maximum demonstration. Not only must the improved services be effectively publicised, but a continuous programme of sophisticated public relations should be undertaken to explain the logic of public transport's argument for preferential treatment.

There are a number of specific research, planning and promotional ways in which marketing might be expected to make a real, immediate and long term contribution to the successful management of large public transport undertakings. Firstly, it should play a major role in selecting those segments of demand which offer the relatively greatest potential. Secondly, in conjunction with the transport planners in the medium to long term and the operational staff in the short run, marketing should formulate and appraise the passenger service mixes for each segment of demand. This will involve, for bus and rail and other forms of urban passenger transport services, influencing the fares policy and design of product-service specifications — covering such matters as scheduling, length of traffic day, frequency vehicle details, fare collection systems, passenger facilities on and off the vehicle, etc. In determining the quality of service a number of phases are implied: (a) identifying travel needs and patterns and determinants of modal choice; (b) devising new concepts for improved mixes both derived from, and validated by, secondary and primary research data; (c) conducting a series of experiments and carefully monitoring the results; (d) in the case of service innovations which are adopted operationally as well as for traditional elements of the mixes which are retained, measuring in-service performance on a continuous basis; and (e) promoting the services available. Thirdly, public transport marketing should undertake public relations activities through the mass media and by lobbying special and influential groups external to the organisation, and internally so as to inculcate the operations staff with a sense of the customer public relations roles which they should be fulfilling.

Evidence of marketing practice in the PTEs — some international comparisons

The case for applying marketing has been stated. When, in 1973, the four PTEs and the London Transport Executive were examined for the way they were practising marketing, it was noticeable how in these organisations — even four years after their establishment[6] — relatively little progress or clarity of purpose had been achieved in adopting the concept and tools of marketing. Supplementary evidence supplied by selected major North American and Western European operators[7] tends in most cases to support the view that its neglect is by no means confined to the PTEs. This section limits itself to a brief examination of some of the more obvious indices of marketing effectiveness; a more detailed coverage of how the operators determine the various elements of the marketing-mix is given in chapter 6.

Marketing's neglect in this industry is amply demonstrated by reference to the promotional budgets of the PTEs in 1972. Table 4.1 expresses these as percentages of passenger receipts for both the PTEs and their North American and Western European counterparts. Although the PTEs seem to appropriate less than several of the foreign operators surveyed, the sums budgeted by nearly all the undertakings would appear to be ludicrously

Table 4.1
Expenditure on promotion as a % of passenger receipts for the PTEs and
selected North American and contintental Western European transit
organisations (1972)

Range of percentages		
PTEs including LTE (total = 5)	North America (total = 8)	Western Europe (total = 20)
0·02—0·50	0·05—5·92	0·04—1·10

Source: The operators

inadequate in relation to the informational and persuasive tasks involved.

The types of information available in the PTE areas demonstrate a patchwork quilt of differing policies. They are indicated in table 4.2. All of the PTEs provide general service timetables and charge for them. Most of the route maps have been specially commissioned and designed and are generally much brighter and more attractive than traditional literature available; none of the PTEs, however, has conducted research on the customer acceptability of these. Merseyside PTE is experimenting with individual British Rail 'Inter-City' style route cards giving timetable and other relevant details, some of which are of a promotional nature relating to their new city centre services and the sale of multi-journey tickets. Household leaflet distribution has in most cases only been used to announce and explain the reasons for conversion to one-man bus operation. Information at stops seems to be very limited and very poor in all areas. A market research study commissioned by the LTE[8] suggested a number of improvements, including: maps in bus shelters to show route location in relation to other routes; place names on bus stops; bus route maps; and prominence for such information as service frequency and times of late night services.

Of the twenty operators, including three PTEs, who provided a breakdown of their 1972 promotional budgets, half of them appropriated more than 50 per cent for publicising service data (30 per cent of these undertakings allocated more than 75 per cent of their expenditure in this way).

Closely allied to information dissemination, but with an element of salesmanship, persuasion is required to retain the loyalty of existing market

Table 4.2
Availability of particular information sources in PTE area

	London	Merseyside	Greater Manchester	Tyneside	West Midlands
General service timetables	Charge	Charge	Charge	Charge	Charge
General route map	Free	—	Charge	Charge	Free
Individual route timetables	—	Experimental	—	—	—
Individual route maps	—	Experimental	—	—	—
Household leafleting	O.m.o. Introduction only	Experimental	Limited	—	O.m.o. Introduction only
Information at stops	Limited	Limited	Limited	Limited	Limited
Official information centres other than at garages or administrative offices	Yes	Yes	—	—	—

Source: Individual executives, 1973

Table 4.3

Types of marketing research undertaken/commissioned by PTEs, North American and Western European transit organisations

	PTEs including LTE (total = 5)			North America (total = 8)			Western Europe (total = 20)		
	Frequently	Infrequently	Not at all	Frequently	Infrequently	Not at all	Frequently	Infrequently	Not at all
Modal-split preference	1	3	1	1	6	1	3	8	9
Factors underlying modal choice	1	2	2	1	5	2	0	11	9
Journey purpose	2	2	1	1	6	1	3	9	8
Origin and destination patterns	1	3	1	1	5	2	3	10	7
Measuring price elasticities of demand	0	2	3	2	3	3	1	6	13
Measuring passenger satisfaction with: (a) existing services	1	2	2	2	3	3	0	9	11
(b) experimental services	1	2	3	3	3	3	1	6	13

Source: The operators

segments, to stimulate more intensive use in these and to induce users of competitive modes to switch to using public transport. Given the small amounts spent on all forms of promotion — in 1972 the maximum PTE expenditure was £75,000 and in North America, where promotional spending by some of the operators was much higher, it did not exceed $750,000 for any one of the organisations surveyed — it is not surprising that the industry as a whole is making little headway with these kinds of communication.

If customer needs are to be identified and translated into improved product and service offerings they must be thoroughly researched. For example, in urban public transport marketing data is required on modal-split and the factors determining choice, journey purpose, journey origin and destination patterns, price elasticities, and on passenger satisfaction with existing and experimental services. Reference to Table 4.3 suggests that these quite basic marketing research tasks are claimed to be done by only a very small number of operators on a regular basis and on a wide enough scale, and by the majority of survey organisations infrequently. Table 4.4 provides evidence of the 1972 research expenditures expressed as percentages of passenger receipts by some of the more progressive concerns.

The ultimate test of marketing effectiveness is normally the way customer patronage is increased in line with certain corporate turnover and profitability goals, and that in highly competitive situations achieving these targets will demand a high rate of product and service innovation. In this industry with its long term background of declining passenger revenues and mounting operating deficits it may well be unrealistic in most cases,

Table 4.4

Expenditures on marketing research projects as a percentage of passenger receipts for selected PTEs, North American and Western European transit organisations (1972)

PTEs including LTE	North America	Western Europe
0·20	1·03	1·12
0·15	0·68	0·70
0·13	0·53	0·22

Note: The percentages quoted are the three highest per group
Source: The operators

and certainly in the short run, to speak of aiming for increased profitability, but the requirement to innovate is even greater if only to reduce the rates of decline in passenger receipts.

In chapter 6 we assess a number of market-oriented product innovations introduced in North America and Western Europe. Collectively they represent a considerable range of experiments, several of them apparently successful. However, as the evidence contained in table 4.5 would indicate, the innovatory contribution made by any one operator surveyed is a relatively small one. The pattern which emerges is that while some amount of experimentation has taken place it has been on a piecemeal basis and most noticeably there has been a reluctance to move from the experimental stage to full scale and regular adoption. We would be the first to agree that in the case of some of the experiments introduced, if the results are properly assessed, the operators would be justified in not moving on to the adoption stage.

The organisational acceptance of the marketing function

The reasons for the neglect of marketing become more understandable after examining the numbers of marketing executives employed by each of the PTEs, the organisational status accorded to the marketing function itself and how it relates to others, especially transport planning and operations. The information obtained as a result of conducting extensive personal visits to the English executives will be supplemented in certain instances with data received from selected major North American and Western European operators.

Marketing executives and their organisational status

In two PTEs, Tyneside and West Midlands, no marketing personnel had been appointed and no appointments were envisaged for the future; but in the case of the former, which has a comparatively strong transport planning section, there is some awareness of the marketing environment.

The Merseyside PTE had one marketing officer operating within the 'planning and development' directorate. This officer was originally appointed as an economic analyst but through his own initiative he had created his present post. His main activities have been largely concerned with promoting a few quite successful but nevertheless minor experimental services; a hoped-for byproduct is that these will serve as a means of gaining credibility within the organisation so that marketing can be applied gradually on a much wider scale.

104

Greater 'Manchester PTE has endeavoured to be somewhat more ambitious in introducing the function. In 1970 a senior non-directorial post, with reporting responsibility to the director general, was established. Shortly following the appointment of the second and present incumbent in October 1972 a firm of management consultants was invited to recommend how, among other things, marketing should relate in organisational terms to the large and highly regarded transport planning department and the day-to-day operations. The first marketing manager had not, it was claimed, been given the opportunity to establish meaningful relationships in this respect and had certairily not been able to secure any staff. The terms of reference given to him on appointment bore little resemblance to the organisational realities then prevailing. At the time of our initial discussions with all those concerned the problems had still to be identified and resolved. Towards the latter part of our research programme in June 1973 the consultants engaged had succeeded in drawing the Executive's attention to the main questions at issue and they were persuading it to regard with some favour recommendations which should enable marketing to play an effective role in Greater Manchester in the future.[9]

A similar but more complicated situation was found to exist in London Transport. A small marketing department containing nine personnel headed by a 'director' (a non-Executive board oppointment situated at the third level in the organisational hierarchy) had been set up in 1970. At the same time five cognate, but in many respects independent, planning 'directorships' had also been established and made responsible for corporate planning, transportation planning, transportation policy, commercial policy, and operational research. The fact that the various planning directors reported to different board members, hardly helped to create a co-ordinated planning function. In addition to the new directorial inputs, traditional departments such as finance and public relations continued to operate under chief officers who were senior to the new 'directors'. Predictably the results were a duplication of effort and a lack of clarity on departmental boundaries. Changes of title and titles that sounded similar to one another, but which did not accord with the normal acceptance of the hierarchical order, added to the confusion. The newly formed departments were, not surprisingly, resented, either because the reason for their creation had not been understood or because they had in theory, or in practice, assumed responsibilities for some functions previously vested in traditional departments, but without formal cessation of responsibility by the original ones or any transfer of staff. As with the Greater Manchester PTE, the terms of reference covering the marketing director's duties were, because of their breadth of scope, not only meaningless but exacerbated the problems of achieving the acceptance of the marketing function. As Landsberger[10] points out, when there are both role conflict and ambiguities in the definition of work responsibilities the dissatisfied departments tend to engage in offensive manœuvres and the 'offending' unit is forced to adopt defensive ploys. Thus while London Transport has attracted some well-qualified marketing personnel who have been responsible for a considerable volume of marketing research and have spawned several useful ideas on product and service improvements. especially during the initial period after their appointment, many of their findings and suggestions have either been opposed or ignored: latterly they have tended to adopt more defensive postures and concentrate increasingly on less sensitive areas which have been regarded as somewhat peripheral by the better entrenched staff members. However, the senior management are to be congratulated for having diagnosed most of these problems for themselves after conducting an exhaustive enquiry as part of an internal organisational audit in 1973, and there are indications that a more viable accommodation of the marketing function will emerge. On the other hand, being a larger organisation, servicing the travel needs of an international metropolis and, as a result of its antecedents, having a long-standing commitment to a particular managerial style — thus in many respects London Transport remains *sui generis* — the attitudinal changes required to integrate marketing might be more difficult to effect than in, say, the Greater Manchester PTE.

Table 4.6

Number of transport planners and marketeers in the PTEs and major North American and Western European transit organisations (excluding clerical and secretarial staff)

	PTEs including LTE		North America		Western Europe	
	Transport planners	Marketeers	Transport planners	Marketeers	Transport planners	Marketeers
None	—	2	1	4	1	10
1—4	2	2	1	2	8	8
5—9	2	1	3	2	6	2
10 and over	1	—	3	—	5	—
Total	5	5	8	8	20	20

Source: The operators

Although we were not able to make the same depth of analysis for the North American and Western European public transport undertakings included in our survey, indicators were received from these which point to a universally poor representation of the marketing function, especially when a comparison is made with transport planning. Tables 4.6 and 4.7 convey the imbalance existing in 1973. Each PTE has a transport planning function; only one North American and one Western European do not provide for it. No specific provision has been made for marketing by two of the five PTEs, four of the eight North American transit organisations and half of the twenty Western European operators. Roughly 50 per cent of the chief senior marketing executives engaged by the remaining undertakings report in a formal sense direct to the chief executive, whereas nearly 80 per cent of the chief transport planners have this right and furthermore nine of them (nearly 30 per cent) are directors; only in one North American organisation is the chief marketing executive part of the directorate.

Table 4.7

The organisation status of the senior transport planner and the senior marketing executive in the PTEs and major North American and Western European transit organisations

	PTEs including LTE		North America		Western Europe	
	Transport planner	Marketeer	Transport planner	Marketeer	Transport planner	Marketeer
A director/vice president who reports direct to the chief executive (formal procedure)	3	—	3	1	3	—
A non-director/vice president who reports direct to the chief executive (formal procedure	1	1	2	1	12	5
A non-director/vice president who reports to a lower level in the hierarchy (formal procedure)	1	2	2	2	4	5
Total	5	3	7	4	19	10

Source: The operators

Organisation factors inimical to the successful introduction of public transport marketing

The following is based on an analysis of the five English executives and concerns itself with a number of issues which we regard as being inimical to the successful introduction of urban public transport marketing. While a few of these are particular to the PTE type structure adopted as a consequence of the implementation of the 1968 Transport Act, many of them we believe relate to the general nature of the industry and its effect on the marketing process, and thus, we contend, have general relevance to the management of major metropolitan undertakings.

In all the organisations studied, the overwhelming majority of the respondents, who were not marketing executives, had little understanding of the way marketing should be employed. There were notable exceptions. Certainly several of the chief executives brought in from outside the industry, for example, in London, Greater Manchester and Tyneside, were quick to display an appreciation of the benefits to be gained from adopting a more marketing-oriented approach. However, these important opinions apart, marketing as a separate function was generally seen by most of the senior managers interviewed as having a 'promotional' role only — and, as we have seen, in public transport circles, this is interpreted in the narrowest sense possible. Whenever attempts have been made to introduce marketing the central difficulty has always been to convince other departments of the importance of the contribution it can make towards public transport's problems.

(a) *Marketing—transport planning relationship* The organisational standing of transport planning is an especially strong one. In three of the executives, Merseyside, Greater Manchester and Tyneside, the function has been headed by a member of the executive board. London, Greater Manchester and Tyneside have each attracted sizeable teams of well-qualified transport planners with the design of the future public transport infrastructure as their main objective. From this position of organisational strength these teams have in some cases tended to extend their planning influence by laying claim to fulfilling other tasks, such as those concerned with formulating the quality of the passenger service mix; for example, route scheduling, length of service day, vehicle frequency details, fare collection systems and passenger facilities on and off the vehicle. Qualified transport marketeers should expect to assume a prime responsibility for many of these while for others, e.g. frequency specifications which affect capacity and thus modal split, might be shared tasks (see chapter 5). There are several reasons accounting for the transport planners' favoured position which has contributed towards the difficulties of establishing professionally staffed marketing functions in the PTEs.

Firstly, the White Paper (Cmnd.3481)[11] provided authoritative backing for the transport planners when it stated an Executive '. . . must employ staff skilled in the latest techniques of transport planning and development, not only by road but by all means of transport' (para.24).

To underline the importance of the point the White Paper (para.25) went on to instruct that 'A first Plan for the development of public transport must be prepared by the Executive for approval by the Authority and for publication within two years. Such a plan . . . will help the . . . Secretary of State in deciding on the capital grants to be made . . .'

The time allotted for formulating plans and the purpose for which they had to be prepared leaves little doubt about the importance which the Government wanted the PTEs to attach to transport planning.

Secondly, the transport planners were able to establish themselves quickly in that they were able to build on the various detailed land use and transportation studies undertaken in the late 1960's and have had a natural access to, and rapport with, the many planners employed by local authorities and, more particularly, those working for the Department of the Environment. In contrast marketing personnel in the PTEs have few experts in official circles connected with urban policy with whom they have had any professional affinity: the Expenditure Committee's report[1] talks of only one such individual working for the DOE and makes a firm recommendation that competent 'market researchers' should be engaged in urban transport planning.

Thirdly, organisational momentum for some of the transport planning teams has been maintained further because, in contrast to marketing they have not been opposed by the operational staff; the conflict between the marketeers and senior members of the operational staff will be discussed below. Given that the planners have been preoccupied with having to produce infrastructure plans, functional time scales have tended, up to now, to differ considerably. There has, therefore, been little opportunity for conflicts of interest to arise (this may change to a certain extent once the long term plans have been laid). Moreover, the end product of planning has been seen by the operational executives as a likely means for enhancing their position; they stand to inherit a modern integrated bus-rail system which promises to have priority over private modes.

The emphasis which some PTEs have placed on transport planning has been both necessary and commendable, and clearly in London and Greater Manchester the intention is not to restrict innovatory zeal to this function.

However, the considerable encouragement given to the planners has to some extent been at the expense of short to medium term marketing activities. For example, the transport planning teams have a tight control over the systems for collecting and analysing environmental information. If public transport marketing is to make any headway it must have a direct access to the inputs and outputs of these data systems. It has also been common practice for the transport planners to adopt a general planning and marketing role. The fault lies not with the transport planners but with the PTE directorates who have, as we stated in chapter 3, made little attempt to differentiate between the various types of planning and marketing. Not surprisingly, apart from the transport planners, few specialist staff have been recruited and thus vacuums have existed, into which transport planners have been able to move. As the final deadlines for publishing the first long term transport plans have been met, so the planners involved have begun to turn to matters more immediate — some of which marketing would normally expect to deal with. They have also assumed some corporate planning tasks.

(b) *Marketing—operations relationships* Among the senior public transport staff interviewed, the operational staff were the most hostile towards the introduction of a marketing function. Much of their hostility seems to stem from a reluctance to have their role confined to a logistics one, providing services to the public in accord with passenger standards laid down and publicised by marketing staff.

Apart from the special and exclusive relationship which operational personnel (the drivers, conductors and inspectors) have with passengers, many of the more senior members can justly claim from their considerable experience an intimate knowledge of the service network and all the associated problems. In fact most of the senior executives, e.g. the directors of operations and the heads of divisional networks, have been general managers of large municipal undertakings, and as such have gained a certain amount of commercial expertise and some have even been responsible for the introduction of a small number of innovations. They argue that experience thus gained enables them to define and fulfil customer needs better than marketing staff, especially as the latter tend to be new to the industry.

In this context it is immaterial whether or not such perceptions are justified. What is apparent is that operational staff are in a dominant position organisationally to express their attitude forcibly. They command all but an insignificant proportion of the total labour and capital resources. To a large degree their organisational standing has been further boosted by the initial effects of implementing the strategy contained in the 1968 Transport Act. At the outset operational staff had the responsibility of taking over all the municipal bus undertakings in their area. Thus at a stroke their geographical and resource span of control was dramatically increased; for example, in the area for which Greater Manchester PTE is now responsible there were no less than eleven municipal undertakings. The implementation of cost-minimising policies has been greatly facilitated by the enlarged scope of operations, e.g. purchasing and maintenance economies have been achieved, many of the illogical route patterns resulting from competition between municipal operators have been removed, and the incentive for applying operations research techniques to give better scheduling and traffic control priorities has arisen. Given the financial situation such policies have gained more support from influential colleagues and from councillors charged with the responsibility for overseeing the policy of the Executives, than those which attempt, more radically, to match up to what are seen as nebulous market needs. Furthermore, cost-reduction schemes have been given short term priority because small but tangible benefits have accrued to passengers. For example, in Greater Manchester lost mileage has been reduced by half; the result of better maintenance procedures and improved crew supervision.

Admittedly, it is clear from Government policy documents and the 1968 Act that the task of an Executive must go beyond the logistical role of running buses, and the acceptance of broader strategic obligations has resulted in far-reaching organisational consequences. However, these have not, as yet, led to any noticeable diminution of the operational staff's position, primarily because the new managerial functions introduced either have dealt with entirely new and somewhat mutually exclusive areas of responsibility, e.g. financial control, and/or with different time scales, e.g. long range transport planning. Had a strong marketing function been created at the time the PTEs were established the operators would have had less licence to stray from what we consider should be, very largely, their logistical brief.

(c) *The nature of the public transport marketing process* Apart from the more specific constraints resulting from the way the transport planners and the operational staff have acquired a dominant status in the English Executives, the organisational development of professional marketing seems to have been inhibited by a number of factors which relate to the general nature of the marketing process in this industry.

In chapter 3 we drew attention to the way public transport's parameters of policy formulation are far more circumscribed by governmental and local authority controls than, for example, are those of most commercial firms. As such the areas of discretion which public transport marketing planners can exercise is considerably curtailed. As already stated, to a large extent the PTEs are precluded from diversifying beyond their conventional and well-delineated product-market scopes; it is often difficult to effect major rationalisations of existing networks of operation, and regulatory bodies have the effect of blunting what is for many products and services one of the most powerful elements in the marketing-mix, price. Thus, by not being able to make the kind of major contribution to overall strategy formulation which his counterpart in the private sector can do, the public transport marketing planner is less able to attract the corresponding organisational authority.

In most commercial situations marketing attracts considerable strength and largely owes its 'power base' to the fact that it has control over those, especially a large sales force, who *implement* the demand creation and fulfilling elements of the marketing-mix. Perrow,[12] in an analysis of departmental power in twelve US industrial firms, found that the sales (marketing) department was in a dominating position. While all departments in an organisation might be expected to contribute towards customer satisfaction, it is sales (marketing) that has the most direct contact with this important group. Sales (marketing) management, acting as a 'gatekeeper', is able to determine:

> . . . how important will be prompt delivery, quality, product-improvement, or new products, and the cost at which these can be sold. Sales *(marketing)* determines the relative importance of these variables for the other groups and indicates the values which these variables will take. It has the ability, in addition, of changing the values of these variables since it sets pricing (and in most firms adjusts it temporarily to meet changes in opportunity and competition), determines which markets will be utilized, the services that will be provided . . . As a link between the customer and producer, it absorbs most of the uncertainty about the diffuse and changing environment of customers (p.65).

Because the functions of actually consummating passenger need satisfaction and 'production' (the actual supply of services) are performed simultaneously by the bus crews, operationally marketing in public transport can only have direct responsibility for advertising and public relations. It is denied, in all but a few minor areas, the opportunity of making a two-way sales communication. Even the bus crews who are involved in this process simply act as 'order takers' and are unable to exert

113

any pre-sales influence — except very indirectly in a minor public relations role. The nature of public transport's demand for most of the main segments makes it unfeasible for any sales force accountable for desired levels of turnover to make contact with all those who might be persuaded to buy seat space in advance of making their journeys. Among the more obvious reasons for this are the large numbers involved, their geographical dispersion, their low values of unit purchase and the difficulty of identifying individuals as potential customers.

The circumstances described are, of course, by no means unique. Most manufacturing companies when faced with similar problems of making sales contact with prospects comprising a mass market work through channel intermediaries, who sell on their behalf. Service companies offering, say, insurance, inter-city and, especially, international travel, use specialist agencies. Both types of organisation can exert sales pressure on channel members. However, willingness to act as intermediaries and the principal's effectiveness in applying sales pressure to these will be a function of, e.g. (i) the percentage discount/commission allowable; (ii) the amount of the discount/commission per sale; (iii) the volume of demand for the products and services involved; and (iv) the attractiveness of the franchise in generating complementary demand (cf. newspaper and sub-post office franchises). Against such criteria it is not surprising that urban public transport operators have not made much headway with this type of selling.

Thus apart from undertaking some specialised selling (e.g. coach hire, parcels service, etc.) and possibly providing sales training to selected crew personnel and inspectors, the main marketing 'line' responsibilities can only be for advertising specific services and products, projecting a corporate image and putting over public transport's case for preferential treatment. The difficulty which public transport marketing faces is to persuade senior management, against a background of declining passenger revenues and mounting operational deficits, to appropriate sums of money for this type of promotion which must seem astronomical set aside previous puny budgets. This difficulty is exacerbated enormously when consideration is given to the resources required to carry out the prime role of the undertaking's promotional task, namely bringing about a fundamental shift in the community's attitude towards public transport. As with all innovatory marketing, one is concerned with attitudinal and behavioural change, but unlike most consumer marketing the concepts to be explained and the attitudes and behaviour to be fostered are complex. Rather than just requiring, say, a minor adaptation to an existing life style, the issues involve promoting intangibles such as optimum land use relationships and encouraging the very reluctant acceptance of restrained car use. In the former case reinforcement of favourable attitudes may be sought, and the inducements promoted will invariably relate to positive, personal and immediate benefits to be gained by adoption; in the latter an infinitely more difficult task is involved.[13] In one sense the enormity of the objective should strengthen marketing's organisational position; however, in practice this has not been so, since there are few planners in central and local government circles and in the industry who have clarified their own thinking about the concepts to be communicated and even fewer who seem to appreciate the part modern promotional techniques can play in the communications process.

Some specific reasons why marketing personnel should be given a strong organisational role

We therefore posit that up to the present time marketing exists as a nascent, largely misunderstood function in urban public transport management. Some of the causes for the current situation have been examined, but we do not feel these adequately justify neglecting marketing in the future.

It could be argued that if the existing transport planners and the operational staff wish to take over marketing tasks, the former extending their brief — as they are beginning to do — to embrace the planning functions involved, and the latter assuming the more immediate aspects concerned with the present network of services, then they should be given every encouragement to develop them. We reject this argument.

Marketing needs to be concerned with customer problems, competitive activities and other market-place events. Having objectively assessed the true nature of these and evaluated the risks and opportunities involved, marketeers must be instrumental in seeing that the organisation's demand-influencing resources, i.e. the product or service offer and the means for communicating with and supplying the market, can react quickly to seize the opportunities available or withstand the threats posed.

The transport planner's relatively long term focus, his particular brand of analytical skills and his attitudes towards and knowledge of marketing procedures would seem to preclude him from being an effective marketeer. As already stated, his main task is to plan ahead for the public transport infrastructure which will best meet certain land use, demographic and transport technology criteria. Given that existing urban land use

115

relationships are not easily changed in the short run, demographic change is slow, and technological break-throughs related to service vehicles cannot, in reality, be expected during the next decade or so, his time scale — if he confines himself to his speciality — is a very extended one. While the planning dimension of marketing also calls for a forward looking perspective, many of its problems require a rapid feedback and relatively short term focus. Other issues apart, it is unlikely that the transport planner could gear himself to deal with these very much reduced time horizons. This time dimension and a set of analytical skills, which tend to make him more interested in the broad symmetrical interrelationships within the total transport system, than with the more individual needs of customer segments, differentiate him. Certainly our discussions with senior PTE transport planners suggested that most of them are not very familiar with marketing procedures as they might properly apply to public transport management and some expressed mild disdain for what they considered to be modern marketing practices.

Operational staff would not appear to be well-suited to perform marketing tasks either. On several occasions we have referred to their preoccupation with cost-reduction and running a service network which from their own point of view offers the least scheduling and manning problems. The evidence of several studies[14] indicates that this is a natural preoccupation for those in a 'production' or logistics function to express.

The skills and attitudes required for marketing, described above, are not those which operational staff normally share. Enough has already been said to indicate that most operational managers do not have the marketing research and promotional skills, to name two, which are required for public transport marketing. Their present attitudes have been largely conditioned by their service in municipal transport departments. Most of the present senior operations executives were recruited in the late 1930's and 40's, a time of demand expansion for public transport. This, combined with the effects of working in an industry protected by monopoly franchise and enjoying security of tenure, tends to make them somewhat resistant to change.

Today marketing is not generally considered to be an innovatory managerial function, but an exception can certainly be made for three of the five PTEs examined, who have either ignored it totally or adopted it only to discontinue or maintain it on a token level: in the other two there is evidence of a stronger intention to adopt and integrate it. In the next chapter we study organisational methods by which marketing can be successfully adopted and integrated with the corporate and transport planning functions and operations.

116

Notes

[1] See para.162 of the House of Commons Expenditure Comittee's report on *Urban Transport Planning,* HMSO, 14 December 1972.

[2] *London Transport Executive's Annual Report for 1972,* published 26 April 1973.

[3] See M. Fishbein, 'Attitude and the prediction of behaviour', in M. Fishbein (ed.) *Readings in Attitude Theory and Measurement,* Wiley, 1967, pp. 477—92.

[4] C. A. Insko and J. Schopler, 'Triadic consistency: a statement of effective cognitive — conative consistency' *Psychological Review,* vol. 74, 1967, pp. 361—76. The rationale for the laws designed to improve, say, race relations is based on this particular prediction.

[5] See, for example, L. Festinger, *A Theory of Cognitive Dissonance,* Stanford University Press, 1957.

[6] London Transport, of course, considerably antedates the London Transport Executive, which was restyled in 1969. Although distinct comparisons can be made between the two, the organisational objective and structure, in essence, remain largely unchanged.

[7] Thirty-two major public transport organisations serving metropolitan areas in North America and continental Western Europe were approached and twenty-eight of these agreed to complete and return questionnaire forms sent to them. For further details, see note 1 to chapter 3, p. 92.

[8] Erwin Wasey, *Report of a Study into the Motivation and Attitudes of Passengers and Potential Passengers of London Transport Buses,* London Transport Executive, September 1968.

[9] Among the principal and relevant recommendations it is proposed that there should be one 'executive policy board' which in addition to the director general should comprise seven 'directors' and 'chief executive officers' representing such major functions as: finance and administration; transport planning; operations, to be sub-divided into five new divisions; personnel; and marketing. It is stressed that the distinction between directorial and chief executive officer status is based on personal considerations (e.g. seniority) and does not reflect the importance of the function. Directors, it is recommended, should lead finance and administration; transport planning, and research and development; while those heading operations, marketing, personnel and integrative operations (PTE-BR-NBC) should be chief executive officers. Additional directors might be appointed in the future. Corporate services, also to be headed by a c.e.o. would be placed in a director general's 'secretariat'. It is proposed that marketing should be undertaken at both an HQ and an operations

divisional level. Central marketing staff would formulate the basic 'principles' of quality of service, communications and sales promotion and these would be interpreted in a more localised manner by divisional traffic/ marketing managers. In the main marketing research would be done centrally and all pertinent performances would be monitored and appraised by HQ personnel.

[10] H. A. Landsberger, 'The horizontal dimension in a bureaucracy' *Administrative Science Quarterly,* vol. 6, 1961, pp. 298-333.

[11] The White Paper on *Public Transport and Traffic,* Cmnd.3481, 1967.

[12] C. Perrow, 'Departmental power and perspective in industrial firms' in M. N. Zald (ed.) *Power in Organisations,* Vanderbilt University Press, 1970.

[13] Some parallels might be the Heath Government's attempt in 1971 to swing public opinion in favour of its EEC policy and the Wilson Government's comprehensive secondary school education policy as it was probably perceived by a large proportion of the middle-class electorate in the late 1960's.

[14] See, for example, R. M. Cyert and J. G. March, *A Behavioural Theory of the Firm,* Prentice Hall, Englewood Cliffs, N.J. 1963; and P. R. Lawrence and J. W. Lorsch, *Organisations and Environment,* Irwin, 1967.

5 Structuring the Organisation for Planning and Marketing

The organisational problems of the PTEs in perspective

In the two previous chapters we have criticised the five English Executives examined for not having made a more positive commitment to comprehensive and integrated planning and marketing. However, such criticism needs to be seen in perspective. There are several indications which suggest that many of the North American and continental Western European metropolitan organisations also surveyed, albeit not as extensively as were the PTEs, were not noticeably more successful in the way they had introduced and integrated these important functions. Furthermore, any strictures made should be viewed in the light of the quite considerable tasks which have been thrust upon the senior managements involved.

In the UK the main managerial preoccupations over the last four years have been to implement the foundation requirements of the 1968 Transport Act — namely, taking over the municipal bus undertakings, grouping them into viable units and co-ordinating them with those suburban services supplied by British Rail and the National Bus Company, which serve the needs of the metropolitan areas; producing an infrastructure plan; and introducing certain new managerial activities. Changes of this order do not take place overnight. As Ginzberg and Reilly stress: 'Large scale change is never an event but always a process and the history of an organisation . . .' (in this context, the legacies inevitably inherited from the municipal traffic departments) . . . 'largely determine the nature and limits of changes'.[1]

The Executives' problems were probably exacerbated by the initial hostility expressed by a wide spectrum of local interests and directed at what was perceived to be an attempt to impose 'nationalised area passenger transport boards' by the Government. In those conurbations where the subsidiaries of the National Bus Company had — and still have in some cases — extensive networks operating within and across PTE boundaries it has been difficult to draw up what both parties regard as equitable agency or acquisition agreements which integrate bus operations. Being able to decide on formulae for compensation and the eradication of wage differentials have been some of the main issues at stake. These and other problems have occupied much of the Executive's thinking on

Tyneside, where until recently about 49 per cent of the bus services were supplied by NBC companies; in the West Midlands the protracted negotiations with the Midland Motor Omnibus Company ('Midland Red') have not enhanced the area PTE's image. It was not until June 1973 that the West Midlands PTE was able to absorb Midland Red's network of services operating within its area at a cost of £3·6 million.[2] Similar but somewhat more complex issues have arisen when the PTEs have sought, through agency agreements, to determine the frequencies, fares and other standards for British Rail's commuter services.[3]

Comparable difficulties have and will continue to beset the senior managements of some of the metropolitan transport organisations established in recent years in North America and continental Western Europe.

In 1959 the Transit Division of the Port Authority of Allegheny County (which includes Pittsburg) was created by the Pennsylvania State Legislature, but it was not until 1964 that thirty-three independent bus and trolley companies had been acquired and their operations consolidated: even so there are still some bus and all the rail commuter services which remain elusively and annoyingly outside the system. The New York Metropolitan Transportation Authority (MTA) has had to pursue a similar approach in fulfilling its role of providing a unified system for about twelve million New Yorkers travelling within an area of approximately 4,000 square miles. At its inauguration in 1965 the MTA became the parent agency for such concerns as the existing New York Transit Authority, but its progress in establishing leasing and acquisition agreements with other rail and bus independents, which it was empowered to do, has been slow, piecemeal and time consuming in managerial terms, and part of the designated network still remains outside the Authority's control.

In most European conurbations, where the complexities of securing an integrated public transport network might be expected to be less, the transitional organisational problems are still very much in evidence. For example, Helsinki City Transport, which has sought since about 1964 to achieve full co-ordination of all metropolitan public transport modes, including those operated by the Finnish State Railway and five private undertakings, only anticipates accomplishing this goal by 1978. The Greater Stockholm Passenger Transport Company claims that since 1973 it has acquired a monopoly but it took eight years and no less than twenty-five agreements to arrive at complete integration. It is probably true to say that Munich's advanced, lavishly endowed and highly integrated public transport system, which emerged after only three years of planning and negotiation — between 1969 and 1971, owes much to the very special impetus provided when the city was selected to stage the 1972 XX Olympiad and the 1974 World Cup soccer finals.

Most of the reforms of the 1960's concerned with the reorganisation of public transport in conurbations called for a radical adaptation to an administrative ethos developed by competitive and political considerations very different from those prevailing today. In the UK, prior to 1968 the organisation of municipal transport, outside London, had been largely unchanged since the 1930 Transport Act which introduced the road licensing scheme. Until the car posed a real threat, from the 1950's onwards, the obvious weaknesses of the type of organisation to be described were masked.

The traditional city transport department, which our research indicates was essentially representative of many major European urban traffic departments to be found until recently, would include three principal functions in its organisational structure: administration, traffic operations and engineering. Although full-time executive staff were employed, both the strategic and day-to-day management was tightly controlled by the transport committee of the local authority. Lambden[4] provides the profile when he writes:

> The general manager will have to confer with his transport . . . 'committee chairman at least weekly, perhaps several times a week, and will certainly meet the full committee, apart from any subdivisions of it, once a month'. In terms of capital expenditures he . . . 'might well have to specify each item and receive not only prior sanction from the transport committee but also from the estimates and finance committees' . . . He 'can have the bitter experience of seeing his development or economy plans vetoed simply for political reasons . . .' While he . . . 'will be responsible for all his system, much of the municipal accountancy side is dealt with by the town or city treasurer; again the town clerk will look after legal matters and so arrange, for example, the presentation of cases to the Traffic Commissioners'

While a sympathetic chairman might be able to promote the operational interests of the transport department, especially if he were influential within his committee and political party, the system was hardly conducive to innovatory styles of management. Under this scheme of things no marketing personnel, as such, were employed and as one ex-general manager respondent put it, 'the management was concerned with one product and no gimmicks'. This concept of the single product reflects the lack of sophisticated market analysis in the industry. Again little, if any, long term planning was conducted and all managerial emphases concerned · short term factors such as marginal route changes following, for example, shifts in population or the general decline in demand. The organisation would be heavily dependent upon the planning and highways departments of the local authority to provide their longer term operating environment.

With the creation of the PTEs in 1969 several functions had to be imported, in particular those relating to the areas of general policy and administration, finance and transport planning. However, the task of integrating them was not made any easier by the fact that the objectives and much of the broad strategy to be pursued were prescribed by the legislation creating these organisations. Thus, while we consider the UK Government's legislative reforms of urban public transport in major conurbations have been imaginative in their design, those charged with their implementation did' not have very much opportunity to develop, through what is normally an extended mental gestation process, a sense of conviction in the new order at the time it was inaugurated in 1969. In spite of the fact that several senior executives had been brought in from outside the industry and some of these had acquired relevant experience in one or two important facets of the new situation (e.g. those with transport planning backgrounds), the managements of the PTEs were unable to work out in advance, by internal examination, consultation and experiment, the organisational consequences.[5] Thus the attempts to structure the organisation had to be made on a trial and error basis at a time when the directors of the newly established Executives were having to familiarise themselves with their obligations and were, understandably, preoccupied with discharging the most pressing of these. In this respect Greater Hamburg's public transport undertaking offers an interesting contrast. The transport Executive for the Greater Hamburg area — which one British observer has described as having the most commercially successful and 'the finest integrated passenger transport system'[6] — was formed in 1965. However, in Hamburg's case the Executive was voluntarily created by the three principal operators, providing bus, tram, rail and ferry services only after the meticulous preparations had been undertaken by the participants involved.

Organisational criteria

Clearly, then, many of the metropolitan transport Executives have had to implement large scale changes. However, while acknowledging that very special difficulties have existed — and that many still do exist — the nature of both the obligations and the environments of these large public transport organisations make it imperative that they adopt appropriate organisational structures.

The purpose of any organisation is to achieve chosen objectives. These objectives will be accomplished by fulfilling tasks designed to convert resources into products and services and supplying these to meet selected customer needs. In terms of the organisational structure the tasks should be so defined, designated and co-ordinated as to promote: (a) the best possible accommodation with the external environment; (b) a measure of flexibility which will permit successful adaptation to change induced by external and internal factors; (c) collaboration between and within departments, while at the same time reducing conflict and tension in these relationships to a minimum; and (d) accountability of task performance.

A number of points emerge when this view of organisational effectiveness is applied to the various aspects of public transport planning and marketing. The English PTE type of organisational structure will serve largely as the point of reference but because, as has been shown, there are many similarities between this form of organisation and those adopted by most of the foreign metropolitan public transport operators, the observations and recommendations arising will have relatively widescale application.

Corporate, project and operational planning, and marketing are among the prime instruments available to the Executives for coping with their external uncertainties, especially those relating to the political and competitive environments which impact upon the rational pursuit of goal accomplishment.

As Thompson[7] and Lawrence and Lorsch[8] suggest, the more organisations become involved with the external environment so their structures assume a more segmented form due to the greater number of specialists that need to be engaged. These trends, in varying degrees, are reflected in the organisational structures being adopted by the executives. In London Transport, in particular, and the Greater Manchester PTE, the tendency is evident and has reached a relatively high level of sophistication, indicative of the stronger commercial responses which these two organisations have developed.

If organisational goals are to be achieved then the concomitant of increased skill differentiation is integration. However, specialisation tends to engender differences in professional attitudes and behaviour. Given these differences and because modern planning and marketing processes call for greater task interdependencies, there is both the incentive for collaboration and the occasion for internal conflict between the various specialisms.[9] Chapter 4 makes mention of some of the manifestations of organisational discord consequent upon the introduction of certain categories of planning and marketing. The main concern of this chapter is to study a number of ways of facilitating the successful integration of such functions with an emphasis on 'conflict resolution' and task performance. Some obvious measures can be taken to foster a better climate for task co-operation and achievement.

As a starting point, the directives contained in the 1968 Transport Act and subsequent governing legislation need to be interpreted, and where necessary, amplified so that they are operationally meaningful as objectives. This will highlight the main problem-solving areas and suggest the range of functions and specialisms required and indicate the relative contributions each might make. More specifically, an exercise of this kind will allow the necessary organisational tasks and the patterns of joint decision making to be identified, but in both cases prescribed definitions should not be in such detail as to be incompatible with other criteria stated below. There must, of course, be a commitment from the chief executive downwards to ensure that there is an adequate balance between task responsibility and the resources essential for its performance.

Where possible cognate tasks should be grouped together under one head, especially those which are highly interrelated and where, because of the requirement for constant co-operation between the participants involved, close locational proximity is desirable. The need to share information and other resources provides additional support for this proposition. However, the issue is by no means a clear cut one. There is an obvious requirement for a good working relationship to exist between corporate and transport planning and marketing. In the case of some decision-making areas, personnel engaged in all three will be required to make joint contributions and there will be occasions where the same sources of information will be employed. Thus, *a priori,* there seems to be a good case for grouping these functions within one department. Yet each adopts different emphases, orientations and procedures; and given the perceived status differences now existing, each is in need of differential organisational support. We shall be taking account of these factors later on in the discussion.

It is also most important that there should be ample opportunity for informal communication to take place between those responsible for corporate and transport planning and marketing, however these activities are assigned to particular departments. Relatively flat hierarchies, characterised by their flexibility and informality would seem to facilitate the free exchange of information and viewpoints.[10] This kind of collaboration, if it is to make the fullest use of, and co-ordinate, the different areas of expertise, should focus on specific tasks to be performed. Special purpose, inter-disciplinary task forces and project groups can be useful media for handling the dialogue, especially between those located in different departments. However, what needs to be emphasised here is that a balance must be struck between promoting good and tension-free exchanges across departmental or sectional boundaries and achieving accountability for task performance. Important as are excellent informal communications, formal arrangements must always exist, otherwise the decision-making process loses its edge and becomes very protracted.

Koontz and O'Donnell[11] offer some practical advice on how to get the best out of task force systems by stressing, for example, the importance of: unambiguously defining their authority and scope; restricting their use to certain types of subject area (e.g. policy formulation); and having a size and composition of membership conducive to reaching well-informed decisions based on integrating group thinking rather than on compromise or on organisational strength.

Those guiding task-oriented systems have a special responsibility to promote a more symmetrical form of interrelationship between specialist groups. Dalton[12] found that where a staff group is expected to understand the problems of another and establish a special rapport with it in addition to promoting its own ideas and having to justify its existence, but none of these relations was a reciprocal requirement, conflict ensued. As we have seen, an analogy was found to exist in those PTEs where the marketing function had been introduced and where the marketeers had had to expend great energy — perhaps unproductively — in creating relationships with transport and operational planning staff.

Similarly, care should be taken to see that the sequential pattern of task initiation and influence accords with the perceived status ordering. Seiller[13] argues that conflict arises when a lower status group attempts to initiate and influence events. Several good marketing ideas associated with improved standards of service operation have been generated in London Transport but have failed to make the impact they deserve because they have emanated from what has been seen to be non-influential positions in the hierarchy. Such evidence suggests that if an important function like marketing is to flourish it must be represented at the highest levels in the organisational structure. A *cri de coeur* along these lines was included in a conference paper given by London's head of marketing.[14] He says:

 . . . The development of services is a natural part of these (marketing)

125

responsibilities, but if such development is carried out in isolation without the co-operation of other departments, and in particular with the service operators, it has little chance of success. This cannot be overstressed: a marketing department with the unique opportunity to acquire a comprehensive market understanding, and with the resources to communicate within the market, must be seen to take part in the day-to-day management process: marketing can thus ensure that its major aim of ensuring that management takes proper account of market factors is indeed achieved.

It is not within the scope of this paper to discuss the position of the marketing department in the organisation chart. All that need be said is that the head of the department must have direct access to the chief executive, and work closely alongside the operating and other managers . . .

The principle might have been put more forcibly. Any department which is expected to set standards for another to follow must have, and be seen to have, the ultimate authority and resources to establish them and control the implementation of those standards. However, realisable targets are more likely to emerge after a two-way dialogue has taken place between those, on the one hand, who have the ultimate responsibility for establishing standards and controlling their implementation and those, on the other, who have to implement them. It should be a process of critical examination based on what the former desire and what the latter feel they can achieve. Only in this way will effective accountability, participation and goal accomplishment be harmonised.

Organisational tasks and information requirements

Before considering some of the ways in which PTEs might incorporate the several categories of planning and marketing into their organisational structures according to the criteria outlined above, it is appropriate to synthesize the analysis of these functions, as examined in chapters 3 and 4, and express them as a series of specific tasks and related information requirements. From these we can devise a number of organisational options to facilitate them.

Corporate planning tasks

Corporate planning as it might be applied to urban public transport is restricted to determining and selecting options which will best accomplish largely predetermined objectives within a predefined product-market scope. More particularly, because of the somewhat vague nature of the socio-political and financial constraints often contained within those broad objectives, energy must be directed towards interpreting these and making them applicable for the various managerial functions. The more specific tasks which arise can be listed as follows:

1   Interpreting and amplifying the directives contained in the relevant legislation and determining the parameters for generating strategic options in terms of modal split per main corridor and segment of demand, degree of road-rail integration, service network quality and financial policies.
2   Devising planning processes and the means for preparing and testing the options.
3   Selecting from the options generated the strategy which it is thought will provide the optimum targets, consistent with the fulfilment of the legal requirements.
4   Seeking internal and external authority and finance to implement the strategy and consequent plans.
5   Planning the implementation of the selected strategy by translating the objectives into quantifiable targets for each of the main functions.
6   Developing procedures for preparing and evaluating and co-ordinating project and operational plans.
7   Ensuring that the organisational structure assists rather than hinders the strategy implementation.
8   Monitoring how far implemented strategic and operational plans achieve their aims and adapting these where necessary.

Given the relative inflexibility of existing urban land use patterns and the length of the gestation period for developing a commercially viable new transport system which incorporates technology radically different from that included in the present one, the ultimate planning horizon will be, perhaps, twenty years or more. Naturally, over such an extended period of time the external contingencies can be considerable: the history of unexpected changes in seemingly established market trends, not to speak of the examples of dramatic modifications to political ideology, is extensively documented. Yet none of this invalidates the need for taking the long range view in planning, especially in the public transport industry; rather it strengthens it since the rationale for long term corporate planning is indeed conditioning the enterprise for handling uncertainty. A series of short term perspectives by themselves, that is to say unlinked to the achievement of some realistic and more acceptable future state, will in all probability result in planning adopting a defensive role and being 'retrospective' in its orientation, dealing with the deficiencies. of short-sighted decision making conducted in previous periods.

This said, it must be recognised that corporate planners will inevitably devote much of their effort to shorter range forward planning, covering periods of, say, three to five years. Certainly in the PTEs there is a pressing need to establish comprehensive operational planning, which as we stated in chapter 3 requires to be centrally guided and co-ordinated. Fresh operational and long range strategic plans should be prepared annually, rolling the entire programme forward by a year.

Transport planning

Indisputably, the transport planners have enjoyed a considerable expansion and influence in most of the PTEs. The reasons for this have been examined, the primary one being the statutory requirement to produce a long range plan and the interpretation this has been given by the Executives.

Within what we consider to be its appropriate parameters the tasks of transport planning can be stated as follows:

1 *Long and medium term infrastructure planning*
(a) Inside the limits prescribed by corporate planning, generating long term infrastructure options for review.
(b) For the chosen infrastructure, developing medium term project plans *in conjunction with* marketing personnel, so as to (i) test the concepts inherent in the long range plan, (ii) establish the future service-mix, and (iii) phase the implementation.
(c) Updating the infrastructure plan in accordance with environmental and political changes and the assessments of the medium term project developments.
2 *Short term planning*
In conjunction with marketing, financial and manpower planning and operations, formulating the most cost-effective operational network plan consistent with the development of the selected long term infrastructure and corporate objectives, on the one hand, and customer needs and the financial and manpower resources, on the other.

It might seem that the distinction between the long term aspects of both corporate and transport planning are academic, especially as the corporate plan cannot be formulated without an important input from the transport planners as to the technical possibilities relating to the options under consideration. However, given the relatively sophisticated nature of the social cost/benefit analysis and mathematical modelling involved in transport planning, there is a real danger that the contributions of other functional areas, financial and marketing and even operations, will be understated unless the differentiation is made and acknowledged in the organisational structure.

Marketing tasks

In contrast to other forms of planning, marketing is by far the most radical departure as an organised and formalised PTE activity. In the public transport context, both because of the nature of external controls and the industry's unique features, marketing's parameters are somewhat constrained. Despite these constraints a number of very important tasks remain:

1 Selecting those segments of demand with the relatively greatest potential for public transport as the basis for formulating marketing strategy.
2 Within the selected infrastructure and *in conjunction with* the transport planners in the long and medium term and the senior operational staff in the short run, determining passenger service mixes for bus and rail and other forms of urban passenger transport for each segment of demand. This would include:
    (i) influencing the pricing policy, and the tactics to be adopted, e.g. special fares for selected homogeneous groups, differential fare levels by time of day and so on;
    (ii) influencing detailed product and service specifications covering such matters as scheduling, length of traffic day, vehicle frequency details, fare collection systems, passenger facilities on and off the vehicle, etc.; and
    (iii) promoting the services.
3 Undertaking public relations, e.g.
    (i) using mass media to argue public transport's case for preferential treatment,
    (ii) lobbying special and influential groups in order to secure support for public transport, e.g. the Press, political parties, civic conservation groups, etc., and
    (iii) dealing with the enquiries and complaints of the travelling public.

4   Promoting a corporate image for the Executive.

5   Inculcating operations staff with a sense of the public relations role which they inevitably have to fulfil.

6   In special segments of demand, e.g. coach hire, plant contract work, parcel delivery and collection, carrying out more direct sales promotion.

It is important to stress once more that marketing task performance is not just confined to the short term, but involves a phased implementation over planning cycles which should extend to the most distant time horizons adopted by the transport planners. Accordingly, it can be argued that marketing should have a total responsibility for all facets of planning, including transport planning, which relate to fulfilling the needs of the urban traveller.

Certainly this contention accords with established marketing theory which unequivocally designates the formulation of new product and service concepts as a marketing task on the grounds that by locating the new product planning section within the marketing department a better customer perspective will result.[15]

In many ways the transport and new product planning functions are analogous. For the former the length of the planning cycle may extend much further into the future and there may be considerably more environmental constraints with which to contend, but these are primarily differences of degree rather than principle. However, in spite of the fact that an increasing number of highly successful firms — especially those in the consumer industries — have adopted an organisational pattern where the planning of new products is subsumed under marketing, we hesitate to suggest its formal adoption by the PTEs at this stage. For them to do so now would demand a complete and sudden reversal of the status order, a situation which has been reinforced by several substantial factors and one which is not confined to the English PTEs. Furthermore, there are probably not the staff currently available who are capable of combining both perspectives. In the long run when marketing has established itself the natural similarities of two functions will doubtless become apparent and the change can be a 'process' rather than a 'resented revolution'.

We now turn briefly to the organisational relationship arising from the juxtaposition of marketing and operational tasks. If marketing is to determine most of the standards for the service mix — certainly in the short and medium terms — it might seem reasonable to suggest that the function should also be vested with formal line authority over operations which has, with the exception of promotion, the responsibility for achieving these standards. The planning, implementation and control elements must be

130

properly integrated; and operations, dealing directly as it does with the customer, would appear to be an essentially logistical dimension of marketing strategy. Perhaps the argument has appeal. However, for a number of practical reasons we do not favour this course. Chapter 4 makes the point that marketing in this industry is unable to apply any real sales leverage. Without a sales force it is unlikely to have sufficient organisational 'muscle' to exercise realistic line authority over operational staff who have at the managerial levels an extensive public transport experience and a largely unsympathetic attitude towards modern marketing methods. Having a direct relationship with the public is only part of the operational task: other aspects, such as engineering, maintenance and crew supervision do not usually fall within the scope of marketing personnel's experience or competence.

Information requirements

In any organisation the vast majority of decisions are facilitated by formalised information flows which seek to minimise the degree to which executives rely on judgement alone. Many of these channels involve information internally essential to the administration and financing of the business, and without which the organisation cannot perform legally required procedures such as accounting or company secretarial activities. In contrast, the emphasis for the planning and marketing functions under consideration will be primarily on tapping the flow of relevant external information. In broad terms the information sought by corporate and transport planners and marketeers will relate to:

1   Long term trends, e.g. socio-economic, demographic, employment, legislative and technological, which are likely to impinge on, and influence, land use patterns and modal split preferences.
2   Factual and attitudinal data which will help to identify and define segments of demand which offer the greater potential for public transport: for example, journey purpose(s), origin and destination patterns, including traffic volume data by time, journey purpose, etc., and preferred mode of travel and factors underlying choice such as directness, speed, frequency, reliability, comfort, price/cost, accessibility and on- and off-vehicle facilities.
3   Empirical data to aid in the formulation of optimum mixes.
4   Measures of passenger satisfaction with existing services against established service-mix standards. Such monitoring would need to be undertaken on a very regular basis.

131

Comparing the sets of tasks stated, with the information requirements listed, it is evident that certain data inputs exclusively relate to specific functional tasks while others would be shared by all three groups of specialists. For this reason we have not attempted to present the information requirements under separate headings.

Organisational structure options

There is an infinite number of structures which could be adopted but it seems sensible to concentrate on what would appear to be the most practicable. We make the distinction between the actual provision of services by operational personnel (a 'line' responsibility) on the one hand, and the 'staff' functions who formulate the overall strategy and service specifications and assess performance, on the other. In this respect we recognise that for the former the traditional organisational pattern is divisionally based. An examination is made of the extent to which staff functions should be centralised, confined to a headquarters directorate as opposed to being placed under the control of operations. Finally, we assess alternative structures for establishing interrelationships between the various staff specialisms and co-ordinating these.

The degree of centralisation for staff functions

In each of the PTEs an executive director has overall responsibility for operations, but the detailed supervision of service provision largely devolves upon the heads of divisions, whose boundaries have been determined by 'political', geographical and fleet size considerations. Given this control structure for operations, three broad options might be contemplated with regard to locating corporate and transport planning and marketing: namely, 'complete' centralisation, 'minimal' centralisation and 'partial' centralisation.

(a) *Complete centralisation* The basic concept behind a completely centralised structure would be that operations should lose all planning authority and simply be viewed purely as a logistical arm of the business. All planning and marketing would be carried out at PTE headquarters, the assumption being that only through such a move could the 'production-orientation' of the traditional management be overcome and the new managerial functions introduced gain the emphasis they deserve. Operations, though divested of its customary managerial discretion, would

132

be completely free to deal with the extensive problems of staff control in a highly labour-intensive system and matters associated with the employment and maintenance of service vehicles. Therefore, while it would retain full administrative responsibility for all operating installations such as garages, workshops, stores and stations, duty rosters, the recruitment, training and supervision of crews and engineering staff, collection of fares and the security of passengers and their luggage, operations would not have jurisdiction over route planning, establishing frequencies, length of the traffic day, fares policy and all forms of publicity. All corporate and transport planning tasks as well as those concerned with financial control and with salary and wage structures would be centralised.

This option does have some strong adherents in the PTEs. The Hamburg operation, referred to earlier, has been put forward as a highly successful example of a centralised structure. The Hamburger Verkersverband (HVV), the transport Executive, has total responsibility for every aspect of planning, organising and financing mass transport within its area. The operation of services, to the exact specifications drawn up by the HVV, is left to the operating companies. Thus the relationship between the HVV. and its operators, who are reimbursed out of the revenue collected for the services provided, is a contractual one. To reinforce the contract's effectiveness, the compensation paid to the operating 'agents' relates not only to the costs of service provision but also to the way the quality standards decreed by the HVV are actually met.

Those who wish to see such a pattern of organisation and planning applied to the PTEs underline HVV's impressive record as supporting evidence; for example, between 1965 and 1970 passengers carried and passenger kilometres covered rose by 6·3 and 5·6 per cent respectively; and the financial situation was correspondingly good. It must be pointed out that this operational success probably owes much to the very high rates of investment in that city's public transport network during the 1960's. However, UK advocates of the scheme place considerable emphasis on the importance of the contract which binds the operators. Certainly the principle of divorcing widely divergent activities as operations, planning and control accords with many of the organisational criteria we have suggested. One important qualification to adopting the HVV model is that we have already stressed the need to establish a consciousness of the marketing concept throughout the organisation and that operational personnel be trained in the public relations role which they ought to fulfil. Total and rigid separation of these functions may well make this sort of activity difficult. Similarly, ongoing market research activities will require considerable help and co-operation from operational staff and this again

133

militates against too rigid a divorce of these functions. Given that the member companies of the HVV themselves took the initiative in forming the current organisational structure, it may well be that they have attempted to overcome potential problems of this nature. In the UK, however, where the level of investment has been much lower, where public transport has declined much further and where existing organisational structures have been externally imposed, in some cases adversely affecting staff morale, very careful attention would have to be given to these areas before the adoption of a similar structure could be advocated.

(b)   *Minimal centralisation* Near to the opposite pole of the spectrum of possible approaches for assigning staff functions is a structure which, because it would seek to consolidate rather than undermine operations' planning discretion, has its strongest proponents among senior operational staff. Under such a scheme responsibility for most of the planning and marketing of services would rest with senior divisional managers. Perhaps only corporate planning and financial control and co-ordination of the marketing-mixes between divisions would be carried out at headquarters which would act very much in the capacity of a holding company, primarily concerned with corporate strategy.

The corporate planning group would be responsible for longer term transport planning while shorter range projections, such as the redesign of the existing network and contributions towards the formulation and implementation of demonstration experiments would be the responsibility of the divisions. To avoid duplication at divisional level, macro-environmental forecasts (with reference to population, employment and other land use patterns) would also be carried out by the corporate planning group who would service divisional marketing and planning departments. Liaison with central and local government for the purpose of obtaining plan approval and financial backing would also be retained by the headquarters' directorate.

In the divisions the chief operating manager would be accountable for profitability, quality control of the services provided and for liaison with headquarters about the corporate plan and also with other divisions on joint services and schemes. Preparation of the divisional transport and operating plans for bus and rail would be delegated to an area planning manager. Determination of the marketing-mix most likely to meet corporate and divisional objectives and responsibility for service advertising and general area public relations would be assigned to a divisional marketing manager. Marketing research would also be one of his duties.

This structure does seem on the face of it to satisfy the requirement that those who implement plans should be part of the planning process. If planning and marketing are to make an impact their importance must be believed in by those who have the most direct control over the provision of service sought, the divisional managers. It can be reasoned that if divisional managers are charged with wide-ranging responsibility for creating and applying plans and marketing ideas, tangible improvements at the point of service supply will materialise more quickly than if the new activities were infused at a senior and central location in the hierarchy. The proposition is in part a tenable one. Applying the same rationale many large commercial firms have successfully adopted this 'from the ground up' approach to planning and marketing. But the degree of autonomy being proposed here can only be justified where planning units are characterised by considerable product-range diversity and spatial separation. These features do not apply to PTE divisional structures.

The amount of delegated planning discretion which this proposal advocates in order to obtain the necessary co-operation of the operating staff is excessive. The disadvantages that are likely to ensue would surely represent too high a price to pay. Those whose prime task it is to supply services to the public would be largely free to determine their own standards and judge their own performance. Apart from violating an important principle, it is doubtful whether the act of conferring responsibility for policy formulation, even if it is backed up with adequate technical assistance (no mean feat), would make divisional managers sufficiently sympathetic to the needs of planning and marketing. Their lack of appreciation of, and declared hostility towards, marketing has been demonstrated. Just assuming that they are able to develop more favourable attitudes in time, an objection can still be made about duplicating planning and marketing resources; the demand and operational differences between most divisions are not great enough to warrant the duplication which would arise. Furthermore, this proposal, if adopted, would not be conducive to maintaining a flexible divisional structure. Without a strong initiative from the centre it would be less easy to promote interdivisional co-operation over trans-conurbation schemes, e.g. a rapid transit system; and such a structure would very likely perpetuate a pre-1968 style autonomy rather than promoting the integrated conurbation-wide public transport system required by the Act.

(c) *Partial centralisation* The drift of our argument is clear. We contend that most of the planning and marketing staff functions should be centralised at PTE headquarters.

Corporate planning by definition must be a centralised activity. The design and testing of infrastructure concepts — both long and medium term ones — should in no way be decentralised. Failure to centralise would undermine the fulfilment of one of the 1968 Transport Act's basic requirements. The centralised aspects of marketing should be: undertaking marketing research; determining criteria for the quality of service required throughout the PTE and formulating proposals for service-mix changes and demonstration projects; monitoring performances against detailed standards agreed with operations; conducting external communications such as advertising, general public relations and promoting corporate identity; and acting as an exchange desk for new service ideas obtained from both external and internal sources.

In addition to being represented on the Executive by a director — and thus sharing in strategic decision making — we feel that operations should make a technical contribution towards short term transport planning and marketing. Admittedly the extent of its delegated powers would be limited, but it is essential for some autonomy to be exercised by operational staff if they are to become psychologically committed to the need for improving customer satisfaction. Furthermore, with their detailed knowledge of the local scene the operators can make important planning and marketing contributions.

It is in the area of 'short term (transport) planning' — planning the future development of the existing operational network in the most cost-effective manner (see p.128) — that there exists some scope for involving the senior operating managers in the decision making, although the headquarters' staff must retain ultimate responsibility for initiating and co-ordinating the process. Decentralised marketing tasks would involve modifying and applying headquarters' recommendations and would largely turn on defining divisional scheduling and frequency specifications and local stage fares, publishing timetables for services run by the division and performing limited public relations confined to local services.

The number of staff required would be extremely small. For example, within any division one staff member should suffice. Preferably he should have an extensive operational background and be sufficiently senior in status to make an impact; his planning and marketing skills might be acquired through a suitable period of training provided by headquarters' staff. He would report direct to the division's general manager, but also he would have a staff relationship with the chief marketing executive at headquarters. To ensure that serious consideration is given to all headquarters' proposals and that the divisional adaptation of any of these does not undermine the essentials of the standards prescribed, it would be necessary for the divisions to submit detailed plans annually. These should itemise which proposals are to be applied, explain how local conditions are being accommodated and justify the exclusion of others recommended by headquarters. In addition, the plans might include details of locally generated schemes. Through consultations with the operations director and the divisional managers, central staff could assess and pass annual plans and these could be processed by the corporate planning machinery. Plans once accepted would form the basis for monitoring performance which would be done centrally.

Structures for accommodating planning and marketing at HQ

Below we propose three alternative structures for accommodating corporate and transport planning and marketing activities at PTE headquarters within the framework of partial centralisation. The objectives are to suggest ways of placing corporate planning and, in particular, marketing on a better footing and promoting interrelationships between these and the already established transport planning function which will be more conducive to all three achieving their tasks as specified earlier. None of the structures to be examined purports to be ideal; each has merits in relation to different sets of circumstances prevailing in the PTE organisations surveyed.

In all three models the recommendations with regard to corporate planning are identical, as the case for this function's position at the head of the hierarchy is decisive and unambiguous. The major inputs will come, as stated, from the transport, financial and marketing planners and, therefore, only a small corporate planning staff is required as part of the director general's secretariat. Such a position in the hierarchy, apart from emphasising the chief executive's role in corporate strategy formulation and implementation, also makes the point that corporate planning must be concerned with the strategic development of all functions and not just transport planning.

We now turn to our main concern, the effective integration of transport planning and marketing. To a large extent we shall be looking at the problems of co-ordinating transport planning and marketing from the latter's viewpoint. This does not represent any bias on the authors' part, but it is merely a reflection of the organisational imbalances existing between the two functions. With very few exceptions transport planning has a strongly established position and marketing a very weak one in PTEs. Given the vital role which transport planning has to play towards formulating a more competitive public transport system its present standing in the hierarchy is in most cases justifiable. Marketing's contribution is no less important and its prescribed tasks are designed to make it an effective bridge between the relatively long range activities of the transport planners and the largely logistical duties of the operational staff. If it is to fulfil this requirement its organisational status must be enhanced and its resources greatly expanded.

In view of the measure of centralisation proposed for marketing, there will be several groups of specialists, marketing researchers, marketing strategists, communications personnel and so on, whose work needs to be co-ordinated. Three possible ways of arranging the specialist sections involved and integrating these with the transport planning function will be analysed.

One approach would be to assign the groups of marketeers to an existing directorate, the obvious one being transport planning. Within this framework the heads of the transport planning and marketing sections might report direct to the Executive member for say, 'network' planning (see Fig. 5.1 — Model A). Alternatively, the transport planning and marketing sections could respectively be unified by, on the one hand, a transport planning manager and, on the other, a marketing manager, and both would be responsible to the same Executive member (see Fig. 5.2 — Model B). Another option is to create a separate directorate of marketing (see Fig. 5.3 — Model C).

Model A more than model B, and certainly more than model C, should encourage lateral communications between the transport planners and the marketeers, on the assumption that these will be promoted more than when formal divisions exist between them. In the same vein model A permits all network research activities to be concentrated under one head. This we consider to be an advantage: the distinctions between information required for transport planning and marketing are far from being clear cut and it would be wasteful and disruptive from a decision making point of view to have separate locations for gathering, analysing and interpreting data.[16] For the benefits of model A to be realised, the director co-ordinating transport planning and marketing must have a good understanding of both areas and, in view of the way the latter has been neglected, he must be prepared to correct the imbalance between the two. For example, he would have to increase considerably research budgets and recruit additional specialists if the information necessary to mount an effective marketing programme was to be forthcoming. Similarly, to conduct promotional campaigns on the scale recommended would call for enormously expanded appropriations and new posts to be established. However, in practice directors charged with responsibility for both transport planning and

138

Fig. 5.1 'Network' (marketing and transport) planning HQ directorate

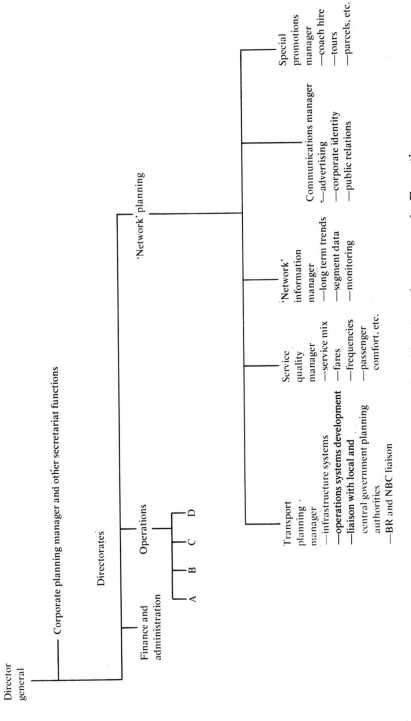

Model A — Marketing and transport planning sectional heads each report to the Executive

Fig. 5.2 'Network' (marketing and transport) planning HQ directorate

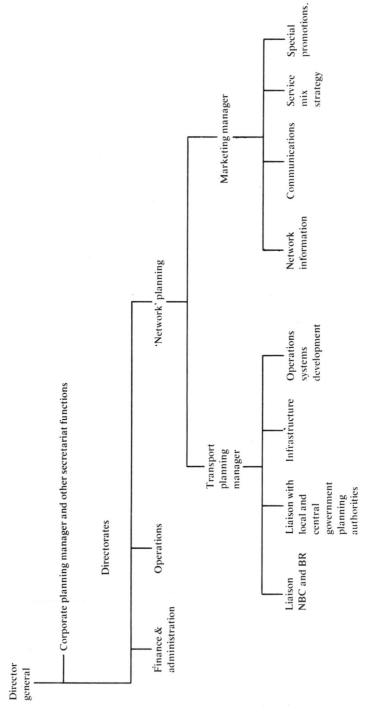

Model B — Marketing and transport planning sections co-ordinated by a marketing manager and a transport planning manager respectively

Fig. 5.3 Separate marketing and transport planning HQ directorates

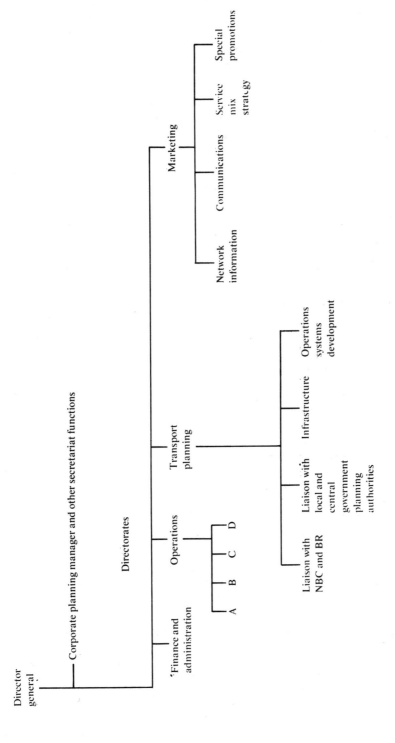

Model C

marketing and co-ordinating the two will themselves be transport planners: three of the four PTEs have directors of (transport) planning[17] and while these are all capable of exercising wider perspectives it would be unrealistic to assume that they have the full appreciation of marketing necessary to give the function the considerable support that it now requires. Thus, while proposal A offers many potential benefits, in the present circumstances prevailing it is likely to only enhance marketing's role and influence marginally.

In comparison the model B structure might allow a slightly more cohesive strategy to be established and with marketing personnel coalesced under a manager a better opportunity might also exist for attracting additional resources.

In these respects, the model C approach might offer distinct advantages. Having directorial status the head of marketing should be in a better position to demand the resources required. However, with a separate directorate of marketing there is likely to be a potential loss of informal communication, especially compared with the degree of lateral interchange possible under the model A structure; and, in particular, some problems may arise in connection with the management of network research. We still maintain that as an activity data collection and analysis should be perceived and managed as an entity. Setting up a corporate network information office might offer a solution but there are strong reasons which can be weighed against this proposal. In volume terms the detailed information required to fulfil the marketing tasks specified should exceed that demanded by the corporate and even transport planners. Besides which only a very small proportion of the total data requirement can be regarded as exclusive to the needs of the corporate and transport planners. Therefore, it is recommended that responsibility for obtaining and analysing network intelligence should be vested in the marketing department. Pettigrew[18] makes the point that 'information control' is an important 'power resource'. Thus a PTE marketing department which has full responsibility for network intelligence may be able to establish organisational credibility, even if it is denied the considerable influence which normally stems from directing a large sales force. By assuring that other interested departments have good access to the data collected, the marketing director would help to create a more favourable image for his department in the minds of his PTE colleagues, as well as a sense of dependence on his staff.[19]

For a large PTE at least, a model C structure has another merit. Marketing must not only have a good rapport with transport planning but, in particular, it has to foster the full co-operation of the operational staff.

142

As a separate department with its own director and a well-defined identity, and having adequate resource support, marketing should be better placed to 'liaise' on both fronts and thus act as a bridge between the two.

Once the bridgehead has been properly established, and we recognise this might take some time to achieve, it should be possible to bring about a more cohesive integration of marketing and transport planning tasks by transferring the responsibility for the latter to the marketing director. As we argued earlier, new 'product' planning, which in this industry is the activity currently undertaken by the transport planners, should be subsumed under marketing. Thus by first building up marketing's organisational role through the creation of a separate directorate, which has full responsibility for network intelligence, the practical prerequisites for reaping the potential benefits attributed to the model A structure may be realised by another route. Under these conditions the senior marketing executive should be capable of appreciating the technical needs of long term infrastructure and network planning so as to guide the work of the specialist planners involved, and under his direction the urban traveller's needs would be more sharply in focus.

The various structures proposed, although not related to specific PTEs, implicitly took account of some of the major differences between them. However, no allowance was made for the attitudes and skills of the senior executives within the PTEs. It is not our wish to comment here on particular individuals but we do recognise that personal attributes inevitably play an important part in determining the nature, extent and consequences of organisational change. If the benefits of change along the lines recommended are to be realised a reorientation of senior managerial attitudes will be necessary in many cases. Furthermore, improvements in functional skills will also be required in some instances.

Notes

[1] E. Ginzberg and E. W. Reilly, *Effective Change in Large Organisations*, Columbia University Press, 1966.

[2] The West Midlands Traffic Commissioners in their contribution to the *Annual Report of the Traffic Commissioners for 1971/72*, published March 1973, regarded earlier failures to integrate part of Midland Red's network as being one of a number of factors accounting for the WM PTE's poor performance — as they appraised it in their outspoken report.

[3] From the PTEs' point of view some of the main bones of contention have been: (i) British Rail's insistence that a fixed fee should be paid for the

services provided, whereas the PTEs would like to receive the revenue from the services offered and reimburse BR with the costs involved, according to a formula which is based on marginal costs, and which reflects the quality of the performances achieved; and (ii) British Rail's refusal to consider the possibility of vesting in the PTEs the infrastructure and rolling stock for local rail services, even where this is technically feasible, e.g. as it seems to be to a large extent on Merseyside.

[4] W. Lambden, *Bus and Coach Operation: principles and practice for the transport student,* 4th ed., Iliffe, 1969, p. 15.

[5] See the prerequisites of successful organisational change as recommended by L. R. Greiner, 'Patterns of organisational change' *Harvard Business Review,* May—June 1967, pp. 119—130.

[6] D. S. Hellewell, in an unpublished report for the Greater Manchester PTE, written in February 1972 after he had made a tour of inspection of West German and Dutch passenger transport organisations.

[7] J. D. Thompson, *Organisations in Action,* McGraw-Hill, 1967.

[8] P. R. Lawrence and J. W. Lorsch, *Organisations and Environment,* Irwin, 1967.

[9] In addition to the Thompson, and Lawrence and Lorsch theses in this respect, see R. E. Walton and J. M. Datton, 'The management of interdepartmental conflict: a model and review' *Administrative Science Quarterly,* vol. 14, 1969, pp. 73—84.

[10] T. Burns and G. M. Stalker, *The Management of Innovation,* Tavistock Publications, 1961.

[11] H. Koontz and C. O'Donnell, *Principles of Management: an analysis of managerial functions,* 5th ed., McGraw-Hill, 1972; see ch. 19. These two authors have recommended that when task forces or committees are established their broad objectives should be specified as should be their investigatory parameters, time scales of deliberation and the types of conclusion to be established, e.g. decisions, recommendations or observations. The authority and scope should be determined preferably by an executive holding office at the next highest point in the hierarchy to whom all the task force members, or their immediate superiors are accountable. On size Koontz and O'Donnell suggest between about five and eight is an ideal number; where the facets of the problem demand a larger membership they advise on the use of subcommittees. All those comprising a task force should have roughly equal status, have authority to take decisions without recourse to their superiors and have the appropriate social skills to make contributions to a decision making process aimed to culminate in integrating group thinking.

[12] M. Dalton, *Men Who Manage,* Wiley, 1959.

[13] J. Seiller, 'Diagnosing interdepartmental conflict' *Harvard Business Review,* Sept.—Oct. 1967, pp. 121—32.

[14] A. C. N. Brown, 'The development and marketing of public transport services', Proceedings of the symposium: *Promoting Public Transport,* University of Newcastle-upon-Tyne, April 1973.

[15] See P. Kotler, *Marketing Management: analysis, planning and control,* 2nd ed., Prentice Hall, 1972.

[16] See K. P. Uhl, 'Better management of market information' *Business Horizons,* Spring 1966, vol.9, pp. 75—81.

[17] The Director of planning of the Merseyside PTE resigned at the end of 1974 and it was decided not to appoint a successor, thus discontinuing this important Executive post.

[18] A. M. Pettigrew, 'Information control as a power resource' *Sociology,* vol. 6, 1972, pp. 187—204.

[19] G. Strauss, in 'Tactics of lateral relationship: the purchasing agent' *Administrative Science Quarterly,* vol. 7, 1962, pp. 161—86, illustrates how purchasing agents were able to increase their organisational standing by favourably influencing the terms of acquisitions.

PART III

Towards a More Competitive System of Urban Public Transport

6 Using Market Research for Service Improvements: the Existing Evidence

There can be no doubt that without explicit support at senior managerial level marketing will not prosper and the prophesies of those who are especially sceptical of it will be self-fulfilling. Senior managerial support is naturally a requirement for the successful organisation and operation of any facet of business but, as we have seen, the need is exaggerated for the marketing function in this industry not only since it has been sorely neglected but also because of the lack of a sales force to give marketing its traditional base within the hierarchy. Further, its interrelationship with the expanded and well-established transport planning function and corporate planning is extremely complex and must be carefully structured if all three are to perform effectively and create a more competitive public transport system. We have, therefore, sought to make some recommendations to ensure that corporate and transport planning and marketing are properly represented and complement rather than conflict with one another.

Having proposed the managerial structures best able to encourage marketing, we now examine the process itself which we have defined as a composite of market planning, information services and marketing promotion activities. The process commences with the systematic collection and analysis of data concerning current and anticipated market needs which then require translation into short, medium and long term marketing plans. Once implemented, these must be closely monitored to ensure that where trends deviate from those forecast the proper adjustments may be made. Recognition and fulfilment of the need for such data collection is a prime characteristic of any market-oriented company, but its importance for a large urban passenger transport undertaking is underlined because of the complexity of the demand determinants, the social importance of the product, and the predicament caused by a rapidly declining demand.

Marketing research projects usually have two phases; firstly the analysis of all relevant secondary data and, secondly, the conduct of primary or original research. This chapter examines the first of these, while in the next we report on research conducted by ourselves in the North West of England. Unlike many research topics, reviewing the secondary material as it relates to public transport marketing is a considerable task in itself for it involves collecting data from scattered sources in the United Kingdom, Europe and America. No such review exists and only now are attempts being made to establish an agency with responsibility for collecting and disseminating research information.[1]

There are a number of methodological approaches to which the marketing manager must pay heed, particularly demand modelling, market research survey and experimental approaches. Findings from the first two have been presented in chapter 2 when assessments were made of the competitive attributes of urban transport modes, and we therefore present only a summary here. This chapter largely concentrates on published empirical research data which transport marketeers should evaluate when considering how to improve the various elements of public transport's service-mix. In the next chapter additional evidence, derived from the authors' research programme conducted in the North West of England, is presented.

Demand modelling and market surveys

In chapter 2 the reasons for urban passenger transport's declining market were explored and in this context public transport was analysed in comparison to the major competitive alternatives. Use was made of the findings of market research surveys and demand modelling exercises. Both sources are important to the marketing manager seeking to improve existing services and planning innovatory ones.

The considerable research effort applied to determining the value of time savings, much of it government sponsored, has been primarily motivated by the desire to employ social cost-benefit analysis for investment appraisal, but there are also a number of 'spin-offs' for the marketing manager. Two studies[2] have clearly disaggregated the values attached to walking, waiting and in-transit time; the much heavier disutilities attached to the first two activities suggest that expenditure should be concentrated on improving these journey attributes rather than improving vehicle speeds. Other studies[3] also show that the value attached to time savings increases with income, although there may be a barrier at approximately the £3,000 mark (at 1966 wage levels) where the relationship no longer holds. The implication to be drawn from such findings is that premium priced services differentiated on the basis of time savings will find greatest support among the medium and higher income groups. The importance of the political environment to public transport has been similarly demonstrated by Quarmby[2] and McGillivray,[4] whose respective models suggest that the disincentive of higher parking costs has a greater effect on modal choice than the incentive of reduced fares. Both variables are important to the demand for public transport, but only by indirect action does the marketing manager have any influence over the former.

A number of market research surveys, also reviewed in chapter 2, reveal broadly similar findings concerning the priorities people perceived to be most important in a public transport system.[5] These are valuable both for understanding modal choice and as a tool for management decision making, since they provide a starting point for considering improvements to public transport's competitive standing. A number of operators have indeed commissioned their own surveys for this purpose, usually seeking to elicit the features of the system perceived to be in most urgent need of improvement.[6] In methodological sophistication they do not approach the studies referred to in chapter 2 and in particular one might mention their failure to analyse the perceptions of particular subgroups as determined for example, by use or non-use of public transport and access to car. They merely present results as global totals and, therefore, may miss highly individualistic profiles for such subgroups. That such differences can exist is attested by the General Motors study (again referred to in chapter 2).[7] In the UK London Transport is developing a 'trade-off'/games theory approach to try and inject contemporary consumer preferences and priorities into the investment decision-making process for specific projects, but as yet this may only be regarded as experimental.[8]

All these studies reveal a consistently high priority attached to reliability, frequency and the avoidance of transfers, and although one must concede that it is most unlikely that the ideal can be met in all respects, guidelines are thus provided for the concentration of effort. In particular, Wilson's study[9] indicates meaningful ways in which an operator might segment his market as a basis for determining market strategies. Degree of accessibility to the car provides a useful primary analytical unit in this respect because the major strategic possibilities are to win back car users and to improve satisfaction for, and increase patronage of, existing users. His study also provides insights of the contrasting needs and perceptions of commuters to central and non-central locations in two very different urban environments.

Monitored and controlled changes of the mix

Examination is now made of the evidence concerning transport characteristics from two empirically based sources, transport operating statistics and demonstration or experimental project data. The major source of the findings quoted are the US demonstration projects which have been financed by the American Government via the 1960, 1964 and 1966 Highway Acts in a programme of research which in dollar expenditure far outweighs anything attempted in the UK. Between 1961 and 1969 central and local agencies jointly contributed £262 million to such research. In this country a working group was established in January 1969 with the following terms of reference: 'To consider what can be done in the shorter term to facilitate the operation of buses in cities, whether by way of changes in traffic policies or by different kinds of bus operation; and to recommend a series of demonstration projects.' The agreed expenditure was £550,000. Apart from the obvios disparity in resource allocations, the UK studies appear far more limited for, of the eleven projects, seven concern bus lanes, two concern operational and locational control and only two projects in this initial programme were concerned with measuring the demand effects of new kinds of bus operation. These two market-oriented schemes cost less than £28,000, just over 5 per cent of the total. This first generation of projects has been complemented by further programmes such as those in Stevenage and on Merseyside which go some way to meet these criticisms.

It might also be asked what it is that these projects are supposed to 'demonstrate'. Are they primarily intended to demonstrate success by increasing usage of the public transport system, or are they more concerned to demonstrate the nature of demand for public transport by manipulation of particular variables? If the latter, one would naturally expect effort to be expended in distinguishing the experimental variable's related effects from the secular trends, seasonal variation, weather effects, or from variations in supply. However, this rarely seems to be the case, particularly with the American programmes which were often experiments where a number of different variables are altered at the same time and, therefore, they seemed more concerned with patronage improvement than with the derivation of demand functions. The analysis presented below is, therefore, often interpretative on the part of the present authors rather than the original commentators, because we are attempting to fit these results and their implications into a framework for which many of the experiments were not devised. The framework referred to is once again that of the marketing-mix presented in chapter 2, with the addition of a third dimension, as outlined below:

1　Product attributes: (a) price; (b) in-vehicle time; (c) mesh density; (d) frequency; (e) reliability; (f) comfort.
2　Promotion.
3　Fare scales and labour productivity: the introduction of one-man bus

operation and the ensuing serious time delays have necessitated experimental changes to the fare system which inevitably affect the marketing-mix. Assessments of these fare systems, primarily designed to meet 'production' constraints, are therefore given separately in this third section.

1 Product attributes

Price Consideration of the pricing of transport services impinges on the most traditional domains of the applied economist, but for marketing management the problem is wider than consideration of price elasticity of demand alone. For example, the interrelationship between price and speed of boarding is one extremely important interface, while the promotional effectiveness of the adopted fare structure is another. However, most of the evidence below relates to the more traditional concerns.

Elasticity measurement

(a)   *System-wide elasticities* The natural starting point for an examination of the empirical evidence is the measure of elasticity most widely accepted in the United States and which is commonly used to make *ex ante* assessments of the level of fare increase necessary to produce a required increase in revenue. By collating evidence of the ridership loss associated with fare increases from public transport systems throughout the United States, Simpson and Curtin[11] derived a short run elasticity of 0·33. Schneider[12] quotes this figure as the accepted norm in the US, although he sets out to undermine it by showing that different segments and end-uses react differently to price changes. In the UK London Transport has made conscious efforts to determine price elasticities through analysis of operating statistics and the Fares and Charges Department use a figure of 0·3. In further research, using passenger miles rather than passenger trips as the expression of quantity sold, London Transport estimated an elasticity of 0·2 following a fares revision in 1970. The discrepancy between this and the previous figure is accounted for by the fact that the subsequent fares revision concentrated on longer journey lengths which are considered likely to be less elastic.[13]

In the US, studies have been completed in Boston[14] to analyse, among other things, the effects of fare reductions, but as the programme introduced major price and frequency modifications simultaneously, the combination of these two elements made it difficult to isolate elasticity figures. In the few instances where price decreases were made with no accompanying increase in frequency the results were disappointing. For example, on the Bedford and Hudson line fares were reduced by an average of 28 per cent for a period of seven months, but the small passenger improvement at the start of the experiment was not maintained and the line's decline was continuing by the end of the experimental period. Four lines on the New Haven Railroad, where fares were reduced by an average of 10 per cent, produced similar results.

The most adventurous experiment directly concerned with price elasticity of demand was conducted in Rome in 1972 where for a period of just over a week the municipality offered free fares. It carefully monitored demand patterns, comparing them with the equivalent period of the previous year, continuing to issue tickets of the current denominations for this purpose.[15] Table 6.1 indicates the effects of the experiment on passenger numbers. Figures covering fifteen representative services for the most typical day of the no-fare scheme, 7 January 1972, are compared with those for the most comparable day in the previous year when normal fares were charged.

Table 6.1
Rome's free fare experiment: comparison of tickets issued
January 1971 and 1972

	Tickets issued		Difference (%)
	1971	1972	
First service to 09.00 hrs	89,776	79,558	—11·38
09.00—11.59 hrs	57,851	70,357	+21·62
12.00—14.59 hrs	61,696	80,449	+30·40
15.00—19.59 hrs	108,432	148,852	+37·20
20.00 hrs to last service	22,957	33,795	+47·20
Total for day	340,712	413,011	+21·20

Source: *Motor Transport*[15]

The decline in early morning use demonstrates that at this time the scheme failed to reverse the annual expected decline. Indeed it may have exacerbated it, for early morning fares were traditionally cheaper and after the abolition of them some switching to more convenient times of the day may have occurred. Incremental rush hour use may have been seriously limited by capacity shortages. Perhaps the most significant result is the greater than average increase in evening leisure traffic. There were wide variations between routes and the increase after 20.00 hours was as much as 111·5 per cent on one of these. The responsiveness of demand at these times should be compared with similarly encouraging increases in our own work in response to a price decrease on Merseyside and a frequency increase at Bolton (see chapter 7). Of those using public transport Table 6.2 breaks down journey reasons by use. Significantly, only 1·7 per cent of users could be positively identified as having been attracted from their cars by the provision of free transport, while a further 8·2 per cent, who though preferring the car were pleased to accept free transport, should probably be included in the same category, giving a total of 9·9 per cent attracted because of free transport. The main purpose of the experiment was to see how free fares would contribute to the reduction of peak hour congestion, but we have already suggested that peak hour capacity on public transport may have been a major impediment. Of the journey-to-work riders surveyed only 7·5 per cent had been attracted because of the abolition of fares. Shopping and leisure trips were the categories most successful in attracting car users and for both the increase may perhaps be partly accounted for by journeys that would not otherwise have been made.

It would appear that the experiment was highly contentious from the start. After a week of free fares throughout the day the concession was extended until 2 July 1972, with free travel during the peak hours only. However, there was no significant effect on the numbers of cars commuting into the centre. Rome has since attempted to counter its congestion problems by increasing its bus fleet by 50 per cent and by introducing more bus-only lanes in central streets.

(b) *Off-peak elasticities* Schneider's[12] hypothesis that the elasticity of demand will vary according to trip purpose is supported by several studies, a number of which demonstrate higher elasticities for a variety of off-peak trips. The Rome experiment, though subject to a number of methodological problems, has already provided elementary support for this, given the much higher response of evening patronage to the free fares trial. Several authors have analysed data from New York fare increases and Kemp,[13] reviewing these, shows an elasticity range for the period 1948—70

Table 6.2
Rome's free fare experiment: relationship between reasons for using public transport and journey type (percentages)

	'I could not arrange car transport'	'Though preferring the car I was pleased to accept free transport'	'Had I to pay for my ticket I would have used the car'	'I would have used public transport in any case'	Other	Total	Percentage of journey for different reasons
Work	18·26	5·97	1·53	72·57	1·67	100·00	55·1
School	22·91	9·20	0·54	64·06	3·29	100·00	5·2
Shopping	21·31	10·54	1·72	64·71	1·72	100·00	13·3
Visiting	22·49	7·60	1·74	65·96	2·21	100·00	13·5
Leisure	18·24	22·17	2·27	52·20	5·12	100·00	6·0
Other	25·11	9·86	2·59	59·33	3·11	100·00	6·9
Total	19·94	8·21	1·65	68·06	2·14	100·00	100·0

Source: *Motor Transport*[15]

of between 1·0 and 0·17 for rapid subway transit and of between 0·13 and 0·34 for surface lines. While it is always difficult to measure the effects of price change because of extraneous factors, e.g. the incidence of strikes and organisational changes, it would nevertheless appear that surface level traffic is consistently more elastic than subway traffic. Furthermore, off-peak social and leisure trips were similarly more elastic, as reflected both in the greater decline of weekend compared with weekday traffic, and the greater relative decline of off-peak weekday *vis-à-vis* peak weekday traffic.

Experiments by British Rail in the UK have achieved mixed results, but in certain cases have been particularly encouraging. In 1970, on the St. Helens-Liverpool line, off-peak fares (i.e. after 09.30 hours) were reduced by 22 per cent (from 22½p to 17½p). The service operates from Monday to Saturdays only. The experiment lasted a year and was successful to the extent of reversing a 1 per cent secular decline (Table 6.3). The result seems extremely reassuring even though some of the traffic may have been drawn from competing bus services, which unfortunately were not monitored during the experiment. Two earlier experiments by British Rail on lines in the same region were limited to evening travellers only (Table 6.4). The experiments offered substantial reductions on return tickets after 16.00 hours, Monday to Friday only and achieved markedly different results for the two separate trials.

The West Kirby experiment which commenced in May 1970 was discontinued in September of that year due to the poor response, although passenger numbers were rising. The New Brighton line provides an example of an unconditional success. Passenger numbers increased 173 per cent and revenue 67 per cent. The price elasticity was thus 1·67 which was achieved with relatively little publicity. The experiment started in February 1970 and was finally terminated in March 1972 when British Rail converted to a completely different fare structure. Thus, off-peak rail price experiments have been successful in certain locations in stimulating substantial numbers of additional passengers and also increases in net revenue.

Bus experiments have been less successful in effecting revenue increases although encouraging elasticities have been demonstrated for particular segments. Bus trials conducted in Los Angeles during the early sixties provided evidence that elasticities for particular passenger subgroups may be much greater than 0·33. In 1961 the Los Angeles Metropolitan Transit Authority instituted a reduced fare for senior citizens applicable to an extensive off-peak period, namely 10.00—15.00 hours and 19.00—24.00 hours on weekdays, 19.00—24.00 hours on Saturdays and all day

Table 6.3
British Rail's St. Helens — Liverpool off-peak fare reduction experiment: passenger and revenue analysis

	Special off-peak return		Regular off-peak return[a]		Cheap day return		Singles		Total	
	Ticket volume	Revenue (£s)	Ticket volume	Revenue (£s)	Ticket volume	Revenue (£s)	Ticket volume	Revenue (£s)	Ticket volume	Revenue (£s)
1969	—	—	66,257	13,501	17,288	4,750	13,761	2,269	97,306	20,520
1970	59,477	9,711	27,670	5,800	15,153	4,395	12,975	2,262	115,275	22,168
Difference	59,477	9,711	(38,587)	(7,701)	(2,135)	(355)	(786)	(7)	17,969	1,648
Percentage of difference									+18·4	+8·0

[a]Saturdays only, 1970

Source: British Rail, Liverpool

Table 6.4
British Rail's New Brighton and West Kirby line reduced evening fare experiment

	Off-peak return reduction		Frequency (mins)	Demand per 'typical' week (passenger numbers)			Revenue per 'typical' week (£s)		
	Range (%)	Average (%)		Before	After	Change (%)	Before	After	Change (%)
New Brighton line	27—44	32	30	770	2,100	+173	120	200	+67
West Kirby line	27—56	43	30	1,610	1,700	+6	244	166	—33

Source: British Rail, Liverpool

Sundays.[12] Revenue for this segment fell by only a small amount, from $1,838,868 per year to $1,708,593. The operators claimed that the reduction caused a shift of riders from the peak to off-peak as well as generating extra traffic and trips, although the measurement of these two sub-effects was insufficient. Some operating cost savings might have occurred from this shift in passengers which will have reduced the net deficit even further; however, these were not quantified and are not included in the above figures. A limited experiment in Newcastle, Pennsylvania demonstrated that cost savings may be achieved through the transfer of passengers from peak to off-peak.[16] The experiment studied the effects of reducing a 25 cent fare to 15 cents during the shopping hours of 10.00 to 14.00. Passenger counts were taken before, during and after the test period. Total ridership did not increase but sufficient redistribution of passengers occurred to decrease fleet and driver costs per passenger by 2 cents. The Boston programme[14] provides two further examples of off-peak fare experiments for buses. Fares on all services north of Boston (i.e. from the cities of Lowell, Lynn, Salem, Marblehead, Swampscott and Lawrence) were reduced by about 30 per cent in order to equate bus and rail fares. The fares were applicable on all trips between 09.30 and 16.30 hours, after 18.30 Monday to Friday, and all day Saturday and Sunday. The reduction resulted in increased patronage for the bus company with revenues reaching 96 per cent of the base figure. In the second case an off-peak fare of 25 cents was reduced to 10 cents for all trips originating between 10.00 and 15.00 hours (Monday-Friday) and within 1·5 miles of Kearney Square, the focal point of Lowell City centre. Off-peak passenger volumes increased by 79 per cent, but this was insufficient to offset the cost of the fare reduction and produced an elasticity of 0·64.

(c) *Elasticities as affected by distance* The hypothesis that shorter distance riders are more sensitive to fare changes than those making longer journeys is supported by Van Tassel's analysis[17] of reduced tariffs for short distance services in several American cities. Again the results are very mixed and there are some notable exceptions where reductions in short distance fares produced hardly any passenger effect. Most of these results confirm *a priori* notions about elasticity as they relate to different trip purposes, user segments and trip lengths.

In-vehicle time The bus, with no fixed track of its own, has suffered heavily because of car-induced congestion. In chapter 2 we have already noted the relative decline of bus speeds and the way earlier traffic management schemes tended to favour the private motorist with their accent on vehicle mobility. In the late sixties a second generation of such schemes recognised that flows of people rather than of vehicles might be a better criterion and sought to give positive help to public transport by granting it priority. This may be achieved in a number of ways. Buses may be given exclusive use of a lane or indeed a street, or they may be given priority at intersections. Bus lanes seem to have met with success in many places. In Reading, England, a series of contra-flow lanes resulted in peak journey time savings of up to 40 per cent and, even more important in the view of the operators, a vast improvement in reliability.

Experiments in France were discussed in an OECD report by Frebault.[18] He showed the effect on bus operating speeds along selected routes in Paris and Marseilles before and after the incorporation of bus-only lanes. In Paris time savings of up to 100 per cent were made, while in Marseilles the routes selected improved journey speeds from a pre-experimental level of 2—7 km. per hour to 15—20 km. per hour. The bus lanes were created by banning parked cars on the boulevards and therefore did not really deprive other mobile traffic of road space. Unfortunately not many cities have such reserves of road space that they can afford to risk increased congestion in the non-bus lanes. In this respect, while the bus lane over London's Vauxhall Bridge (where it replaced a central reservation) was successful in reducing bus time, the experimental lane in Brixton, London,[19] if initially enforced would have brought sufficient congestion as to deny access to the bus at the commencement of its lane.

All these and many other measures are currently being applied, as throughout the world local governing bodies seek to proffer assistance to public transport.[20] This represents a considerable change of policy. In the UK, for example, the police have often insisted that bus stops should be located some way from intersections, which, while permitting freer flows for cars, reduces the convenience of the bus particularly for interchanges.

Improved vehicle power itself offers little opportunity for time savings and expectations are low in many cases anyway; the older and female respondents in one survey[21] even expressed fear about the present speeds at which buses are driven.

Time savings are possible by varying the number of stops, and thereby offering stage carriage, limited stop or express services. United Kingdom examples of improved commuter services through the introduction of express bus services are provided by Leeds' 'Fastaway' and Merseyside's 'Rapidride' services. In both cases selected stage carriage services have been converted to express during the peak, picking up at a limited number of stops in a residential zone and travelling non-stop to the city centre. The limited pick-up and alighting zones give the operators flexibility of route and in the Liverpool situation drivers are given discretion so that they may avoid the worst congestion points. The time savings in Liverpool are as much as 10 minutes off a traditional 40 minute journey time. On-bus surveys indicate a high degree of satisfaction with the 'Rapidride' services and they may therefore represent an important tactic for retaining existing users even though few car commuters have been attracted to the new services.

In America a number of demonstration projects have included the introduction of express bus services. The 'Metro-Flyer'[22] is an express service which first picks up passengers in a high income, low density suburb some 2·75 miles long and then proceeds non-stop over 11 miles of interstate highway south to the Baltimore centre. The journey times achieved were 30 minutes off-peak and 35 minutes during the peak. Regular stopping services were continued and the 'Flyer' charged a slightly higher fare. The study claims that 63 per cent of the riders were new to public transport and over 50 per cent were 'choice' travellers with access to a car. However, over 91 per cent were work journeys and revenue did not cover operating costs. Factors other than time were vital (although this was cited in surveys as being the most important factor). Extensive 'park-n-ride' facilities were available, the buses had reclining seats and air conditioning and the service was heavily promoted.

Chesapeake, the US equivalent of a British 'new town' organised a bus service similarly conceived, with journey time and frequency improvements compared with its predecessor.[23] Journey time over the 13·9 miles of the route was cut from 42 to 35 minutes, while frequency on weekdays was increased from 8 to 27 round trips. Improvements were also made to evening and Sunday services. While patronage increased to 2½ times pre-project levels, revenue only covered 50 per cent of costs. Although air conditioning and feeder services were again included, promotion was not as aggressive and extensive as is usual in such projects and this may have adversely affected results.

Probably the most successful of these schemes are the St. Louis Radial Expresses[24] which were devised to determine the criteria influencing bus patronage, in particular competitive and socio-economic factors. Perhaps the most important characteristic of the St. Louis corridors along which these services operated was the extremely high level of car ownership; in these areas 86—92 per cent of residents went to work by car. Despite such adverse conditions at least four of the seven routes covered costs and contributed towards overheads. A premium fare of 35 cents was charged compared with 25 cents for local services and this project adds further evidence therefore, that premium services may permit premium fares to be charged and, given the right service mix, attract car users.

A US rail experiment successfully and dramatically showed that time savings on commuter rail journeys may be extremely important in attracting passengers.[25] The 'Skokie Swift' service is a revamped version of a rail service abandoned fifteen months earlier after suffering a steady annual loss of passengers in spite of a growing population in the catchment area. The 5-mile non-stop run to Chicago's express rapid transit line took 6½ minutes in contrast to the approximate time for the predecessor of 12 minutes. This advantage was supplemented by others — extensive parking facilities were made available, a feeder bus route was integrated into the service, and through-booking with one fare covering the whole journey was offered. Most importantly perhaps, the service received unprecedented promotion; as much as 20 per cent of the first year's projected revenue was budgeted for this purpose, in addition to which extensive free public relations activity was undertaken.

The results of the 'Skokie Swift' service have been well publicised. Whereas it was forecast that the reopened line would take some time to reach the daily total of 1,400 passengers carried by its waning predecessor, the service carried 5,000 passengers per day within one month and this continued rising to reach 7,500 passengers per day three years later. The previous modes of travel by those who used the new service are shown in Table 6.5.

The success of the 'Swift' is stated in these figures particularly in the attraction of 45·5 per cent wholly or partly from car. So successful has been the service that it has even brought about a redistribution of destinations and there is record of travellers having actually changed residences so as to take advantage of it.

Table 6.5
Chicago's 'Skokie Swift' service: modes foregone by users

Mode	Percentage of users
Automobile to rapid transit line	26·8
Bus to rapid transit line	36·0
Automobile to work	18·7
Bus to work	7·4
Rail to work	11·1

Source: Buck[25]

A final area for discussion when considering in-vehicle times is the effects of one-man bus operation. While improving labour relations and decreasing labour costs, this mode of operation has brought disadvantages which may well have been unforeseen or underestimated by sections of the industry. The passenger has experienced much longer stopping times and the delays have added as much as 14 per cent to scheduled running times.[26] The perceived delay may well be out of proportion to the actual times involved because it is composed of numerous small waiting times which are known to be particularly onerous to passengers. The associated problems of such delays have been well documented by Fishwick[26] as higher fixed costs because of increased vehicle requirements, lost passengers, increased congestion and greater strain on the driver. The lower utilisation of vehicles and the loss of passengers have not made it possible to realise the reduction in operating costs that were anticipated originally. The problem may be tackled by experimenting with vehicle design to determine the best width, and opening and closing mechanisms, for doors and to determine the costs and benefits of two rather than one door vehicles. Additionally the fare system may be re-oriented so that the driver's time undertaking tasks other than driving is minimised. Experiments with fare systems for this purpose are considered later in this chapter and our own primary research involved experimentation in this area (see below and chapter 7).

Mesh density Route or mesh density determines the level of passenger accessibility to a public transport system; the denser the network the less will be the walking (or cycling, etc.) time incurred for any door-to-door journey, although obviously this is also affected by the number of boarding and alighting points. The evidence examined in chapter 2 has clearly indicated the high disutility attached to activities such as walking and waiting.

The Maryland Study[27] found that to 'avoid walking more than a block' was an important attribute of a public transport system for 65 per cent of the respondents, and the factor under which this item was subsumed, 'convenience', was one involving the greatest differentials in satisfaction between the private car and public transport.

It should be noted that continuing urban sprawl is disadvantageous to public transport in this respect and makes it increasingly difficult for operators to provide dense route networks. The importance of this factor is acknowledged and countered in public transport planning in many new towns where the objective is often established for all residents to be within a defined walking distance from a bus route. The public road transport system in Stevenage, for example, is planned on the basis of an average walking time of either 3·3 or 2·5 minutes (depending respectively on whether Stevenage Development Corporation's or a scheme originally proposed by London Transport is finally implemented).[28]

Substantial efforts have been made recently to improve accessibility for rail and bus, both at the origin and destination points of the journey. For the bus a number of demand-activated systems have been proposed, and in some cases tested; these seek to take advantage of the bus's flexibility to minimise access time. In 1965—66, the private bus companies of Peoria, East Peoria and Decatur inaugurated a door-to-door peak hour service for employees at several industrial plants.[29] Buses stopped at or near to the rider's home for regular users, and seats were available for everyone and bookable. Riders used passes and were invoiced monthly. The number of buses and the routes were determined, as much as it was practicable, by those intending to use the service on a regular basis. The effect of any single element is difficult to determine in a complex programme which included the provision of uniformed hostesses to ride on the buses and administer the service, the development of a cordial 'club-coach' atmosphere, and the availability of a telephone service at the bus company designed to handle messages and complaints quickly and the provision of taxicabs should the buses break down. The importance of the accessibility factor, however, is indicated in responses to a questionnaire asking passengers what they liked about the service. Responses are shown in Table 6.6.

The service was financially viable while retained in this form and attempts to achieve a similar success have been made in the UK with the Hale Barns' executive service in the Greater Manchester area,[30] which has essentially comparable features. Details of the Hale Barns' executive service experiment are given in chapter 7.

Table 6.6
Peoria and Decatur premium coach service: questionnaire survey

	Percentage of approval
Convenience of service	12
Door-to-door service	22
Speed, timing, reliability	23
Avoids driving, parking, carpool	18
Savings in transport cost	14
Other	11

Source: *Passenger Transport*, May 1967, pp. 183—87

However, success is not assured, even for well researched services. A service similar to that at Peoria and Decatur was attempted at Flint, Michigan.[31] The town is dominated by just a few work locations, largely owned by General Motors, and in this respect closely resembles Decatur. The service was rigorously researched in terms of the potential market. The close imitation of the Peoria and Decatur services may be seen in the creation of a 'club-like' atmosphere (achieved by gestures such as a free outing to a baseball match), the use of 'bus bunnies', a slick naming policy — 'Maxicab' — and a highly sophisticated promotional launch. Yet the problems in Flint were enormous. The high wages of the automobile industry induced a high turnover among the bus drivers, which in turn adversely affected schedules. The nature of the main industry served meant periodic lapses in demand caused by labour lay-offs during annual model changes and by the occurrence of occasional major strikes. An additional damaging factor was a widespread belief among customers, existing and potential, that the project was an experiment and would inevitably be terminated. All these factors contrived to weaken the service's brand loyalty and to make an imaginatively designed project unprofitable.

Extending the ideas inherent in such services, a number of proposals and tests of 'dial-a-bus' concepts have been made; these utilise minibuses whose drivers respond to telephone requests for service, picking passengers up at their door. In its most sophisticated form a small computer would be used to determine vehicle route scheduling which would then be conveyed to the driver. One possibility is the use of differential fare scales determined by the length of wait the prospect is prepared to accept. Roos[32] reviews a number of schemes which have been tried in America and is optimistic about their potential. Although none of them has fully covered its operating costs, some (particularly those services offering a multi-origin and multi-destination type service) have attracted new riders, and users have been willing to pay a premium for a higher quality service. A number of 'dial-a-bus' experiments have recently commenced trial in the UK.

Another closely related innovation which has been strongly advocated from some quarters[33] is the relaxation of the laws controlling taxis and minicabs so that they may combine fares (i.e. carry more than one fare-paying passenger at a time)· and thus compete more directly with public transport. In some cases these 'jitneys' (as they are popularly known) operate along fixed routes with flat fares but with the additional advantage of being able to pick up and set down passengers at any point. Where they have been introduced (for example, in Istanbul and Teheran) they are reputedly highly successsful. The 'jitney' concept obviously mirrors that of the dial-a-bus and one issue arising from its introduction may well be whether or not such schemes should be publicly or privately owned. The latter would seem to be preferable if the peak hour fixed cost requirements of public transport can thereby be reduced and the utilisation of resources in the public sector likewise improved. Given the flexibility available to the private taxi-driver, successful peak hour operation combined with the possibility of other kinds of off-peak work may make this a very attractive proposition.

For rail, which is inherently less flexible, there are two possible strategies for improving access: the encouragement, on the one hand, of 'park-n-ride' and 'kiss-n-ride' facilities and, on the other, the provision of feeder-bus services. All the PTE transport plans so far adopted for implementation in the UK conurbations include substantial upgrading of the rail network; the importance of the access problem has been acknowledged by making available government grants to finance a series of demonstration projects at a number of stations on Merseyside so that these alternative strategies may be adequately tested. The results of this programme should be available shortly, and are awaited with considerable interest. The major area of uncertainty concerning the rail-oriented strategies adopted by the PTEs is public acceptance of multi-mode journeys. There seems to be a general dislike of changing vehicles, given the reluctance to accept the extra walking and waiting times involved. Lansing[34] found that having to transfer seems to have a depressing effect on the use of public transport. National Analysis,[35] in an attitude survey in Washington DC, found that 30·3 per cent of its sample objected to the general idea of transferring while another 51·4 per cent objected to specific transferring situations. However, where an ideal transfer situation was described, 88·8 per cent indicated they would accept it. One experiment so far conducted should provide operators with encouragement. In the UK the Formby Bus-Rail Feeder Service,[36] one of the eleven demonstration projects cited at the beginning of this chapter, has enjoyed considerable success. Details of this project are given in chapter 7.

Provision of parking facilities is another tactic which may be employed to encourage the use of public transport. The provision of easily accessible, inexpensive parking facilities at suburban stations encourages commuters to trade off high, city centre parking rates, plus any delay in finding a space, against a less comfortable but faster trip. Such a policy has been successful in America and Schneider[12] cites two parking lots provided by Cleveland Rapid Transit where 3,800 free spaces are filled daily, and of those using the car parks, 30 per cent formerly drove into the centre of Cleveland. The Boston demonstration programme[14] provides a further example; when parking fees at certain stations on the Boston rapid transit lines were reduced, substantial increases in ridership and net rail revenue increased. Another experiment in New Brunswick, New Jersey, involved the construction of a commuter station 1½ miles from the main suburban one.[37] The new station, which included free car parking facilities for 300 vehicles, attracted a substantial patronage.

For rail journeys originating or terminating in the city centre, accessibility to public transport has become progressively poorer as the modern commerical centres have gravitated further away from the rail termini. Thus in Manchester the northern network, based on Victoria Station, is separated by approximately a one-mile gap from the southern network, based on Piccadilly. Underground terminal link projects are contained in the Greater Manchester, Merseyside and Tyneside PTE plans to rectify these problems by joining such stations and adding additional ones convenient to the contemporary commercial centres.

Accessibility may also be facilitated in town centres by the provision of city centre bus services to connect with radial trains and buses. Such services have been introduced in Birmingham, Leeds, Liverpool and Manchester, but indications from the operators suggest that these are not viable on a financially based analysis alone. However, one demonstration project of this kind in Washington DC has proved highly successful.[38] The project, initiated in 1963, used small eighteen-seat buses, operating on a nineteen-mile round trip route in the retail core of the city. Service was provided at a frequency of 2½ minutes, six days a week from 10.00 to 18.00 hours. The project was financially successful. Time savings and the low fare were the major factors attributed to the success of the service, but frequency was surely also important, for it is the primary differentiating factor between this project and similar trials in the UK.

The Greater Manchester PTE is additionally considering alternatives to a minibus system which include: directing radial route services as they cross an inner cordon line near to the city centre to a variety of destinations; and the route scheduling of radial services into clockwise and anti-clockwise loops in the city centre or the extension of termini so that all radial services terminate on the far side of the centre.[39] The limited data available suggest that although there is no strong demand for services connecting different suburbs via the city centre, significant demand does exist for services to the far boundary of the central area, e.g. north to south. An evaluation of how best to meet this demand is being made.

Facilities for suburban car parking are particularly required where a rail line serves a low density area, although these are generally needed with all rail traffic. Where city centre congestion is a problem and parking facilities have been reduced in the central area, a combination of car and train modes often offers a faster and cheaper form of commuting. Similar reasoning would also be valid for the bus, particularly where the major part of the journey is by car and the bus is used for the last stage only. Both Leicester and Leeds have tried operating non-stop buses at frequent departure times from extensive car parks situated on the edges of the city centre. Neither of these attempts has been financially successful but Leicester is to persist with the experiment, absorbing the cost from its profitable services. A US demonstration project[40] introduced similar bus services to and from car parks just outside the centre of Atlanta; ridership steadily increased until a 50 per cent fare increase (50 cents—75 cents for the bus-parking charge) brought the service into near parity with the cost of car parking in the centre. Net costs were claimed to be 80 per cent covered prior to the increase and nearly all the riders had previously used their car to the centre, thus contributing to congestion. On the face of it, bus 'park-n-ride' of this nature would appear to be at a disadvantage to the train, since the bus itself is slower than the car, and when parking is subsequent to a longer car trip, the motorist must be tempted to continue by the same mode to his destination. However, this may become less the case as city centre congestion and parking problems develop further.

Frequency Frequency has already been established as a particularly important characteristic of a public transport system since it affects: (i) total journey time — the more frequent a service the greater the probability that public transport schedules and desired arrival time will harmonise, and the lower the safety margin of time that the traveller need allow to avoid missing a bus and incurring a long wait; (ii) convenience — the more frequent a service the less is the need for expensive route schedule information and the lower the probability that a trip will have to be planned by the traveller in deference to the operator's schedules; and (iii) reliability — frequency lowers the rider's dependence on reliability and particularly his susceptibility to considerable inconvenience as caused by missed schedules resulting from breakdown or crew shortage.

A number of experiments have been conducted to test whether extra passenger demand may be generated by increases in frequency such that incremental revenue outweighs the incremental costs.

The Boston programme[14] was perhaps ultimately more oriented to gauging the effects of frequency increases than of any other variable. The two main phases of the rail experiment were as follows:

Phase 1   January—July 1963
1.1   89 per cent increase in frequency — weekday 92 per cent; peak 82 per

Table 6.7
Boston and Maine frequency experiment: average passengers carried per month

	1962 numbers (base)[a]	Phase 1 nos.	% change against base	1962 numbers (base)[b]	Phase 2 nos.	% change against base	Net % change, phase 2 against phase 1
Peak	325,080	380,507	+17·0	314,812	384,579	+22·1	+ 5·1
Off-peak	103,293	157,937	+52·9	105,723	176,593	+67·0	+14·1
Total	428,373	538,444	+25·6	420,535	561,172	+33·4	+ 7·8

[a] Equivalent months in 1962, January to July.
[b] Equivalent months in 1962, August to December
Source: J. Maloney[14]

off-peak 96 per cent (i.e. 386 trains per day, 182 more than in 1962).
1.2   28 per cent reduction in fares, ranging from 12 to 72 per cent for both one-way and twenty-ride tickets.

Phase 2   August-December 1963
2.1   Frequencies maintained at phase 1 levels.
2.2   Commuter fares raised pre-phase 1 levels.
2.3   Further reduction of one-way off-peak fares.

A major objective of the programme was to test the willingness of peak period commuters to pay fares close to pre-demonstration project levels for improved frequency of service. Passengers carried for both phases of the programmes are shown in Table 6.7.

The frequency increases coupled with fare decreases brought substantial passenger gains for both peak and off-peak in phase 1. However, in phase 2, for the peak, when fares were reverted to 1962 levels and frequencies maintained at phase 1 levels, there was in fact a further net patronage gain of 5 per cent compared with the phase 1 improvements. This is sufficient evidence of the primacy of the frequency factor. As can be seen from the increased revenue receipts (see Table 6.8), passenger gains were more than sufficient to offset the fare decreases.

But despite the highly successful stimulation of incremental passenger trips resulting in an increase in revenue of 20 per cent by the end of the second phase, the contribution was insufficient to meet the extra costs involved in improving the frequency of service.

	Phase 1	Phase 2
Incremental costs	$700,000	$500,000
Incremental revenue	$200,000	$284,000 (57% costs)

It is at this point that social cost-benefit criteria became essential to an evaluation of public transport effectiveness, for by any wholly commercial analysis the incremental services are not profitable and therefore not justifiable. However, traditional accounting criteria make no allowance for the congestion cost savings of the 1,590,000 extra rail journeys, most of which would have been made by car at peak time.

The same programme included a number of frequency improvements to bus services. These were not as successful as rail in generating extra patronage and typically additional revenue only reached 20—50 per cent of incremental costs, although there were exceptions to the general rule. For example, frequency on a service between Milford and Boston was increased from nine to sixteen trips, resulting in hourly arrivals in Boston from 07.00

Table 6.8

Boston and Maine frequency experiment: total revenue earned

	1962[a] revenue in $'000 (base)	Phase 1 revenue in $'000	Change (%)	1962[b] revenue in $'000 (base)	Phase 2 revenue in $'000	Change (%)	Net % change, phase 2 against phase 1
Weekdays	1,765·6	1,776·9	+0·6	1,263·4	1,556·3	+23·2	+22·6
Weekends	207·8	217·7	+4·8	152·0	142·9	−6·0	−10·8
Total	1,973·4	1,994·6	+1·1	1,415·4	1,699·2	+20·0	+18·9

[a] Equivalent months in 1962, January to July.
[b] Equivalent months in 1962, August to December.
Source: J. Maloney[14]

to 19.00 hours. Patronage increased and additional revenue offset incremental costs at the rate of 25 per cent in the first month but rose to 50 per cent in the twelfth month. The service operated on a 33-mile route which took 90 minutes from terminus to terminus. There was no other public transport system available to the commuters concerned; private car travel time was only slightly less than for the bus. Another service increase was introduced on a 17-mile route from Uxbridge to Worcester, linking three small urban areas (populations 7,000—10,000) to a regional centre. Again patronage increased, but was only sufficient to cover 30 per cent of the incremental costs.

One exception to these bus experiments contained in the Boston programme, was a frequency increase on a suburban service through three small interconnected urban areas — Williamstown, North Adams and Adams (population 7,000—19,000). Despite interruption to the experiment through the financial difficulties of the operator, the increase from fourteen to twenty-four round trips daily brought passenger increases such that the ratio of incremental revenue to incremental cost varied from 79 per cent to 147 per cent. Overall, nearly 50 per cent of the incremental costs were met by incremental revenue. The best performance seems due to seasonal factors, although the report itself provides no analysis of this variation. While the report concluded that carefully selected service improvements from suburban commuter to the city core can be self sustaining, the majority were not. However, such US services do not seem typical of UK bus operations; the American ones usually operate on much longer routes, have much lower frequencies, and operate in predominantly car-using areas.

Reliability While reliability is a key element in the marketing-mix, it is particularly difficult to assess, comprising as it does: punctuality of vehicle arrival at the embarkation point; punctuality of vehicle arrival at the destination; and avoidance of periodic and unpredictable breakdown of the public transport system.

Car-induced congestion, as well as slowing down buses, as we have noted, also interferes with their reliability. Some indication of the seriousness of this interference is shown in the Greater Manchester area, where the PTE calculated that buses take an average 20 per cent longer to complete an itinerary than the scheduled times during the peak. The nature of this problem is reflected to some degree by the numerous complaints which operators receive, or by uncomplimentary letters to the Press; increasingly the assertion is made that the public transport system in major cities has collapsed or broken down. Considerable inconvenience is caused to passengers, particularly where services are not very frequent.

Further problems have been caused by the poorer standards of mechanical reliability associated with rear-engined vehicles. Since the widespread adoption of these to assist one-man bus operation, many of the major UK operators have had to increase the size of their spare vehicle fleets by a substantial amount. This is obviously a high cost to pay for mechanical unreliability and the onus is obviously with the operators to assert the importance of this factor with manufacturers.

The priority schemes outlined under in-vehicle time, not only improve bus speeds, but are also a crucially important aid to reliability. As well as schemes of this sort a number of other policies and experiments have been pursued and conducted in an attempt to increase flexibility and improve reliability in the face of highly congested road conditions. There has been a considerable increase in the provision of radio links between drivers and operating headquarters so that the position on the road at any particular time may be known. (Such links also afford some protection for drivers in the face of increasing vandalism and thuggery, especially on late night services.) Similarly, some cities operate a TV scanning system in the central areas adding a visual to the aural links. The crucial issue is the use to which this information is put, and it does seem that in many cases any potential benefit the information may have is not realised, since little managerial action is taken on the basis of the incoming data. There are one or two exceptions, and a good example of managerial ingenuity Exists at Leicester, where, in combination with TV and radio surveillance, a fleet of some six vehicles forms a mobile reserve in the city centre during the peak hours. On the basis of incoming information reserve buses are radioed into action wherever critically severe gaps in service occur.

A most sophisticated example of the same idea exists in electronic fleet location systems which, if fully developed, could provide minute-by-minute information on the position of all vehicles in the fleet and not just in city centre locations. Such a system is being tested currently as part of a demonstration project at Bristol. The phenomenon of the 'bunching' of buses in congested conditions is well known by management and aggrieved passengers alike. Congestion delays a particular bus which, in running later than scheduled, inevitably picks up a larger number of passengers, and is therefore further delayed at stops. The next scheduled service, setting out on time, will also by delayed by congestion, but this will be countered by smaller numbers of passengers boarding and alighting, because of the increased demands on the delayed bus ahead; thus the second will tend to catch up with the first vehicle.

Fleet location aids could identify many of these situations, and by giving instructions to drivers together with the judicious use of reserve fleets, ameliorate their effects. However, there seems little promise for the immediate future. The system being tested at Bristol, one developed by Marconi, has encountered a number of teething problems and is highly expensive.

Comfort Comfort is the least easily defined element of the marketing-mix and possibly the most neglected. The difficulty in adequately defining passenger comfort in part stems from the number of elements it comprises and their interrelationships. Table 6.9 demonstrates these numerous elements which were described as early as 1949, but few authors writing since then cover more than a few of these factors.[41] Similarly, there is no research which has demonstrated the priorities to be attached to the factors nor qualified the interrelationships between them.[42]

If the attitudinal findings quoted in chapter 2 are accepted, it would seem reasonable to afford comfort a low priority in relation to reliability and frequency, but we would argue that it remains important in an absolute sense for a number of reasons. Few of the studies analyse comfort in any depth, and global use of the term, in view of its complexity, seems inadequate.[43] Where specific subfunctions of comfort have been researched they have assumed some importance as, for example, in social and community planning's priority evaluation, where overcrowding in London's underground system was found to be a factor for which many people sought improvements.[8] Further, motivational research has shown distinctly different tolerances for individuals in relation to the degree of crowding acceptable.[44] In those cases where congestion reduces time differentials between public and private transport and perceived cost differentials are blurred, comfort may be intuitively expected to be an important contributor to modal choice. The evidence cited below indicates that some substantial improvements in comfort may be bought relatively cheaply.

Most of the published research relating to comfort specifically concerns rapid transit design. Here, research has concentrated on particular facets: (i) motion tolerances,[45] where 'jerk' — the rate of change of acceleration — has emerged as the most sensitive component; (ii) vibration; and (iii) noise, where attempts have been made to establish riding comfort indices.[46] There is much more agreement between researchers about acceptable temperature and ventilation levels, although as Schneider[12] argues, operators have been slow to accept these findings. The importance of seat availability and crowding for the user of the London tube system has already been cited. It has also been an important criticism of American rapid transit systems, for example, in Washington DC[34] and in Philadelphia.[47] In the former study

Table 6.9
Passenger comfort criteria

1 *Motion*
acceleration
rate of change of acceleration
duration
direction
effective wind pressure

2 *Vibration:*
amplitude
frequency
duration
direction
intensity

3 *Noise:*
speech interference
sound pressure ratio
frequency
duration

4 *Visual disturbance:*
vibration
flicker vertigo
eyeball movement
illumination levels

5 *Ventilation:*
temperature
humidity
air composition
odour, taste

6 *Air pressure magnitude:*
rate of change

7 *Body fatigue:*
inclination and position
seating
standing
walking

8 *Electrostatic charge*

9 *Space:*
privacy
crowdedness

10 *Amenities:*
aesthetics
orientation

Source: K. M. Soloman, R. J. Soloman and J. S. Silien[42] based on the earlier work of Dr Ing. Carl Pirath, *Die Grundlagen der Verkehrswirtschaft* (Fundamentals of Transportation Management), Springer Verlag, Berlin. 1949, p. 166

overcrowding was a source of criticism of public transport by 60·2 per cent of respondents. Lansing[34] also specifies this factor in his study of modal choice, when he states: 'The most important factor in determining comfort seems to be the availability of seats. 57 per cent of positive comments about comfort relates to getting a seat.' Schneider[12] in his analysis of four modern rapid transit systems in America showed that there was a high proportion of 'standees' (buses offering limited seat capacity) on all the systems at peak times and that standards on new systems which had promised 'jet age travel' did not differ much from traditional systems. The operators argue that 150—200 per cent load factors are acceptable at peak times where many of the journeys are short ones, but undoubtedly the most important factor is the cost that a seats-for-all policy would entail. Higher frequencies provide one means of improving seating availability as well as attracting incremental trips but, as the Boston programme[14] demonstrated, such a policy is unlikely to be commercially viable. Increasing train lengths is the major and probably the least expensive alternative.

Published research specifically relating to bus operations is much sparser. Until British Leyland's recent attempts to rationalise its market, bus design has been largely the product of the quirks of the chief engineers employed by the operators. A standard chassis would be chosen but the body building would reflect the individual preferences of the operators' chief engineers and few, if any, examples can be found relating to market research findings or product tests. In one reported interview it was difficult to impress that a customer existed beyond the engineer himself! Again, the major design changes of recent decades have stemmed from production or cost-oriented decisions, in particular the introduction of one-man bus operation which caused the switch to rear-engined, front loading vehicles.

The most recent addition to British Leyland's stable, the Leyland National, was designed largely to bring bus design within the scope of modern production techniques and this was achieved by the elimination of the chassis. However, it also included a much greater input of passenger comfort considerations than ever before and a considerable emphasis was placed on the flexibility of seating arrangements so that various permutations may be offered according to the purpose to which the vehicle would be put. The Leyland National presents an interesting example of the physical/psychological links in the perception of comfort. Sheehan[43] remarked that:

> If the passenger is presented with a cheap looking but well designed 'comfortable' seat, he may be dissatisfied and uncomfortable; provide him with an expensive looking but less comfortable seat and he will

probably be happier and more comfortable notwithstanding that the 'cheap looking' seat could be more expensive.

The negative aspect of this phenomenon was demonstrated at the launch of the National; despite Leyland's assurance that the seats had been very carefully designed, reporters had difficulty in accepting this in view of their hard and uncomfortable appearance.

The importance of seat availability in bus operations, especially if car users are to be attracted back to public transport, is strongly emphasised by Schneider,[12] who attributes the success of some of the US express bus demonstrations partly to this factor. In the UK a similar policy has been adopted in two schemes.[48] Schneider's biggest complaint in this area is that US operators have been very slow to adopt air conditioning. He considers this one of the easiest and cheapest ways of improving public transport's image. A questionnaire sent to a number of operators showed that in the event of the finance being available most would prefer to make capital improvements. This, the author claims, further emphasises the production orientation of the industry, particularly as the incremental costs of air conditioning, at approximately 2·4 per cent of the cost of non-air conditioned equipment, is not great. Given the milder weather conditions, this particular consideration is, perhaps, of less importance in the UK.

Few controlled experiments have specifically sought to test improvements in comfort and where such improvements have been made they have usually been part of a wider package. In certain respects operators and designers seem to understand their market and show concern for design features which will make boarding and alighting easy for elderly people. In other respects they seem completely out of touch. When London Transport introduced 'standee' buses on suburban routes they found them vehemently rejected by passengers. One or two PTEs have shown a willingness to experiment. Merseyside, for example, introduced 'Muzak' on test routes but this was withdrawn after an extremely mixed reaction.

In conclusion, it may be said that comfort standards are poor, particularly in urban bus operation. Nowhere does the quality of ride approach that of the car, particularly in relation to seating design and space, and vibration.

Promotion

Promotion comprises sales, advertising, public relations and control of the corporate image. While sales, as embodied in a sales force, is not relevant in this particular industry,[49] the other functions are among the most neglected marketing areas, for production-oriented transport managements have taken a highly conservative and outdated view of them. This neglect was demonstrated when reference was made in chapter 4 to the ludicrously low advertising budgets of the PTEs and of the majority of their counterparts in North America and Western Europe. The level of expenditure is derisory, not simply by comparison with contemporary expenditure in other commercial fields, but essentially because of the need for extensive advertising, especially of an informational nature in the urban passenger transport industry. Ultimately each service on the timetable on the same route may be considered as a different product because of its non-substitutable nature, particularly for journey-to-work segments.

A further reason for castigating operators in these areas is that where material has been published it is often of a poor quality and difficult for the public to interpret. The reasons for these deficiencies are numerous. Some operators still persist in taking a very optimistic view of their custom and among the attitudes expressed is that the public know about their local services anyway. Alternatively, it is said that advertising material is unnecessary because the public can enquire of drivers, conductors or inspectors. Other operators have cut information to a minimum because service reliability is so poor that such information only antagonises their public further, while still others take a very defeatist view in the face of continuous vandalism at stops and shelters. This conservativeness finds still wider expression in the view that advertising is wasteful in some undefined way. Undoubtedly the caution arises out of the character of the industry which fears the public criticism that might stem from an adventurous policy, although it is also linked to the belief that advertising is unsuitable because 'one can't sell journeys like one sells soap.'

The two main aims of advertising in this industry may indeed be categorised as making available service information, and providing persuasive communications in favour of public transport.

One US demonstration project attempted to test the hypothesis that informational aids would increase passenger trips, improve attitudes towards public transport and improve route knowledge. The experiment was conducted in Washington DC,[50] and it was unfortunate that the operators raised fares before a follow-up survey could determine attitudes after information aids, including posters and timetables, had been distributed. The only positive feedback was that public knowledge of sources of information had increased — people knew of the existence of timetables and many had them in their possession.

Publicity with a high persuasive content is required in order to arrest passenger recession in each of the market segments, to encourage existing public transport riders to make more intensive use of the system, and to persuade car users to transfer to public transport modes. Thus for retaining existing business the promotional themes should emphasise the bus's — train's advantages in offering relaxed and remunerative travel and, in the specific cases where it is applicable, the advantages of speed and cost should be publicised. These same themes could be used to recapture markets, particularly where perceptible improvements have been made. In the US it is clear that urban public transport has often ceased to be considered an alternative and it takes a liberal amount of promotion to motivate people to use it. Clearly this was the case with the 'Skokie Swift' experiment where the relatively minor product improvements depended considerably for their attractiveness on the market being adequately informed that they had been made.

Apart from the Washington DC study, the only other US demonstration project which studied advertising effectiveness as its major objective was the Allegheny County Study,[51] designed to stimulate off-peak riding. This latter experiment claimed a 3½ per cent increase in revenue as a result of an extensive household distribution of maps and other supporting literature. The costs were recovered in twenty-six weeks. Radio and TV promotion was used later, but could not be shown to have stimulated much additional business.

3   Fare scales and labour productivity

The introduction of one-man bus operation has ramifications which affect the marketing-mix, and therefore we append to the discussion on product attributes and their promotion a section which considers these, particularly as they affect the design of fare scales.

A number of season tickets and multi-journey tickets have been introduced by operators recently in the UK and elsewhere, most often not primarily as a marketing measure but to overcome the adverse boarding time effects caused by the introduction of one-man bus operation. They must therefore be judged largely by their effect on boarding time as well as by their ability to stimulate trips and/or revenue. The alternatives fall within the following categories:

1   Non-graduated fare scales — coarsened (i.e. a reduction in number of fare stages); zonal; and flat.
2   Automated fare collection — turnstiles; ticket vending/dispensing machines.
3   Multi-journey tickets — pre-purchase tickets; pre-purchase tokens.

180

4   Season tickets.

Coarsened, zonal and flat fare systems have always enjoyed greater popularity in continental Europe and North America than in the United Kingdom, where operators have traditionally preferred graduated scales which more closely match the costs of individual journeys to the fares paid by passengers and are therefore more equitable from an economic viewpoint. However, in particular situations operators have shown themselves willing to experiment, for example, London's 'Red Arrow' services operate with a flat fare system. Most PTEs have recognised the need to rationalise in order to achieve a uniform system for the whole of their area, and to simplify the scales in order to meet the needs of one-man bus operation. Thus the Greater Manchester PTE now only has four scales compared with twelve in 1969 and fourteen standard fares compared with twenty-nine when the executive took over.

Automated fare collection has been tested with limited success. For example, autoslot machines have been used on Greater Manchester's buses, but reliability seems to be a major stumbling block to the use of sensitive machinery on a stiffly sprung moving vehicle. The 'Red Arrow' service in London combines a flat fare with automatic collection through a barrier. In addition to reliability problems, the barrier utilises a considerable amount of space with the attendant opportunity costs of the foregone passengers.

Experience of pre-purchased tickets, either in multi-journey or season ticket form, is extensive in Europe and has been gained in a limited number of UK cities.[52] As early as 1965, sixty-seven of seventy-three urban undertakings in Belgium, Italy, Holland, Austria, Switzerland and Spain used these tickets in some form. They have been tried in Manchester ('cheap travel tickets') but, while it is generally agreed that the experiment failed, no documentation of it exists. Currently they are available in Coventry, Leeds, Merseyside, Nottingham and Newcastle-upon-Tyne in this country, as shown in Table 6.10.

With very limited information about the penetration of, and the boarding time savings effected by, these systems, it is obviously difficult to evaluate them. Merseyside is making efforts to determine penetration levels and is trying to reconcile survey information which suggests a 25 per cent use against gross revenue percentage figures of only 12 per cent. Penetration targets have been established by Coventry and Merseyside of approximately 60 per cent after their own research has shown that two passengers may effectively cancel their tickets in the time taken by one to pay his fare to the driver.

Table 6.10
Characteristics of the UK multi-journey ticket systems

	Coventry [a]	Leeds	Merseyside [b]	Nottingham	Newcastle
General fare structure	Graduated	Graduated	Graduated	Graduated	Graduated
Multi-journey tickets	30p or 40p books	10 journeys	10 journeys	10 journeys	12 journeys
Discount	13—19%	11—18%	20%	nil	20%
Target penetration	$62\frac{2}{3}\%$	—	60% peak	—	—
Actual penetration achieved — overall	—	—	25%	—	—
Actual penetration achieved — peak	—	—	—	—	—
Actual penetration achieved — % gross	10%	—	12%	22%	—
Sales source	agents & machines	on-bus	agents	on-bus	on-bus
Service availability	all services	'Fast-away' routes	all corridors operating a one-man bus service	some one-man bus services	one route
Method of collection:	cancellator	cancellator	cancellator	cancellator	cancellator

[a] Coventry — this operator is currently converting to a multi-journey ticket system rather than books. The tickets will be mostly for twelve journeys and will be sold at an average discount of 16·66 per cent with a narrower range than at present

[b] Merseyside — tickets are not available on any Wirral services

Source: Various operators, Spring 1972

Continental European experience provides more useful evidence. With automatic cancellation and double entry doors, the use of these tickets accelerates passenger loadings considerably. Observations at peak hours in Brussels and Ghent indicated that when 70 per cent of passengers are using multi-ride cards substantial improvements in boarding times per passenger may be achieved.[52,53]

Penetration levels are dependent on the type of fare scale, and the level of discount offered. They will be most limited where a graduated scale exists, where the tickets are for a number of rides of one denomination only when they will be purchased only by those making frequent regular journeys over a set distance. Most UK systems demonstrate these limitations and undoubtedly account for the relatively poor penetration levels achieved. Penetration will be much greater where tickets may be used for a variety of distances. One survey of thirty-two Western European cities with both flat fares and discount tickets showed that in twenty-two of these passengers using pre-purchase tickets were more numerous than those paying cash fares.[54] It is clear, however, that in continental cities both discount and penetration levels tend to be much higher. Strasbourg, for example, offers a 30 per cent discount and achieves 54 per cent penetration. Mulhouse (France) offers tickets with discounts of 20, 28 and 40 per cent and has achieved 36 per cent penetration. In both cases, however, the operators use a zone or coarse fare system allowing greater flexibility of journey length than is available with a graduated scale.

Obviously such high discount levels mean considerable revenue losses, but in effect the discounted fares in these cases are reputed to represent break-even levels and the much higher cash fares represent a penalty for those not purchasing tickets in advance. One would expect such systems to be most effectively introduced at the time of fare increases. Coventry increased its discount levels from 8 to 14 per cent and from 8 to 19 per cent at the time of its November 1969 fare increase; ticket sales rose by 50 and 100 per cent respectively. The revenue loss of the Coventry system, for example, is estimated at £39,000, but the management feel that the introduction of these tickets accounted for the fact that, for the first time in a number of years, little passenger recession occurred at the time of a fare increase. It is hypothesised that the recession would have been much greater were the tickets not available. (The loss in revenue of £39,000 per annum represents a 1·5 per cent passenger recession.)[55]

The most convenient sales method for the passenger is when the tickets are available at the 'point of sale' i.e. either from the driver or from machines at the stop. Selling through the driver is not necessarily incompatible with the purpose of the tickets; if, for example, it involves selling books of ten journey tickets, passengers need only approach the driver once in every ten journeys. Admittedly, demand for tickets may reach a peak, particularly in the case of books of ten-journey tickets, on Monday mornings or on traditional pay days such as Friday evening. But this may be overcome — and the boarding time delays reduced — by having tickets which cater for more than just a week's journeys, e.g. twelve-journey tickets.

Vending machines are subject to vandalism and they require considerable supervision. Agents demand a commission and this, together with the distribution of tickets and collection of cash, adds to the costs.

Cancellation is most appropriately performed by a machine mounted on the opposite side of the boarding platform to the driver. Where graduated systems exist the machine will record on the ticket the stage at which the passenger boarded. It is only by the use of such machines that the dual flow may be created which is the key factor in improving boarding times.

By far the most radical recent innovation has been the introduction by the Stockholm Transport Authority of a monthly season ticket allowing unlimited travel on all buses and trains within Greater Stockholm, an area of more than 6,000 square kilometres. The objectives of this system were to rationalise and simplify a complex system of season, zone and graduated fares, and to achieve some administrative savings. The primary effects were to make the journey to work from suburban to city centre locations much cheaper and thus it was hoped that commuters would be attracted from the car. For short journeys (up to three kilometres) the price of a monthly season ticket is equivalent to the cost of a month's commuting journeys paid for by single tickets, but for journeys of maximum distance, approximately twenty-four kilometres, a saving of 150 per cent is realisable, added to which the ticket provides the opportunity for unlimited off-peak travel. Previously some 30 per cent of passengers used season tickets and 70 per cent paid by single ticket; those percentages have now been reversed. While the scheme has effected a small increase in journeys of 5 per cent per annum, there has been little attraction of trips from other modes. Most of the extra travel is accounted for by incremental weekend and lunchtime travel and extra buses have been required to cope with this increase in demand. Our own research includes analysis of a similar UK scheme introduced on Merseyside, and this is presented in chapter 7.

Notes

[1] The creation of such an agency has recently been called for by the Second Report of the Executive Committee on *Urban Transport Planning,* HMSO, December 1972.

[2] D. A. Quarmby, 'Choice of travel mode for the journey to work: some findings' *Journal of Transport Economics and Policy,* vol. 1, no. 3, September 1967, pp. 273—314; also *Choix du Moyen de Transports par les Usagers,* Institut d'Amenagement et d'Urbanisme de la Region Parisienne, October 1963.

[3] P. R. Stopher, 'Report on the journey to work survey, 1966' *GLC Department of Highways and Transportation Research Memorandum 48.*

[4] R. G. D. McGillivray, 'Demand and choice models of modal split' *Journal of Transport Economics and Policy,* vol. IV, no. 2, May 1970, pp. 192—207.

[5] See chapter 2 for details of these: T. F. Golob, E. T. Canty and R. L. Gustafson, 'An analysis of consumer preferences for a public transportation system' *Transportation Research,* vol. 6, no. 1, March 1972, pp. 81—102; F. T. Paine, A. N. Nash, S. J. Hille, and G. A. Brunner, *Consumer Conceived Attributes of Transportation,* Department of Business Administration, University of Maryland, 1967; F. R. Wilson, *Journey to Work,* Maclaren and Sons, London 1967.

[6] For a review of some of these see R. Bennett, 'Increasing the attractiveness of public transport', *UITP Conference Paper,* Rome 1971; also Research Projects Ltd., *The Importance of Service Features to Passengers and the Effects on Traffic,* London Transport Board, October 1966; Nathaniel Lichfield and Associates, *Stevenage Public Transport: Cost-Benefit Analysis,* Stevenage Development Corporation, October 1969.

[7] T. F. Golob et al., op. cit.

[8] G. Hoinville and E. Johnson, 'Commuter preferences: summary report' *Social and Community Planning Research,* July 1972.

[9] F. R. Wilson, op. cit.

[10] Department of the Environment, Working group on Bus Demonstration Projects: Report to the Minister, 1970.

[11] J. F. Curtin, 'Effect of fares on transit riding' *Highway Research Record 213,* Washington DC, Highway Research Board, 1968.

[12] L. M. Schneider, *Marketing Urban Mass Transit,* Harvard University Graduate School of Business Administration, Boston 1965.

[13] M. A. Kemp, 'Some evidence of transit demand elasticities' *Transportation,* vol. 2, 1973, pp. 25—52.

[14] J. Maloney, 'Mass transportation in Massachusetts' Transportation Commonwealth of Massachusetts PB 174 422, July 1964.

[15] See *Motor Transport,* 2 June 1972, pp. 18—19.

[16] John Blackman Associates, 'Mass transportation in a small city', Newcastle Transit Authority, Autumn 1968.

[17] R. C. Van Tassel, 'Economics of the pricing of urban bus transportation', Brown University Ph.D. thesis. Ann Arbor: University Microfilms, 1956.

[18] J. Frebault, 'Assessment of the effects of introducing reserved bus lanes', Conference of Ministers of Transport, Paris 1969.

[19] L. B. Yates, 'Vauxhall Bridge bus lane 12 months after study' *GLC,*

Department of Highways and Transportation, Research Memorandum 178, July 1969.

20 E. R. Ellen, 'Ways of helping buses in urban areas', papers and proceedings of 9th International Study Week in Traffic and Safety Engineering, Munich, September 1968; also 'Bus priority: proceedings of a symposium held at TRRL, 1972', Transport and Road Research Laboratory, TRRL Report LR 570, 1973.

21 Research Projects Ltd., op. cit.

22 'The Metro Flyer: a suburban express bus service to Downtown Area, Baltimore County — Baltimore City', Maryland Metropolitan Transit Authority, PB 177 030, April 1967.

23 Wilbur Smith and Associates, 'Chesapeake mass transportation demonstration project', Department of Housing and Urban Development, VA-MTD-1, 1969.

24 'The radial express and suburban cross town bus rider', final report, Department of Housing and Urban Development INT MTD 8, 1965.

25 T. Buck, 'Skokie Swift — the commuter's friend', Chicago Transit Authority, PB 175 734, Chicago 1968.

26 F. Fishwick, 'One man operation in municipal transport' *Institute of Transport Journal*, March 1970, pp. 413—25.

27 F. T. Paine, A. N. Nash, S. J. Hille and G. A. Brunner, op, cit.

28 Nathaniel Lichfield and Partners *'Stevenage Public Transport: Cost — Benefit Analysis'*, 1967.

29 See 'The Decatur and Peoria Premium Special Services' *Passenger Transport*, May 1967, pp. 183—87.

30 P. J. Hovell, 'Applying the marketing concept to urban passenger transport' *British Journal of Marketing*, Spring 1968.

31 'Maxi-Cab Commuter Club' Flint Transportation Authority and the American Academy of Transportation Project Technical Managers, MICH-MTD-2, 1970.

32 D. Roos, 'Operational experience with demand responsive transportation systems' *Highway Research Record No. 397*, prepared for the 51st meeting, 'New transportation systems and technology', 1972.

33 *The Economist*, 12 October and 9 November 1974.

34 J. B. Lansing, et al., 'Residential location and urban mobility', Survey Research Centre, University of Michigan, June 1964, p. 88.

35 National Analysis, Inc., 'A survey of commuter attitudes towards rapid transit systems', for the National Capital Transportation Agency (now the Washington Metropolitan Area Transit Authority), March 1963, vol. II p. 15.

36 P. J. Hovell and W. H. Jones, 'The Formby bus-rail demonstration

project: a pre-service feasibility study', University of Liverpool, August 1970; P. J. Hovell and W. H. Jones, 'The Formby bus-rail demonstration project: a study of its effect on modal split for the journey to work', University of Liverpool, July 1971; W. H. Jones, 'The Formby bus-rail demonstration project: a survey analysis of the changed demand pattern' University of Liverpool, July 1972. For a summary of these and an assessment of the service, see *Bus Demonstration Project: Summary Report No. 6, Formby, Bus Feeder Service to the Local Railway Station,* Department of the Environment, 1974.

[37] Tri-State Transportation Commission, 'Park-n-ride rail service: final report', PB 174 740, New York, May 1967.

[38] Washington Metropolitan Area Transit Commission, 'The minibus in Washington DC - final report', DC-MTD-2, May 1965.

[39] SELNEC (now styled Greater Manchester) PTE 'Transport plan for the future', January 1973.

[40] City of Atlanta, Department of Planning and Eric Hill and Associates, 'Town-Flyer: Atlanta's city centre shuttle bus', SA-MTD-1, 2, Atlanta 1972.

[41] L. M. Schneider, op. cit., for example, concentrates on seat availability and air conditioning.

[42] For a fuller discussion of technical research and a literature review see K. M. Soloman, R. J. Soloman and J. S. Silien, *Passenger Psychological Dynamics, H804,* US Department of Transportation, Urban Mass Transportation Administration, June 1968.

[43] But see, J. K. Sheehan, 'A discussion of transit car features' Operations Research Inc., for the National Capital Transportation Agency (CFSTI: PB 176 901), June 1964.

[44] Erwin Wasey, 'Report of a study into the motivation and attitudes of passengers and potential passengers on London Transport buses', London Transport Executive, September 1968.

[45] See, for example, C. F. Hirshfeld, 'Distributing effects of horizontal acceleration', Electric Railway President's Conference Committee Bulletin No. 3, 27 September 1932.

[46] J. P. Carstens, et al. 'Literature survey of passenger comfort limitations of high-speed ground transports', United Aircraft Corporation, for the Office of High-Speed Ground Transportation, Department of Commerce, (CFSTI: PB 168 171), July 1965; also E. W. Davis, 'Comparison of noise and vibration levels in rapid transit vehicle systems', Operations Research, Inc., for the National Capital Transportation Agency, NCTA TR 216, April 1964.

[47] F. T. Paine, A. N. Nash, S. J. Hille and G. A. Brunner, op. cit.

[48] As for example in the Hale Barns service or in Merseyside rapid-ride services.

[49] There are exceptions to this general rule, as, for example, on Merseyside where a small sales force is employed to sell traveller tickets.

[50] 'Transit information aids', Washington Metropolitan Area Transit Commission and Sidney Hollander and Associates, INT-MTD-10, 1969.

[51] Port Authority of Allegheny County and Transport Research Institute of Carnegie — Mellor University, 'Advertising and Promotion Demonstration Programme', PA MTD-7, Pittsburgh 1970.

[52] F. Fishwick, 'One man operation in municipal transport' *Institute of Transport Journal.* March 1970, pp. 413—25.

[53] M. A. Cundill and P. F. Watts, 'Bus boarding and alighting times', Transport and Road Research Laboratory, TRRL Report LR 521, 1973.

[54] W. Latscha, 'Economic viability in public transport undertakings', UITP Conference, London 1968.

[55] D. L. Hyde, 'Multi-journey discount ticket system', report to the Municipal Passenger Transport Association, 1970.

7 Using Marketing Research for Service Improvements: Findings from Experiments Conducted in the North West of England

We now present the findings from experiments conducted in the North West of England on Merseyside, a metropolitan county which has as its core Britain's second largest port, Liverpool, and at Bolton, a comparatively compact industrial town with a population of over 150,000 and which is situated within the boundaries of the metropolitan county of Greater Manchester, some eleven miles to the north west of Manchester's centre. The experiments were designed to test further many of the ideas inherent in the US demonstration projects and, in particular, the hypothesis that the sensitivity of demand for dimensions such as price, time or frequency will vary by trip purpose. The data on promotion effects were found to be particularly poor in our review of the published findings contained in the previous chapter and, therefore, we include an experiment designed, in part, to elicit the potency of this factor. Finally, because of the problematical time delays caused by the introduction of one-man bus operation and the increasing trend to multi-mode journeys (given the acceptance of most PTE plans for upgrading rail systems) we include two experiments designed to test pre-purchase ticket systems.

More specifically, the experiments covered the following mix elements and locations:

1 Three fare reduction experiments:
1.1 Bolton, all-day fare reduction;
1.2 Bolton, off-peak weekday fare reduction;
1.3 Huyton—Liverpool, off-peak fare reduction.
2 An in-vehicle time reduction experiment: the Hale Barns executive express coach service.
3 A mesh density improvement experiment: the Formby bus—rail feeder service experiment.
4 Two frequency improvement experiments:

4.1   Bolton, increased bus frequency;
4.2   Liverpool—Ormskirk, extra peak-time rail express.
5.   A promotion experiment:
Promotion of an off-peak rail fare reduction.
6   Two pre-purchase ticket experiments:
6.1   Bolton, pre-purchase ticket books;
6.2   Merseyside, pre-purchase 'Flash Pass' ticket.

Experiments 1 to 4, therefore, concern the first dimension of the marketing-mix, namely product attributes, 5 concerns promotion and 6 the third dimension, fare scales and labour productivity. With the exceptions of 2 and 3 all the experiments involve changes to a single marketing-mix variable for established services; the two exceptions entailed the formulation of a total marketing-mix for entirely new services.

The obvious rationale for concentrating on single variables is that it becomes possible to attribute any fluctuation in passenger demand and net revenue to the experimental variable concerned. Most US demonstration projects, with the particular exception of some of the Boston experiments, seemed little concerned to distinguish the effects of specific variables. There are, of course, difficulties in isolating the effects of changing individual elements of the mix because of the interrelationships involved. For example, before the effects of a fare reduction or an improvement in frequency become apparent, the public must first be made aware that a change has taken place, and this means introducing another variable, publicity. In those experiments where there was no intention to test the effectiveness of the promotional element, we endeavoured to reduce the interference caused by this dimension by only resorting to minimal promotion, largely of an informative type.

The objective in any experiment involving an adjustment to a single mix element, supported only by minimal promotion, was not to demonstrate that this *in itself* would lead to operational 'success' (e.g. increased numbers and receipts), but rather to determine the potency of that variable, or in economic terms to attempt to derive a demand function for the variable concerned. This knowledge is an essential prerequisite for the marketing manager seeking to manipulate all the relevant variables into an optimum mix that will be 'successful' in meeting his executive's objectives. These experiments, therefore, represent a first attempt to analyse the diverse elements which determine modal choice within the context of the development of an optimum mix. It must be emphasised that in an ongoing research situation it will be necessary to conduct many more controlled experiments, testing the incremental demand effects of introducing a whole range of changes to the relevant variables.

Apart from the difference already stated, the methodology employed to gauge the effects of improvements to established services was similar to that applied to many US demonstration projects, and we were thus concerned with longitudinal data gathered from pre and post-change time periods, and care was taken, where possible, to offset the interference caused by seasonal, cyclical or secular changes in demand. Most commonly this was attempted by collecting as much control data as budgetary considerations would allow.

Obviously, in the case of experiments involving entirely innovatory services (2 and 3 above) it was essential to formulate the total mix before we could begin to test the main objectives, i.e. the importance of in-vehicle time and improved mesh density respectively. It was also advisable, before committing the necessary resources, to make some assessment of the extent to which the proposed service might be self-supporting. Both these concerns suggested the use of market research techniques to forecast the likely demand, and to determine product attribute preferences as an aid to service design. They, therefore, also provide working case studies of the application of the marketing concept and functions to service innovation. In those cases where we were interested in establishing successful services if possible, their launching was accompanied by relatively intensive promotional support. It was appreciated that any definition of 'success' ought to take account of how the new services might improve the total transport system. For example, by how much will they increase the profitability of other parts of the public transport network; and to what extent will they affect levels of road congestion by attracting passengers from the private mode? Some account might also be taken of how future changes in total network infrastructure and service levels are likely to affect such innovations. Although time and budgetary constraints limited our fares to short term innovations the type of methodology adopted will basically be applicable to product preference and demand feasibility studies associated with longer run proposals for infra-structure developments.

1   Three fare reduction experiments

1.1   Bolton, all-day fare reduction experiment
From 14 June 1971, reductions were made to fares throughout the day on a short suburban-city route in Bolton. The route was approximately 2½ miles in length and covered a relatively poor inner suburban district as demonstrated by low car ownership and relatively high bus usage. Only 42 per cent of households in a sample survey owned cars while 44 per cent used

the bus for the journey to work. (The control route demonstrated a comparable pattern in this respect.) The experimental and control routes were one-man bus operated; they were also reasonably self-contained and it was not anticipated, therefore, that traffic would be attracted from other services.

The Greater Manchester PTE already differentiated peak and off-peak fares and promoted them as 'standard' and 'cheap weekday' respectively; the latter were operative from 10.00 to 12.00 hours and from 14.00 to 16.00 hours on weekdays. The experimental fares offered an average 21 per cent reduction off 'standard' time fares and 18 per cent off 'cheap weekday' fares. The data from three passenger counts, one before and two after the change are shown in Table 7.1.

The day totals indicate passenger losses in August (– 1·5 per cent) and October (– 5·8 per cent) rather than gains. When the experimental and control routes indices are compared the position is worse since the latter made gains for the same period. Monitored in this way the experimental

Table 7.1

Bolton, all-day fare reduction experiment: passenger changes on a weekday

Time of day	Experimental route			Control route			Experimental route: net percentage change against control	
	June: passenger numbers	August: passenger index	October: passenger index	June: passenger numbers	August: passenger index	October: passenger index	August	October
06.00—09.00 and 16.00—18.00	3,030	95·4	113·9	3.818	99·1	121·3	— 3·7	— 7·4
09.00—10.00 and 12.00—14.00	1,609	90·1	75·6	1.664	122·2	103·0	—32·0	—27·4
10.00—12.00 and 14.00—16.00	2,194	101·0	81·2	2,306	113·1	90·4	—12·1	— 9·2
18.00—23.00	1,581	103·1	87·7	1,942	104·4	89·0	— 1·3	— 1·3
Total per day	8,414	98·5	94·2	9,730	107·4	104·4	— 8·9	—10·2
Total two-man bus services operated all day	—	—	—	71,160	92·3	104·2	—	—

Source: Passenger counts, single day each month

192

route made net losses of 8·9 per cent, and 10·2 per cent in August and October respectively. Even though passenger demand improved during the former 'cheap weekday' and 'standard' evening periods in August and again during the former 'standard' peak times in October these gains were considerably less than those for the control.

Estimated passenger figures for all two-man bus operated services were also monitored as a further control check, but provide no clue as to why a reduction in the fares operative on the experimental route should cause a reduction in demand during weekdays. This is clearly a perverse finding, one for which we are unable to account. The revenue data relating to this experiment is given in Table 7.2.

The experimental route was similarly monitored for changes in Sunday traffic, when 'standard' fares had applied previously throughout the day, and this provided a test of the propensity for increased social and leisure trips in response to a fare decrease. As Table 7.3 shows, the experimental route performed consistently well, registering absolute passenger increases of 16·7 per cent and 3·4 per cent in August and October, compared with the base month of June, which were, respectively, 18·3 per cent and 13·5 per cent better than those for the control. However, revenue fell by 13 per cent between June and August on the experimental route but remained constant for the control. Using passenger trips as a measure of quantity sold, an elasticity of 0·65 may be derived for this experiment.

Table 7.2

Bolton, all-day fare reduction experiment: revenue changes on a weekday

	Experimental route				Control route				Experimental route: net index change against control
	June		August		June		August		
	£	index	£	index	£	index	£	index	
'Standard' time	193·40	100	159·06	82·3	290·76	100	313·32	107·5	—24·2
'Cheap weekday' time	50·77	100	38·72	76·4	73·25	100	85·45	116·4	—40·0
Total	244·17	100	197·78	81·1	364·01	100	398·77	109·6	—28·5

Source: Revenue counts, single day each month

Table 7.3

Bolton, all-day fare reduction experiment: passenger and revenue data for a Sunday

	Experimental route						Control: All two-man bus services						Experimental route: net % charge against control	
	June		August		October		June		August		October		August	October
	Nos.	Index	Nos.	Index	Nos.	Index	Nos.	Index	Nos.	Index	Nos.	Index		
Passenger total per day	3,459	100	4,040	116·7	3,578	103·4	24,252	100	23,882	98·4	21,822	89·9	+18·3	+13·5
Total revenue per day (£s)	116·19	100	100·53	87·0	*		970·37	100	970·97	100	*		—13·0	*

* Revenue data not computed for October

Source: Passenger and revenue counts, single day each month

194

Data from Los Angeles have shown that senior citizens (i.e. pensioners) demonstrate a more elastic demand than average. In the case of Los Angeles a figure of 0·7 was derived, which is only marginally higher than the overall elasticity in this experiment; however, the Bolton data for pensioners indicate a greater than unity elasticity (1·9), and stimulation of trips by this group was significantly higher than for all passengers. Numbers of passengers carried, by category of passenger, are shown in Table 7.4. Pensioners thus formed a steadily growing segment of this route increasing from 7·5 per cent to 10·2 per cent of passengers carried. More dramatically, trips by pensioners increased by 56 per cent in August and 40 per cent in October. This therefore seems a particularly encouraging result.

1.2 Bolton, off-peak weekday fare reduction experiment

This experiment was similar to 1 above, and commenced on the same date, but the reductions were confined to specified off-peak hours only, namely the 'cheap weekday' time period, 10.00—12.00 hours and 14.00—16.00 hours. Fares at these times already offered an average of 18·6 per cent off 'standard' fares and for this test the differential was widened to 33·3 per cent (a further reduction of 18·2 per cent).

The route selected was a radial one connecting Bolton with Horwich, a relatively high income suburb some eight miles to the west of Bolton. Of the four routes tested in Bolton, this was the most affluent with 54 per cent of households owning at least one car, and of these 12 per cent with at least two cars. Only 33 per cent of respondents used the bus for their journey to work.

Table 7.4

Bolton, all-day fare reduction experiment: passengers carried on Sundays by category of passenger

	Total		Adults			Children			OAPs		
	Nos.	Index	Nos.	Index	% total passengers	Nos.	Index	% total passengers	Nos.	Index	% total passengers
June	3,459	100	2,736	100	79·0	463	100	13·3	260	100	7·5
August	4,040	116·7	3,147	115·0	78·8	487	105·1	12·0	406	156·1	10·0
October	3,578	103·4	2,805	102·5	78·3	408	88·1	11·4	365	140·3	10·2

Source: Passenger counts, single day each month

195

Table 7.5
Bolton, off-peak weekday fare reduction experiment: passengers carried

	Experimental route				Control route				Experimental route index change against control
	June		August		June		August		
	Nos.	Index	Nos.	Index	Nos.	Index	Nos.	Index	
'Standard' time	12,901	100	11,772	91·2	8,172	100	7,201	88·1	+3·1
'Cheap weekday' time	3,560	100	3,804	106·8	2,387	100	2,504	105·2	+1·6
Total	16,461	100	15,576	94·6	10,559	100	9,705	91·9	+2·7

Source: Passenger counts, two days each month

As the figures in Table 7.5 indicate, demand on the experimental route increased by 6·8 per cent from June to August, while a similar but slightly smaller increase, 5·2 per cent, occurred on the control route for the same off-peak segment at maintained 'cheap weekday' fare levels. 'Standard' time traffic for both routes declined over the same period.

On the basis of the experimental figures, demand was not very responsive, given the size of the fare reduction and in view of the favourable change on the control. Elasticity was 0·38 for the experimental route, only 0·09 more elastic than the control. Correspondingly revenue fell by 20 per cent, whereas it increased by 8 per cent for the control, as shown in Table 7.6.

Table 7.6
Bolton, off-peak weekday fare reduction experiment: revenue effects

	Experimental route				Control route				Experimental route index change against control
	June		August		June		August		
	£	Index	£	Index	£	Index	£	Index	
'Standard' time	539·62	100	508·29	94·2	309·69	100	285·42	91·9	+ 2·3
'Cheap weekday' time	108·90	100	86·86	79·8	74·74	100	80·90	108·0	—28·2
Total	648·52	100	595·15	91·6	384·43	100	366·32	95·3	— 3·7

Source: Computed from passenger counts, two days each month

Some analysis of these findings is desirable. They are consistent with our supposition that off-peak trips, where there is a large proportion of shopping journeys, will be less elastic than off-peak leisure and social trips, but the elasticity of demand is far less than one might expect; the low level of responsiveness accords, for example, more with the figures produced for peak hour travel at Stevenage or for all journeys in London. This might be explained in part by the highly restricted nature of the off-peak period and by the car-oriented nature of the catchment area with a relatively high proportion of second cars and, therefore of women with the car available to them for shopping trips.

1.3 Huyton—Liverpool, off-peak fare reduction experiment

Huyton is a large 'overspill' area eight miles to the south east of the Liverpool centre with a preponderance of council housing. Commencing 1 November 1971, fares on a route between Huyton and the Liverpool centre were reduced by an average of 25 per cent; the reduction was available throughout the week except for the periods before 09.30 hours and between 16.30 hours and 18.30 hours on weekdays. This one-man bus service follows a rather devious route to the city centre since it was created to replace three adjacent routes. It is unlikely that a fare inducement would cause people to switch to this route from others since this would incur a considerable time penalty.

Table 7.7 summarises the fare takings during the week prior to the

Table 7.7

Huyton—Liverpool, off-peak fare reduction experiment: revenue analysis

	Weekdays			Saturday			Sunday		
	October (£s)	February (£s)	Index change	October (£s)	February (£s)	Index change	October	February	Index change
06.00—09.29	226·56	168·94	— 25·4	33·22	15·29	— 54	*		
09.30—16.29	444·56	328·32	— 26·1	89·91	73·29	— 18·5	*		
16.30—18.29	157·67	88·80	— 43·7	38·57	27·62	— 28·4	*		
18.30 — last service	60·07	199·42	+232·0	11·53	25·03	+117·1	*		
Off-peak total	504·63	527·74	+ 4·5	173·23	141·23	— 18·5	*		
Day total	*	*					90·91	84·82	— 6·7

*Data not relevant
Source: Waybill Analysis, five day count each month

change in October 1971 and during the early part of February 1972; an intermediate count in mid-January produced similar findings. Unlike the Bolton experiments, it was not possible to conduct passenger counts and any figures for passengers are estimates derived from waybill analyses.

During the weekday daytime off-peak periods revenue fell by 26·1 per cent; evidently, however, there was a substantial recessionary trend since morning and evening peak takings also decreased. The evening figures present a stark contrast for at this time traffic increased by 232 per cent. Assuming a pre-change average fare of 6p and a post-change average fare of 4·5p, passenger trips increased from something like 1,000 to 4,400, and these figures indicate an elasticity considerably in excess of unity. For the daytime and evening off-peak period combined trips increased from some 8,400 to 11,700 approximately, and this generates an elasticity of 1·3, again in excess of unity.

Saturday services had the reduced fare applied throughout the day and overall some 300 incremental passengers were attracted. Indeed, before 18.30 hours usage was actually down, and once again it is the evening traffic that proves highly elastic; evening usage increased from less than 200 to over 500 passengers.

For Sundays when the fare was again available throughout the day the numbers were too small for a meaningful analysis by time period. For the day total, however, some 300 incremental trips were attracted and an elasticity close to unity achieved (0·87).

2 An in-vehicle time reduction experiment: the Hale Barns executive express coach service

Hale Barns is some eleven miles south of Manchester; it seemed particularly suitable for testing an executive coach service, for it is representative of many of the middle class suburbs in the southern half of the conurbation and, in common with some of these, has relatively poor access to good public transport. The nearest railway station at Hale is 1¼ to two miles away and the only bus service to Manchester involves a circuitous route and a change at Altrincham. The area is highly car-oriented, 54·2 per cent travelling to work by that mode in 1966, only 12 per cent by bus and 15·5 per cent by train.

The marketing-mix, especially the service attributes, and the likely demand for the service, were researched in a survey of 400 of the 900 households in the area and particular emphasis was given to timetabling, the siting of stops, pricing and in-vehicle comfort such as availability of a hostess service for the sale of light refreshments, cigarettes and newspapers, and the provision of 'Musak'.

The feasibility study suggested that a viable demand for the service existed and it was launched on 20 April 1970, attended by an extensive promotional campaign. The major features of this were door-to-door leaflet distribution of all households and the placing of posters throughout the area, advertisements in two local newspapers, the provision of specially designed boarding-point signs, a sales drive to all 'sympathetic' respondent households and also to 25 per cent of the total households in the area. Other innovatory features for the UK transport market included the option for regular passengers to be picked up from their own front door within Hale Barns and the use of a hostess to administer pre-booking arrangements and to travel on the coach. There was just one journey in each direction per day and the coach travelled non-stop to the centre of Manchester. A modern luxury coach was used and free newspapers provided on board, reflecting the operators' determination to penetrate a high income segment in a car-owning and commuting community. At the time of inauguration the cost of a return journey was 50p, or alternatively books of ten return tickets could be purchased for £3·50p (equivalent to 35p per return trip).

Demand for the service has been stable since inauguration; based on an analysis made over a six month period average weekly demand was 202 trips, producing an average weekly revenue of £47 (1970 fares). The total costs were estimated to be £61 per week (1970), of which 40 per cent represented a contribution to corporate fixed costs and 24 per cent an allowance for depreciation. Although a depreciation charge is not strictly applicable in the case of this particular test, where the coach is drawn from a coach hire fleet, and therefore represents the utilisation of spare capacity, we have included depreciation as it is unlikely that such a situation would obtain in the more general application of this concept. Revenue, by these rigorous criteria, does not meet the operating costs of the service, but the loss (estimated at £700 per annum) is largely offset by the annual congestion cost savings of the 10,000 car trips removed from the road system at peak hours. These may be estimated at £500, assuming that most of the travellers would travel by car to central Manchester were it not for the availability of this service.

This represents an encouraging attempt to penetrate a highly car-oriented community and it is worth noting that there have been no follow-up marketing campaigns following that which accompanied the initial launch. The promotional launch costs of some £500 may therefore be discounted over a four-year period adding £125 per annum to the costs of the service. Experiment 3 indicates that follow-up promotion may well be beneficial, particularly if it is of a selective kind and that there may be substantial benefits in directing promotional material at new residents in an area of considerable mobility. The marketing-mix in the case of this service would also be more aggressive if a seasonal 'go anywhere', 'flash pass' ticket of the kind tested in experiment 6.2 was made available; the Formby experiment (3) also indicates that it is particularly attractive to commuters living on the periphery of conurbations. There are, therefore, several ways in which the marketing of this service might be strengthened and its market penetration increased, and the idea itself might find extension for both periphery-core and periphery-industrial estate commuting.

3   A mesh density improvement experiment: the Formby bus—rail feeder service

This experiment was designed to assess the viability of, and the benefits to be derived from, the operation of a feeder bus service to a local railway station during the morning and evening peak hours. More particularly, it tested the willingness of the public to accept a transfer as part of their journey and the attractiveness of an integrated bus-rail mode to existing car commuters. It was also intended to measure the net costs and benefits that might accrue to public transport.

Formby, largely a dormitory area, is situated fourteen miles due north of Liverpool. The town is on the Liverpool to Southport railway and the journey to Liverpool's Exchange Station takes 26 minutes by local service or 19 minutes by express. The average frequency of peak hour services is 13 minutes and there are two express services in both the morning and evening peaks. At these times the services are well patronised and Formby is one of the busiest stations on the line. For car commuters the Formby to Liverpool journey takes about 30 minutes; bus provides a further alternative, the stopping service taking 51 minutes and the express 36 minutes. The average peak frequency of the former is 17 minutes and there are two express services during the morning and one during the evening peak. At the time the feeder service was introduced, a day return rail ticket to Liverpool cost 35p, although the purchase of a monthly season ticket would reduce this to 30p; the cost of the equivalent bus journey was 40p. Besides being more expensive and involving a longer journey time, the bus is at a disadvantage because the Liverpool bus terminus, unlike the rail one, is situated 5—10 minutes' walk from the central business district (although the former is more convenient for the main shopping areas). However, in Formby the bus services are reasonably accessible, whereas the location of the railway station was inconvenient for many people.

Prior to the feeder service a local circular bus service passing the station did operate once during the morning and twice during the evening peak but because of its infrequency and the long journey time of 13—19 minutes, the service was little patronised. When this project started, no 'park-n-ride' facilities were available at the station, although on-street parking was possible nearby. Commuters who travelled by train mostly walked to the station. Like Hale Barns, the area is car-oriented and the 1966 partial census revealed that 55·8 per cent travelled to work by car, 29·3 per cent by train and 8 per cent by bus. The feeder scheme was introduced on 2 November 1970 with four weekday morning and four weekday evening services, a frequency of approximately 15 minutes, a 4-minute interchange time between bus and train, and a fare of 2½p. The feeder serves an estate half-a-mile at its nearest and one mile at its furthest to the south-east of the station. Since its inauguration a number of changes have occurred, including the addition of a fifth evening service in December 1970 and a fifth morning service in May 1973; additionally, there has been one feeder service fare increase and four rail fare increases. The Merseyside PTE's traveller ticket (this provides multi-mode facilities and, especially, for commuters living in peripheral areas such as Formby, a considerable financial incentive — see experiment 6.2) introduced in January 1972 has also affected demand.

The launch of the bus feeder service in Formby was accompanied by a substantial advertising campaign organised by British Rail. This included a house-to-house leaflet campaign, the placing of advertising bibs on milk bottles, sales visits to over 200 households and the display of banners and posters at the station and other appropriate locations. All residents new to the estate were, and continue to be, supplied with promotional material. In January 1972 a second promotional campaign was carried out, both as a reminder and to inform residents of the existence of the new Traveller Ticket. Demand for the service has grown steadily from 19,917 passenger trips in the first year to 24,552 in the second and 39,328 in the third, increases of 23·2 and 97·3 per cent respectively. A post-inaugural survey showed that users of the bus feeder abandoned use of the following modes: car 13 per cent; express bus 8 per cent; other means of reaching the station (walking, cycling, etc.) 67 per cent, while the remaining 12 per cent used the feeder for local trips. A survey revealed the considerable popularity of Traveller Tickets with passengers and its financial incentive is clearly important. Further research revealed that a disproportionately high number of new residents were joining the service, which implies that new residents in a community are more 'open minded' about the alternatives available to them. There is no evidence that a higher proportion of new residents than existing ones work in Liverpool, nor that the service is sufficiently attractive to be influencing house purchase. Finally, research also revealed strong circumstantial evidence of the benefits of the advertising.

The operational costs of the service were £792 in the first year of operation and £900 in the second. These costs include the normal operating elements (driver's wages, fuel, tyres, etc.) plus an allowance for depreciation and administration. They do not include the promotional expenses of £520 and £160 in the first and second years respectively which were paid by a central government grant. Arguably these expenses are mostly 'launch' costs and should perhaps be discounted over several years and not just apportioned to the years in which they occur. A proportion of them are also attributable to British Rail for the promotion in effect advertises their services as much as the bus feeder itself.

In both years for which data have been obtained, actual fares collected were insufficient to cover the operating costs, and losses of £249 and £229 were recorded. The figures are given in Table 7.8. The view was taken throughout the study that the cost-benefit situation for public transport is more relevant than the profit or loss of an individual mode. The feasibility study estimated a net annual gain to public transport of £1,552. The post-inaugural survey sought to test this figure by examining the modes abandoned by users of the bus feeder, and showed that, mainly because of the lower than expected numbers transferring from their cars, the total net gain during the first year was only £162·50. Using revenue and cost data for the bus feeder for the second year of operation and applying the post-inaugural survey results to total annual passenger trips in the second year, the marginal revenue gains and losses for rail and express bus are shown in Table 7.9. On the basis of this analysis the service has brought a net benefit to the total public transport system, which increases from £162 in the first year to £513 in the second despite the increase in operating costs. The continued increase of passengers in 1973 will have meant a further substantial improvement in that year. Further benefits derived from the reduction in congestion resulting from the transfer of car commuters to the railway; it was estimated that the benefit in the second year from the elimination of some 3,200 trips would be of the order of £300, bringing the total net annual benefit to over £800.

The primary task of the feasibility study was to forecast demand. A

Table 7.8
Formby bus—rail feeder service experiment: revenue and cost analysis

Year 1: November 1970 — October 1971 inclusive

Revenue	£542·76*
Costs of operation	£792·08
Net loss	£249·32

Year 2: November 1971 — October 1972 inclusive

Revenue	£545·27*	£672·77**
Costs of operation	£900·38	£900·38
Net loss	£355·11	£227·61

* Bus fares only
** Including an allocation of £127·50 from Traveller Tickets

Table 7.9
Formby bus-rail feeder service experiment: total public transport system effects

Item	Value
Marginal revenue to rail from previous car users	£702·02
Marginal revenue to rail from previous bus users*	£432·08
Gain to rail	£1,134·10
Loss on operating bus feeder service	£227·61
Marginal loss from passengers converting from express bus*	£392·80
Loss to bus	£620·41
Overall gain for public transport	£513·69

*982 return trips at the fare in operation on 23 April 1972

prediction on ninety-eight trips per day was made and although the actual demand for the service in the first year of operation was eighty, in the second year the forecast was almost exactly realised. However, the prediction still overestimated the number of car users who would convert to the service. This will probably have been caused by the increase in rail fares between the feasibility study and the introduction of the service and also by car drivers exaggerating the likelihood of their using the service; perhaps motivated by the desire to have a reserve mode for those occasions when the car was not available to them.

4   Two frequency improvement experiments

4.1   Bolton, increased bus frequency experiment

This experiment was devised to measure the incremental passenger and revenue benefits that would be brought by a substantial bus frequency increase similar in magnitude to the Boston rail increases. The route employed for this purpose was about four miles in length, radiating in a north-easterly direction from the centre of Bolton. The route corridor had fairly modal characteristics for the area: 47 per cent of households owning a car and 37 per cent using the bus for their journey to work. The frequency increases introduced were extensive; applied throughout the week, they varied from 33 per cent to about 58 per cent. Thus, for this experiment, weekday peak frequencies were 3—4 minutes, afternoon off-peak 5 minutes and evening off-peak 10 minutes. On Saturdays the frequencies were 3—4 minutes morning and evening, and 5 minutes in the afternoons, while on Sundays the frequency range was 6—20 minutes. The effect of these changes (introduced on 14 June 1971) on weekday passenger trips is shown in Table 7.10.

No clear cut trends emerge from these figures with the marked and important exception of evening traffic, where net increases of 23·7 and 39·5 per cent occurred in August and October respectively. As with experiments 1.2 and 1.3 this seems the segment most responsive to service attribute improvements.

The operators estimated the increase in average hourly costs of these improvements to be £1·70, a figure which included direct operating costs and allowances for depreciation and overheads. As an average it will understate peak and weekend costs which are much higher for the latter periods and overstate weekday off-peak costs. Incremental revenue and increased average cost relationships are examined in Table 7.11. The viability of all time periods improved from August to October, to a range of

Table 7.10
Bolton, increased bus frequency experiment:
passengers carried on a weekday

	Experimental route			Control route			Experimental route: net index change against control	
	June	August	October	June	August	October	August	October
	Passenger numbers	Index	Index	Passenger numbers	Index	Index		
06.00—09.00 and								
16.00—18.00	2,100	104·7	117·6	3,818	99·1	121·3	+ 5·6	— 3·7
09.00—16.00	2,568	105·0	98·2	3,970	116·9	95·7	—11·9	+ 2·5
18.00—23.00	803	128·1	128·5	1,942	104·4	89·0	+23·7	+39·5
Total per day	5,471	108·3	110·1	9,730	107·4	104·4	+ 0·7	+ 5·7

Source: Passenger surveys, one day each month

Table 7.11
Bolton, increased bus frequency experiment:
incremental revenue and cost analysis for a weekday

	Incremental revenue		Increased average costs	Incremental revenue as a % of incremental costs	
	August	October	Both months	August	October
06.00—09.00 and					
16.00—18.00	£6·49	£8·17	£34·00	19·0	24·0
09.00—16.00	—£8·17	£11·40	£35·70	—	31·9
18.00—23.00	£8·54	£18·64	£17·00	50·2	109·6
Total per day	£6·86	£38·21	£86·70	6·9	44·1

Source: Revenue counts and operators, one day each month

24—109·6 per cent, the patronage of evening services improving to such an extent that the full incremental costs of operation were adequately covered and a contribution to profitability made. It should also be remembered that the situation improves still further if the depreciation charge is taken out of account and there is a strong case for this where off-peak services are concerned.

For Saturday traffic the passenger trends were encouraging at most times of the day (see Table 7.12), particularly for afternoon traffic which showed increases of 51·9 and 14·4 per cent for August and October. The net changes showed ranges of 0·7 to 19·3 per cent for morning traffic, and —1·1 to +23·4 per cent for evening traffic and 11·8 to 29·9 per cent for the whole day. The incremental revenue generated by these passengers and the costs associated with the increased services are analysed in Table 7.13. Despite the encouraging passenger increases incremental revenue was never sufficient to cover the associated increase in average costs and for the total of Saturday traffic the percentage of costs covered varied from 39 to 46 per cent. Naturally the best performance in this respect was in the afternoon when 70 per cent of the costs were recovered and at this period the experiment would doubtless have more than broken even if marginal revenue were being compared with the actual marginal costs involved.

Table 7.12
Bolton, increased bus frequency experiment:
passengers carried on a Saturday

	Experimental route			Control route			Experimental route: net index change against control	
	June	August	October	June	August	October	August	October
	Passenger numbers	Index	Index	Passenger numbers	Index	Index		
06.00—12.00	1,691	107·8	105·7	3,091	107·1	86·4	+ 0·7	+19·3
12.00—18.00	2,444	126·6	110·2	5,200	74·7	95·8	+51·9	+14·4
18.00—23.00	1,402	104·1	94·7	2,509	80·7	95·8	+23·4	— 1·1
Total per day	5,537	115·2	104·9	10,800	85·3	93·1	+29·9	+11·8

Source: Passenger surveys, one day each month

Table 7.13
Bolton, increased bus frequency experiment:
incremental revenue and cost analysis for a Saturday

	Incremental revenue		Increased average costs	Incremental revenue as a % of incremental costs	
	August	October	Both months	August	October
06.00—12.00	—£0·47	£18·40	£30·60	—	60·0
12.00—18.00	£43·77	£24·48	£61·20	70·4	39·3
18.00—23.00	£10·89	£4·03	£25·50	40·0	16·0
Total per day	£54·19	£46·91	£117·30	46·1	39·3

Source: Revenue counts and operators, one day each month

4.2   *Liverpool—Ormskirk extra peak-time rail express*

The objective of this experiment was to measure the effects of an improvement in frequency accompanied by promotional support, although budgetary limitations ensured that the latter was at a low level. The improvement was effected by scheduling an existing morning and evening express to stop at Old Roan station on the Liverpool to Ormskirk line from October 1971. This additional morning train for Old Roan passengers left that station at 08.39 hours between two stopping services departing at 08.32 and 08.52 hours. The 08.39 which arrived at Liverpool's Exchange Station at 08.51 hours, was approximately five minutes faster than the stopping services. The evening equivalent left Exchange Station at 17.05 hours and arrived at Old Roan at 17.18 hours, again sandwiched between two stopping services from Exchange Station.

The test only imperfectly met our objective since more than one factor was involved, i.e. an increase in frequency and a time saving. A further complicating factor is that, theoretically, our analysis should also have taken account of the marginal disbenefits suffered by all those boarding the express train in the morning before it reached Old Roan, who consequently suffered small time losses because of the stop added there.

Old Roan station is situated 5¾ miles from the centre of Liverpool and serves large estates, both of council and of private houses. The area is also well served by several frequent bus routes running along a main arterial road to Liverpool. On-street parking is available on minor roads close to the station, but very few 'park-'n-ride' passengers were found to use the train. A household distribution of leaflets was made within the natural catchment area of Old Roan and posters were put up at the station. A station with a comparable socio-economic catchment area and length of journey on the Wigan line, Thatto Heath, was monitored as a control. Passengers boarding the 08.25 hours train at Thatto Heath were compared on a 'before and after' basis with passengers boarding the extra train and the services either side of it at Old Roan. The passenger figures for the experimental station and the control are shown in Table 7.14.

Table 7.14

Liverpool—Ormskirk extra peak-time rail express experiment: passenger analysis

	Daily number of passengers (October 1971)	Daily number of passengers (March 1972)	Change (%)	Expected daily passengers at experimental station *	Estimated daily incremental passengers at experimental station
Experimental station	143	136	− 3·7	124	12
Control station	46	36	−13·4	—	—

*Assuming no experimental changes and applying the trend at the control to the experimental station: $143 - 19 (13·4$ per cent$) = 124$
Source: Passenger counts, five days each month

Assuming a 250 working-day year, some 3,000 incremental journeys per year were generated by this experiment. An on-train survey was conducted in February 1972, with the objectives of determining: the frequency of commuter train usage, particularly of the experimental service; sources of information about the new service; mode usage prior to its introduction; and the most important element in the decision to make use of it. Of particular interest were the modal change data which indicated that only five previous car users had switched to the train in response to a small improvement in service. Posters were the most usually cited source of information, naturally so for existing train users. Of the respondents switching mode, four heard of the service change through household leaflets, one by word of mouth and only two from posters. Of those switching to the 08.39 hours express train from car, three gave convenience of the new timetable as the major reason, one specified a reduction in journey time and the other both factors.

The experimental service did not involve any considerable improvement over its predecessor, yet it was instrumental in generating increased traffic, and it may be that even the most modest promotional support associated with it (£60 total cost) in order to communicate that a change had been made was more effective in stimulating demand than were the quite minor product changes themselves.

5   A promotion experiment: promotion of an off-peak rail fare reduction

The Rock Ferry line runs under the River Mersey along the east side of the Wirral peninsular to connect Liverpool centre with a smaller but fashionable city, Chester, the capital of the adjacent county, Cheshire. This line was selected to conduct a controlled promotion and price experiment because, unlike almost any other rail route on Merseyside, the absence of a competitive bus service can isolate it and ensure that incremental passengers are either rail-borne passengers making additional trips or passengers won from the car. The travellers using this line tend to be oriented towards Liverpool for many of their work, shopping and leisure needs, although Chester, whose importance is growing, can cater for some of these. The concessionary fare was only valid for Liverpool bound trips.

The objective of the experiment was to measure the effect on passenger demand of two elements in the marketing-mix, namely price and promotion. This was achieved by making an off-peak price reduction of 29 per cent with minimal promotion at one station (Port Sunlight) and a similar reduction with medium intensity promotional support at another (Spital); a third station (Bebington) was monitored as a control. For the purpose of this rail experiment off-peak was defined as the period after 09.30 hours, and passengers were 'requested' not to travel back during the evening peak. The off-peak period was also limited by the railway timetable to shopping hours for trains did not stop at the experimental stations after 19.00 hours.

'Minimal' promotional support was achieved by limiting this element to a display of posters at the station, while the 'medium' level of support was achieved with posters and a household leaflet distribution in the catchment area.

The stations selected each had identifiable catchment areas. In this way it was thought that few passengers would switch from non-experimental stations, which they normally use to experimental ones in order to take advantage of the reduced fares available there; a check was incorporated for this factor. The experiment commenced in October 1971 and station counts were made on three occasions and a survey conducted to establish passengers' prior travelling patterns and modes. Passenger changes are shown in Table 7.15.

Table 7.15
Promotion of an off-peak rail fare reduction: passenger analysis

Stations	May 1971	November 1971	Change on May 1971 %	March 1972	Change on May 1971 %
Control	186	154(170)	—17·2(—8·6)	159(176)	—14·5(— 3·4)
Fare decrease plus 'minimal' promotion	358	393(377)	+9·8(+5·3)	417(400)	+16·5(+11·7)
Fare decrease plus 'medium promotion	162	213	+31·5	218	+34·6

Bracketed figures have been adjusted for 'back-tracking', i.e. switching from non-experimental to experimental stations. These were determined by the use of origin and destination surveys
Source: Passenger counts, five days each month

The results show an encouraging rise over the control at both experimental stations. Our surveys provided an indication of the volume of passengers living in the Bebington (control) catchment area who were thought to be 'back-tracking' to Port Sunlight. In Table 7.15, these passengers, constituting nearly 10 per cent of Port Sunlight's volume, were reapportioned as Bebington travellers. It is probable that we have overestimated the 'back-tracking' effect since many of the trips may have been incremental, stimulated by the price concession; thus the inclusion of these passengers within the control station figures probably artificially enhances the volume at that station with adverse repercussions on the comparisons with the experimental stations. Using the control station to estimate expected passenger volumes, Table 7.16 is a measure of the success of the other two.

Our figures indicate that by March 1972 a 29 per cent fare reduction had stimulated a 15·6 per cent passenger increase at Port Sunlight, where promotion had been minimal, and a 39·7 per cent increase at Spital, where more aggressive promotion was employed. These figures produce elasticities of 0·45 and 1·05, respectively, for the two stations. Revenue fell by some 18 per cent at Port Sunlight and, as indicated by the elasticity figure, was maintained near parity at Spital, where revenue returns indicated a drop of 1·3 per cent. The revenue effects of 'back-tracking' only involve a very small loss (2·6 per cent of Spital's expected revenue), and are perhaps unique to an experimental situation as opposed to a marketing promotion where a whole rail line might be promoted in this way. If Spital's revenue is maintained at parity, and Port Sunlight 'covers' this loss, their deficit increases from 18 per cent to 19·3 per cent of base revenue.

The promotional costs have hitherto been neglected. These costs were approximately £150 for Spital (where the more intensive of the two campaigns was conducted); for a small experiment of this nature fixed costs were high and three-quarters of this figure represents the costs of setting up the printing, the run-on costs for additional copies of the promotional literature being negligible. Assuming a campaign life of one year the net deficit is 10 per cent. The implication is strongly presented that promotional campaigns of this nature are not economic as very small exercises and the operator should consider such promotions only on a scale sufficient to justify the fixed costs involved.

The influence of promotion on passengers' modal choice (and a number of other relevant factors) was studied in a survey of those travelling at off-peak hours from the two experimental stations in March 1972. The specific objectives were: to determine regularity of travel to Liverpool and the proportion who have the use of other modes available to them; to estimate the effect of price decreases on regularity of travel; to gauge the numbers who had transferred from other stations; and to identify the importance of the various possible sources of information. With reference to the sources of information, at the 'medium' promotion station 29 per cent had learned of the fare reduction through the household leaflets, 41 per cent through posters and 47 per cent through the ticket clerk; the equivalent figures for the 'minimal' promotion station were 10, 18 and 58 per cent respectively. Clearly there was some overlap between the areas which explains the delivery of leaflets to some houses in the catchment area of the 'minimal' promotion station. The ticket clerk's large influence is to

be anticipated as his natural role is ensuring that all travellers purchase the appropriate tickets. 'Word of mouth' was also important and influenced 21 per cent of the total travellers.

6   Two pre-purchase ticket experiments

6.1   *Bolton pre-purchase ticket books*

Most of the multi-journey tickets at present offered in the UK require relatively sophisticated machinery to cancel them each time a ride is made (see p.182). This self-service element facilitates faster boarding times for passengers on one-man operated buses because passengers may form two streams, one to the driver and one to the automatic ticket cancellator. However, most of these systems are limited in so much as they offer a number of journeys for one distance only and thus are in effect a 'commuter' ticket, appealing particularly to those making regular trips of equivalent length.

The objectives of experiment 6.1 were to evaluate the possibility of devising a pre-purchase ticketing method which would speed boarding times, stimulate extra trips and allow for flexibility of trip lengths by the holder. Such a method would appeal equally to non-commuting segments.

The pre-purchase tickets used for the experiment were handed to, and cancelled by, the driver, thus obviating the need for expensive cancelling equipment in a trial situation. In effect, they promoted a 'correct fare' position which itself saves boarding time. The principle adopted was a relatively simple one involving the sale of books of tickets. With different quantities and denominations of ticket in each, the books offered and the discount on the face value of each are shown in Table 7.17. Such a scheme thus gives a progressively larger discount the greater the number of tickets bought in proportion to the face value of the ticket book.

The books were available from two bus stations and a transport office within Bolton; they were not sold on the buses themselves. Although the radial nature of the network meant that the bus stations were at least reasonably situated, this sales approach was far from ideal. Leeds Transport sell only 1—2 per cent of their multi-journey tickets from their offices, and the consumers' preference for purchasing them at the point of sale, i.e. from the driver, is easily understandable. Restricting sales to these three points was thus seen as a major limitation, but it was accepted with reluctance because of the extra workload already imposed on Bolton staff who were undermanned particularly at administrative levels; it was thought

Table 7.17
Bolton pre-purchase ticket book experiment: the 'saver' book scheme

Book types	Full value	Proposed selling price	Saving	Approximate saving (%)
2p Tickets				
Books of 10	20p	17p	3p	15
,, ,, 20	40p	32p	8p	21
,, ,, 40	80p	54p	26p	35
3p Tickets				
Books of 10	30p	25p	5p	17
,, ,, 20	60p	45p	15p	28
Combined book containing 10 x 3p 10 x 2p	50p	38p	12p	24

Experiment introduced 14 June 1971

that devising methods of administrative supervision and control would be too much of an added burden at the time.

One major shortcoming of other UK pre-purchase ticket introductions is in most cases that they have lacked the support of a suitable brand name. Apart from London's 'Red Rover' and the recently innovated 'Traveller' ticket on Merseyside, most of them are referred to by their generic term, e.g. multiple journey tickets, multi-journey tickets or books. These names are somewhat difficult to remember and fail to connote any of the advantages for the consumer. Even Merseyside's ticket name 'BET' conveys nothing to anyone unfamiliar with it; surveys in Liverpool showed that few people were aware that the letters stood for 'Bus Economy Tickets' for some considerable time after their introduction.

It was thought that a brand name should form a useful promotional feature of the Bolton experiment and help to establish the tickets with the public more quickly. The name 'Saver' tickets was adopted which is simple and easy to say and remember. Advertising stressed the double connotation of the name — 'save money and time'. Minimal publicity was conducted in Bolton, chiefly by the distribution of leaflets to all households along the route corridor concerned.

The penetration of these tickets on the three routes where they were introduced is shown in Table 7.18. Given the limited purchase sources and that the tickets were restricted to three routes only, a level of use ranging

Table 7.18
Bolton pre-purchase ticket book experiment: ticket penetration

| | August | October | | |
	Route 1	Route 1	Route 2	Route 3
Total passengers travelling	18,400	17,659	9,614	16,610
Percentage using tickets	7·4	11·3	7·3	11·4
Time since introduction (weeks)	8	19	8	8

Source: Passenger counts

Table 7.19
Bolton pre-purchase ticket book experiment: passenger analysis

	June: numbers	August: numbers and index	Change against control route 4 (%)	October index	Change against control route 4 (%)
'Saver' routes	18,615	96·9	+6·9	99·4	+2·9
Route 1					
Route 2		10,250	—	94·1	—2·4
Route 3		16,485	—	101·0	+4·5
Control routes					
Route 4	32,750	90·0	—	96·5	—
All two-man operated bus services	429,193	91·4	—	99·0	—

Note: Routes 1 and 4 were introduced in June, routes 2 and 3 in August
Source: Passenger counts

from 7—11 per cent is most encouraging. The two main forms of evaluation established were their potential for stimulating extra trips and their potential for speeding boarding flows. Table 7.19 shows an indexed breakdown of passenger changes.

Two routes, therefore, showed gains as a result of introducing the tickets. The effective rate of discount was established by analysing ticket book sales and determining the average discount of all tickets sold. This was 29·9 per cent. The net loss then depends upon the penetration levels achieved by the tickets and at the levels obtaining on the various routes it is incorporated in the revenue analysis in Table 7.20. As may be seen, all these routes performed considerably better than the controls and the passenger and revenue data indicate that the 'Saver' ticket system was stimulating a sufficient number of extra trips to more than offset the revenue loss incurred through the discount.

Table 7.20
Bolton pre-purchase ticket book experiment: revenue analysis

	June revenue (£s)	August revenue index	October revenue index
'Saver' routes			
Route 1	2,075	105·7 (103·6)	128·9 (125·6)
Route 2	1,100	—	143·0 (140·9)
Route 3	2,355	—	121·3 (117·9)
Control routes			
Route 4	2,380	94·9	112·2
All two-man operated services	14.960	96·3	117·0

Note: bracketed figures are 'net', i.e. allow for effective discount on 'Savers'
Source: Computed from passenger data, seven day base each month

The tickets also meant faster boarding times per passenger, for quick checks on a 'before and after' basis indicated benefits. However, the improvements were not dramatic given the modest penetration levels involved.

216

6.2   Merseyside pre-purchase 'Flash Pass' ticket

In January 1972, the Merseyside PTE introduced a 'Flash Pass' called the 'Traveller' ticket. Essentially this allows unlimited travel by bus, train or ferry within the PTE's area for a weekly payment of £1·95 and is, therefore, similar in principle to the Stockholm ticket described in chapter 6. At the time of our research (June 1972) sales of tickets were approximately 2,600 per week which represented roughly a 1 per cent penetration of passengers travelling to work within the area by public transport. Our major concern was to establish the effects of this system and specifically to determine modal transfers, incremental trip generation and the financial implications for the operators. The results of a survey of some 20 per cent of ticket users, i.e. 518 respondents, is given below.

(a)   *Modal switches from car to public transport* Out of 518 respondents in the survey, 39 (7·5 per cent) had started using public transport for their entire work journey as a result of the 'Traveller' ticket. A further 32 (6·2 per cent) had switched part of their trip from car to public transport. All the respondents switching from car were identified and telephone interviews successfully completed with 28 respondents. They all lived on the periphery of the conurbation and the purchase of the 'Traveller' ticket brought a substantial cost saving; nevertheless, 13 of the 28 respondents cited convenience as a feature of attraction. Most of those converting to the public transport system lived either on the Wirral (River Mersey tunnel tolls at a daily rate of 30p have to be paid by them to reach Liverpool) or at Formby on the northern perimeter of the conurbation (which, as we have seen, has a good rail service and which was the only area wherein the 'Traveller' ticket was vigorously publicised — by a household leaflet distribution campaign (see experiment 3 above). Fifteen ex-car users were identified as regular 'Traveller' ticket purchasers and of these all but one used the train for the major portion of their journey.

(b)   *Switches between public transport modes* The Merseyside public transport system comprises three modes: bus, train and cross-river ferry. The ferry travels from the Wirral to Liverpool's pier head, which is close to the city centre. In general, trains are slightly more expensive than buses, while the ferry is very cheap. Hence, because the 'Traveller' ticket is equally valid for all modes, passenger switching was to be expected. Of the 518 respondents, a total of 447 'Traveller' ticket purchasers were chosen (excluding those converting from car commuting) to complete a special questionnaire by post; the response rate was 75 per cent.

217

Modal changes were claimed by 30 respondents (9 per cent). Only 9 (3 per cent) made a 100 per cent change, 5 from bus to train, 3 from ferry to train and 1 from train to bus. Others made occasional switches to take advantage of a more convenient schedule or to take advantage of a different mode so that, for example, return journeys to and from work could be broken by shopping trips. There were 21 such switches, representing 6·5 per cent of the total sample — 13 of these were from train to bus/ferry, 4 from ferry to train, and 4 from bus to train.

Thus the net effect is small, probably entailing approximately 3 per cent of trips switched from the bus/ferry to the train, offset by about 1 per cent of trips attracted from the train to the bus/ferry.

(c) *Incremental trip generation as a result of possession of the 'Traveller' ticket* Just under 200 of respondents who had not switched to public transport from the car claimed to be making more journeys as a direct result of the possession of a 'Traveller' ticket. Total incremental trips are given in Table 7.21. Virtually all the incremental journeys were undertaken during off-peak periods. Advantage is taken of the increased mobility gained from possessing the pass, particularly for leisure trips made mainly in the evening and for casual shopping trips within working time. Incremental work trips are relatively less frequent and it is difficult to see even how virtually free fares can generate many *more* of these as opposed to modal *switches*. Most of those identified as undertaking more work trips took advantage of bus feeder services where previously, they had walked or motored to the station.

Table 7.21
Merseyside pre-purchase 'Flash Pass' ticket: incremental trips analysis

Incremental Trips	Local shopping	Liverpool centre shopping	Work trip	Short trip within city	Leisure/ visiting	Total
Number	71	88	46	102	188	495
Percentage	14	18	9	21	38	100

Source: Survey analysis

In stimulating such incremental trips the public transport network is augmenting its role as a public service and fostering greater urban mobility. It could also be argued that, in facilitating more convenient and

218

in effect, cheaper, travel the 'Traveller' ticket may lead some customers to put off purchasing cars. This is particularly so in the off-peak period where surplus capacity exists.

(d) *The financial implications for the operators* Respondents were asked to estimate the extent of their savings based on their previous public transport usage. Table 7.22 summarises this for those who had previously used public transport (i.e. excludes those switching from the car).

Table 7.22

Merseyside pre-purchase 'Flash Pass' ticket: respondents' weekly saving (loss) in terms of previous expenditure

	0—10p	11—20p	21—30p	31—50p	51p—£1	Over £1	No savings/ loss*
Approximate mid point	5p	15p	25p	40p	75p	£1·25	(—10p)
Numbers	31	39	39	71	63	43	35

* Some respondents were evidently willing to increase their expenditure in order to benefit from the convenience of the ticket

Multiplying the numbers in each category by their average saving or loss one may derive an average saving over this sample of 44½p which is effectively the revenue foregone by the operators by offering these tickets for sale. However, one must take account of the incremental revenue attracted from car users, which, when averaged over the ticket sales, reduces the net loss to 31·7p. On the basis of sales of some 2,500 tickets per week at the time or our analysis (June 1972), this means revenue of £40,000 per year lost to the PTE. This figure may exaggerate the loss, since the research was conducted early in the life of the 'Traveller' ticket when the majority of those using the ticket would presumably be existing public transport users, to whom the ticket offered a high immediate saving. Car users and public transport users to whom the ticket offered marginal savings would be more likely to adopt it at a later date. Nevertheless, it would seem unlikely that this bias will be instrumental in significantly reducing the net loss.

Compared to the Stockholm experiment, and even the relatively less successful experiment in St. Louis, the Merseyside 'Traveller' ticket has been unsuccessful in significantly gaining favour with public transport users. As in the other experiments, it is only where a financial advantage was markedly apparent that high sales were achieved, although convenience was often cited as a major rationale for the purchase of the tickets.

8 Strategies for Urban Public Transport Management

A wide range of secondary and primary research data relating to service-mix experiments was examined in the previous two chapters. However, before developing the marketing ramifications of these findings it is necessary to establish a total strategic framework within which urban public transport management can formulate more competitive services.

This work has set out to prescribe strategies and recommend organisational structures which will enable large passenger transport undertakings to exploit their market opportunities. Most of these strategies are based on how different demand segments react to changes in the marketing-mix. Public transport could easily operate as a profitable industry by adopting a careful pricing policy and by eliminating unprofitable routes; this largely follows from the price inelasticity of demand for most segments of users. However, public transport must bear social responsibilities as a result of a political choice to preserve some form of balance between town and countryside. In advanced industrial countries the 'natural' trend, given the extent of car ownership and use, points inexorably towards even greater urban dispersal. Most Western European countries have programmes designed to prevent the city's encroachment on rural areas and to foster specific travel patterns. These attempts are less in evidence in the US, but even there State and Federal funds have been allocated for urban renewal and massive sums have been spent on programmes such as the San Francisco's Bay Area Rapid Transit, which alone has received $1,400 million in an attempt to attract much larger numbers of commuters.

Thus public transport's social obligations, and the fact that ultimate control rests with a local political governing authority, mean that conventional profit objectives cannot be employed. When management states its objectives in terms of volume and penetration of different categories of passenger segments, it must do so within specified financial parameters: while management can expect to receive capital grants and subsidies, and even under the most favourable operating conditions that can be realistically forecast these will probably be required, it must still hold itself accountable for achieving optimum operational efficiency. Its planning must obviously be framed within the agreed land use strategy for the area and, in turn, should be finely tuned to local government policies determining freedom of access to the city centre for private motor vehicles, bus priority schemes and car parking. Adaptability will be required in both respects because, given the methodological problems of population and employment forecasting, continuous updating and modification will be necessary. Local government planners may well seek to use the car access factor as a regulator in the achievement of their land use strategy and again close liaison with the operators will be crucial.

Because these factors, particularly the land use structure, fundamentally interrelate with the kind of transport system which is operable, management will be required to provide expertise and judgements as an aid to formulating the broader land use and car access policies of the relevant political authorities. If it were ever the case that management's expertise was not sought, then it would have to establish its right to a part in this process and thus safeguard the interest of its customers and avoid the severe problems that would stem from a land use policy determined with little or no regard for the transport implications. As such, much of the strategic planning, described specifically under the headings of corporate and long term transport planning tasks in chapter 5, will be conducted in the political arena. The operators must, therefore, consciously develop strategic planning and marketing procedures to cope with these demands if the full potential of urban public transport within the conurbation is to be realised.

A 'political' strategy

We have shown how a reciprocal relationship exists between maintaining a relatively compact urban form and operating an effective public transport system. This reciprocity of interests provides both the need and opportunity for large public transport organisations to make their contributions towards the total urban planning process.

The strategy to be pursued

Accordingly, public transport operators must ensure that the transport implications of urban planning are properly understood at the policy making level for the conurbation as a whole. In doing so it should emphasise the economic, social and environmental advantages of: obtaining a better utilisation of existing transport infrastructure; stabilising the centrality of primary urban functions; and preserving the urban-rural balance. More specifically, management should press for land use development which projects urban growth along main corridors rather than in a broad spectrum; for plans which concentrate work locations; for plans which retain the conurbation core as a primary cultural centre and major shopping area for non-convenience goods (e.g. semi-durable and durable products); and where out-of-town shopping and leisure centres are considered necessary, for plans which locate them so that they can be served effectively and economically by public transport.

Within the context of such land use patterns, management should argue for a transportation policy which acknowledges that public transport must cater for much of the intra-urban movement of people, particularly for the journey-to-work. Such a policy is essential to the containment of car-based urban congestion and to the maintenance of a thriving focal centre which is conveniently accessible; this view is now more widely accepted by urban planners. However, we do not underemphasise the importance of car restraint in a market where the externalities of modal choice are so considerable and where actions to redress the imbalance thus caused will be more potent than short term improvements to the public transport system. Among the obvious measures conducive to more profitable transport operations, and which take into account the social costs caused by private motorists, are stricter controls over car parking and traffic management schemes offering priority for buses; in the longer term a centre city vehicle-mileage charge on cars may be possible.

Clearly, managerial attempts to have sterner car constraint measures applied should be made in concert with its efforts to have more effective planning machinery introduced which will forestall the dispersion of work place, residential and shopping locations. For management to concentrate only on the former, because these might appear to affect more directly its operational efficiency, would stimulate greater numbers of car users to orientate their work, and certainly their leisure and shopping activities towards periphery locations. This would result in a further erosion of the market that public transport is technologically best suited to serve.

However, if the community is to accept restrictions on both fronts, it must be convinced of the benefits to be derived. It is unlikely that the majority will readily accept that restraints are necessary in order to prevent the quality of life from deteriorating; by itself too many intangibles are associated with such an inducement for it to have immediate appeal. Of course, creative attempts to persuade the public in this respect must be undertaken, even though the educational process may be a protracted one. Failure to communicate with the public over such issues, apart from being undemocratic, is likely to lead to gross misrepresentation and hostility. For example, as local authorities have decided to reduce city centre car parking facilities little or no effort has been expended in publicising the need for, and possible benefits arising from, such a policy. It is difficult to account for this reluctance to engage in adequate public relations: the authorities may have assumed that the policy would be self evident, or the view may have been held that motorists' opposition would be too entrenched for their attitudes to be amenable to change, or there may have existed a general belief that publicity is wasteful and even unethical. What does seem to emerge from the numerous protest letters published in newspapers is that the policy has been misrepresented; frustrated motorists have cast serious doubt on the technical efficiency of the authorities whom, it has been perceived, have failed to balance the demand for, and the supply of, car parking facilities. Any public relations campaign dealing with the urban environment needs to be complemented by measures likely to produce some early and perceptible benefits. For the majority, the case for sterner controls will be better understood and the restrictions themselves more acceptable if there are tangible signs of an improved public transport system being available.

Therefore, management must press for the resources, capital investment and, in all probability, operating subsidies, in order to achieve the necessary improvements in cost, journey duration time, frequency, reliability and comfort. Bearing in mind the advantages which the car bestows, motorists will only be prepared to acknowledge that real improvements have been made after: large scale infrastructure investments have been undertaken which allow more modern travel modes to be adopted (e.g. rapid fixed-track transit systems); more imaginative services have been introduced to market segments hitherto ignored or sadly neglected; and the mix has been improved as much as possible for the more traditional types of services.

Understanding the decision making process

To pursue its objectives successfully, management must identify all those who influence and shape its political environment, and understand the processes through which the influentials operate. In the UK three levels of influence can be identified. Within the existing legal framework created by the 1968 Transport and 1972 Local Government Acts the elected metropolitan councils formulate land use and transportation policies. Thus for the primary level of influence management should present its case to the senior councillors, especially those occupying, or likely to assume, powerful policy-making positions in their parties. At the secondary level the

224

principal influentials include: (i) the civic planners who, besides interpreting the council's policies, play a significant part in the process of policy formulation by providing important inputs, for example, suggesting the range of options to be considered and technical information relating to their feasibility; (ii) central government (ministerial and official levels), whose influence on the council's planning discretion, in terms of its ability to adapt the urban legal framework, sanction grants and provide specialist planning know-how, is considerable; (iii) the police, who have direct powers for local traffic management schemes and general traffic law enforcement; and (iv) the regional traffic commissioners who administer the road passenger service licensing system. At the tertiary level the main influentials might comprise: (i) organisations representing important local employers and retailers whose policies on, for example, location, business or trading hours, and staff and customer car parking facilities, impinge on many of the central transportation issues; (ii) civic amenity and rural preservation societies who are anxious, at least, to maintain existing land use patterns; (iii) the regional and local media who seek to inform opinion directly or provide platforms for other influentials to impart their ideas; and (iv) the urban general public who as electors, ratepayers and travellers provide the rationale for local government and public transport.

In some respects there has never been a more propitious time for placing urban public transport on a sound footing. There is now a greater appreciation among central and local government policy makers and their planning bodies of the problems which major cities face and a wide measure of agreement exists about many of the solutions to these, including the need to support public transport. The folly of the virtually unrestricted use of roads by private motorists, especially at peak travel time, is generally recognised, as is the wastefulness and counter-productiveness of allocating huge sums for urban motorway construction. However, senior public transport executives should not assume the present climate of opinion will automatically provide them with the optimum operational framework. In a period of economic stringency they will have to assert considerable influence if adequate funds for transforming the system are to be obtained, insisting that negative factors alone, e.g. car use constraints and rising fuel costs, will not be sufficient to reverse passenger recession. Now that the composition of the decision making units has changed, following the introduction of the metropolitan county councils, new relations will have to be forged for such influence to be exercised. Relationships with the police and traffic commissioners are well established and are founded on mutual co-operation. The media are now more sympathetic and it should be relatively easy to cultivate the support of the civic and rural amenity societies. Except through such devices as transport user consultative committees, little positive attempt appears to have been made to foster the goodwill of local employers and traders and the travelling public.

The nature of Executive influence

Some Public Transport Executives may be reluctant to play an active policy-making role, preferring instead the anonymity afforded by a system which gives elected members the exclusive right to formulate policy while they are left to deal with administration. Such a traditional view is far too simplistic and naive in its separation of powers; nor does it accord with the realities of the situation, especially as it has been affected by the latest developments in local government.

In the first place the Maud Committee report explodes the myth of policy being a matter for the elected members and administration a matter for officers, stating that:

> We do not believe that it is possible to lay down what is policy and what is administrative detail; some issues stand out patently as important and can be regarded as 'policy'; other matters, seemingly trivial may involve political or social reaction of such significance that deciding them becomes a matter of policy and *(elected)* members feel that they must reserve to themselves consideration and decision on them.[1]

In the past the problem of distinguishing between policy and administration has probably accounted for an excessive amount of involvement by elected members in day-to-day management. However, with a greatly increased volume of work in the new unitary authorities, accompanied by the growing technical complexity of service operation and the management techniques appropriate to them, the pendulum seems to be swinging in the opposite direction, as manifested in the delegation of decisions to full time professional executives.

Secondly, we cannot accept that management was ever completely passive with regard to policy making, even when its activities were most tightly controlled. There has always existed the opportunity for covert influence to be applied, in particular in a large authority where it was not uncommon for a long working relationship to exist between a transport committee chairman and the general manager of the public transport department.[2] The exercise of a certain measure of covert influence would seem to be an inevitable by-product of organisational decision making

226

structures. However, we suspect that where it is the only real medium by which the operators can express their views, it not only restricts debate but tends to encourage defensive attitudes and policies, ones which give a higher priority to operational convenience than to the needs of the travelling public. Under the new system of local government, especially as it operates in the conurbations, there is likely to be an increasing tendency to acknowledge overtly the contributions which senior officials need to and do make during the discussions *prior to* key decisions actually being taken by elected members who retain the ultimate direction and control. For example, in London, where a metropolitan county council structure predates the one introduced recently for other conurbations, the publication of the Green Paper on public transport[3] presented the problems and stimulated the kind of debate which is essential to 'open government'. More papers of this type are required.

Thus we regard our proposals as being consistent with present trends: in practical terms they accord with a viable system of local democracy in large urban areas; they recognise the value of operational efficiency; and within a desirable social and financial framework they acknowledge that customer needs are of paramount importance. Their basic premise is a simple one, the democratic process is better served when important political decisions are taken, and are seen to be taken, after a critical examination has been made of all the relevant information. Earlier chapters provide evidence of transportation schemes involving vast expenditures being based on too many dogmatic assertions, too few options, too little sound empirical data, and too little informed debate, largely because elected representatives, the media and the general public were not in a position to make detailed assessments of their worth. Large public transport organisations should now be well qualified to make significant innovatory contributions to the processes of formulating land use and transportation policies. By publishing reports, plans and discussion papers which contain well researched proposals they can stimulate a meaningful debate. This was clearly anticipated by the 1967 White Paper for the English PTEs which stated that:

The Executive must comprise men of vision and wide experience . . . (the White Paper makes specific reference to transport planning skills) . . . It will be the job of the Executive to work out with the local authorities a practical balance between private and public transport, to integrate the bus and rail services in the Area and evaluate the costs and benefits of major new investments in public transport, whether in fixed-track systems, reserved routes for buses and by other means. A

227

first Plan for the development of public transport must be prepared by the Executive for approval by the Authority and for publication within two years.[4]

The conditions of appointment, including specified duties and salaries for the directors general and other directors of the PTEs reinforce this expectation which is very much in line with the current trend towards a 'promotional' rather than the traditional 'regulatory' operational setting for senior local government executives. The first plan published by the Greater Manchester PTE[5] seems particularly encouraging in this respect and has provided a useful focus for discussion.

Naturally when management presents its arguments and proposals, especially to primary and secondary influentials, it must display the obvious communication skills; however, its competence in these matters will be judged more on the standard of its corporate, transport and marketing planning. It has not only to convince those with the ultimate authority for policy making to select parameters which provide optimum operational viability and effectiveness, but must also be in a position to spell out the adverse consequences of having to accept sub-optimum ones. In the final analysis management's credibility will depend on its operational and financial performance, and certainly in the case of the former, passengers will judge this on the quality of the service provided.

Marketing strategies

Our major criticism of the operators is that most of them have not actively pursued a policy of market segmentation, other than differentiating between peak and off-peak segments by frequency and very occasionally by price. Our analysis indicates that car accessibility, journey purpose, and origin and destination variables are among the principal influences on demand and, when combined, provide the most fruitful approach to segmentation, as shown in Table 8.1.

The importance of journey purpose, in a market where the demand for transport is almost entirely a 'derived' one, has been demonstrated. Using price as one example of a demand determinant, it can be said that its influence will largely depend on the need to undertake a particular type of journey, the ability to change journey origin and destination points and the extent to which other modes are considered to be substitutes for public transport. For the journey-to-work it was hypothesised that demand would be relatively unresponsive to price changes; for one thing, the cost of

228

can decide on the number of such journeys to be made; increases in travelling costs may induce the selection of closer shopping centres, especially if a reasonable choice is available in neighbourhood areas, or may result in fewer shopping trips being made. Evening and weekend leisure and social trips on both these accounts are probably the most responsive to price change. The significance of car ownership as a determinant of modal choice has been clearly shown and the extent to which access to a car exists for particular household members will be determined by the number of cars and driving licences possessed. In one-car households where both husband and wife have driving licences, the husband's decision as to whether or not to use the car for the journey-to-work work may well decide the day-time use which the rest of the family makes of public transport. The external parameters of car use, i.e. those imposed by local and central government, are clearly vital considerations for a segmentation policy. Both Quarmby's[6] and McGillivray's[7] work indicate the greater comparative benefit of higher parking charges compared with reduced public transport fares. Controls may inflict varying degrees of restriction on car use, ranging from the minor inconvenience of a small parking fee to severe restrictions on parking places, heavy parking charges, or reduced road capacity as a result, for example, of traffic management schemes favouring public transport. Restricted use is theoretically possible for each of the eight journey purpose/origin-destination dimensions, although under present conditions it is not likely to apply to evening or weekend leisure or social trips. Naturally, where the external restrictions are extremely rigorous segmentation by car accessibility becomes virtually meaningless; however, this is presently the case in only very few cities — notably New York (Manhattan) and London (the City and the West End) — where the vast majority of commuters must use public transport.

It must be emphasised that the matrix should only be regarded as a useful starting point for analysis, and other factors should be taken into account, such as stage in the family life cycle, particularly with reference to teenager and old age pensioner groups. Also, more specialised leisure segments could be added, for example, trips to locations of massed gatherings, chief among which would be spectator sports or possibly trips to parks, zoos and other entertainment centres which attract large crowds during concentrated time periods. Management must consider the development of an optimum marketing-mix for each main category and we have defined the mix as comprising a number of product features (price, time, frequency and comfort), promotion and fare scales. While it is axiomatic to say that the quality of all attributes should be improved, limited resources (particularly where subsidies have to be justified) mean that guidelines need to be formulated to determine priorities. In a number of instances, competing demands will have to be reconciled. Familiar examples are mesh density versus frequency, or cost against comfort. In the former case the need for a 'trade-off' might arise where preference for a more frequent service entailing a longer walk or car ride to the network competes with a demand for a less frequent service which more conveniently approximates to individual trip origin and destination requirements. The conflict may also present itself when the standards of comfort sought by some result in incremental fares which others may be reluctant to bear.

Where the availability of the data permits, the end-user categories identified by the segmentation chart given in Table 8.1 are examined in the light of our literature review and research findings so that we may consider the important strategy implications. While we are not able to make a systematic examination of each of the twenty-four end-user categories, we highlight the principal strategies applicable to the major segments which we have regrouped under three primary headings: journey-to-work trips; shopping trips; and leisure and social trips.

Journey-to-work

The journey-to-work is, and will remain, public transport's largest segment, especially given the commitment to maintain a compact city structure in the future. Tyson[8] has shown that peak-time operations as a whole are unprofitable and the fare increases necessary to achieve break-even might be regarded as excessive, particularly for rail, and would probably, therefore, stimulate increased car use. Ambitious strategies which succeed in greatly increasing passenger volumes, primarily at peak times, will exacerbate this problem unless a greater increase in off-peak volumes is also achieved to share the burden of the incremental fixed costs. The short term strategy implied by these market and cost factors is to maintain the existing modal split until such times as major product improvements may be achieved with the implementation of the long term infrastructure plans. These improvements, offering among other things comfortable, rapid and highly frequent fixed-track systems for the main corridors, should provide powerful promotional platforms for winning back large numbers of motorists, and, given the technology they employ, catering for extra peak loads should be far less difficult than under present operational conditions. The immediate problem is thus more concerned with improving public transport's current services in the eyes of existing users, rather than seeking to attract car users. There are exceptions to this in the case of rail, where many suburban services outside London, for example, at Liverpool and Manchester, are under-utilised even during the peak, and here a more aggressive policy must be pursued. Equally. for bus operation, management must assume a highly imaginative customer-oriented approach if the short term objective of maintaining the *status quo* is to be accomplished when car ownership and use are increasing annually.

The most radical policy to be advocated as a means of improving the attractiveness of public transport is that of so-called 'free fares'. Obviously such a decision would fall largely within the sphere of political rather than managerial decision making, for it involves placing public transport, alongside health and education, firmly within the realm of welfare services. Yet this does not preclude a transport management lobbying strongly for it if it feels this policy would enable it to meet its objectives more closely. All the evidence, however, suggests that this is not the case. Quarmby[6] and McGillivray[7] both forecast that 'free' transport would induce about a quarter of car commuters to switch, Lave[9] estimated that 15 per cent of car commuters would transfer, while Charles River Associates[10] suggested that free transport would produce a 9 per cent reduction in morning peak hour car traffic: all the studies contended that similar results could be achieved by service improvements at a fraction of the cost. Empirical data from Rome[11] seems to confirm the limited demand effect of a 'free' fares policy, although the experiment was probably of too short a duration for the full impact of this major change to be thoroughly assessed.

Less radical policies merely call for a cheap peak hour fares policy but the response to any such fare reductions would probably be negligible, and the indications of the Bolton experiment (1.1) verify this. Where price changes have been combined with a service improvement such as frequency, as at Boston[12] and Philadelphia,[13] the price element has demonstrated far less potency than the service one. Thus operators seem justified in their assumption, intuitive or otherwise, of a highly inelastic demand with respect to price for peak hour services. A 35 per cent fare increase in New York[14] brought a decline in commuter traffic of only 2·4 per cent, some of which could have been accounted for by 'normal' long term decline factors. One pattern which may be construed from the New York and Rome findings is the difference between morning and evening peaks; in response to a price increase the morning peak is most affected, in response to a decrease the evening peak showed the greatest benefit. It may be that many travellers are more captive to public transport for the inward journey whereas in the event of a price increase some may take advantage of the opportunity of returning as car passengers in the evening.

Returning to the effects of improved frequencies, American tests such as

232

the.Boston and Philadelphia experiments suggest that much higher returns are obtainable when they are applied to rail rather than bus for outer suburban to conurbation centre work journeys. Under such conditions car owners seem to be more willing to consider the train as an alternative commuting mode because they recognise its fixed-track advantage over the bus which has to share the congested road system. In the US, compared with the UK, the demand benefits to be derived from increasing frequency should be seen in the light of the much lower levels of service prevailing there. Spectacular evidence of this is provided by Chicago's highly patronised and profitable 'Skokie Swift' service[15] which involved a reclaimed rail line, and where it was possible to publicise noticeable frequency and in-vehicle time advantages for those working in central business districts and living in a peripheral suburb.

Where no rail service exists, as will continue to be the case in a number of corridors in most UK conurbations, even after the implementation of the proposed infrastructure, public transport must rely on direct bus services which are almost certain to be slower than the car. St. Louis' 'Radial' routes[16] demonstrate the ability to segment the market for long distance bus travel by offering a faster journey to those who will pay a premium for speed and this can be used to improve operating finances. Such services may be attractive to both car and non-car owners; the figures for St. Louis were 68 and 32 per cent respectively.

In the UK the Hale Barns Express service (experiment 2) has been successful in attracting a wholly car-owning segment by operating an express service from an outer suburb to the centre with a strong accent on comfort and passenger convenience. Although revenue has not been sufficient to cover all the costs assigned to it, with the introduction of sterner parking control and perhaps bus priority measures, this kind of service should not find it difficult to break even. It seems that longer distance bus services to the centre will not attract car owners unless the operators pay considerable attention to comfort and convenience factors. Merseyside's 'Rapidride' express services have not succeeded in this respect. In some instances they have reduced journey times by as much as 25 per cent, but they do not appear to have incorporated other product improvements.

We have emphasised the importance of access time and the high priority accorded to it by commuters. In transport plans designed to transform the rail network attention is being given to the improvement of this aspect which is probably the worst feature of any fixed-track system, particularly for outer suburban locations where residential densities are typically low. Several market research and statistical studies have stressed the high

233

disutility attached to access time. One way to improve the accessibility of suburban stations is to provide feeder bus services, and the Formby experiment (3) has established that their provision can increase utilisation of the rail system and improve the financial viability of the total public transport network. Some 13 per cent of the patronage of the Formby service derives from previous car commuters. While this particular result augurs well for the future of upgraded rail systems, test marketing must obviously be carried out on a more extended basis and on Merseyside the PTE is carrying out such a programme.

The provision of car parking faciiities at stations is a tactic also aimed at improving accessibility. Policies of this kind have been successful in America, particularly when allied to free or cheap parking charges as for example at Cleveland,[17] Boston[12] and New Brunswick,[18] and the concept is currently being tested in the UK.[19] To improve mesh density in central districts, a number of city centre distributor-bus services have been introduced both in the US and the UK, but with the exception of the Washington minibus service[20] they have not generally been commercially successful. However, some evaluation must be made of the extent to which they are attracting car drivers who would otherwise use their cars for trips to, and within, central districts; from the available analysis, information about the social benefits seems to be lacking. Where it has been decided to impose very severe restrictions on city centre car use then these services will be necessary to make such a policy politically acceptable.

The foregoing has primarily discussed longer distance journeys to work; for shorter distance work trips, the experimental studies are fewer in number and their findings tend to be less positive in terms of the attraction of increased patronage. One would expect shorter distance journeys to be more price elastic because of the likely availability of a wider range of substitute modes and the small absolute price differences between them. Van Tassel's analysis[21] of reduced fares for short distance services in several American cities might, despite mixed results, support this hypothesis. Again in New York[14], the price increase curtailed demand at 'low income' (inner suburb) stations to a greater extent than at the more traditional (outer suburb) stations, but this might be due to the greater price sensitivity of the lower socio-economic groups as much as to distance.

The Bolton bus frequency experiment (4.1) on a short-medium length suburban route brought few additional passengers, while the Liverpool-Ormskirk rail experiment (4.2) which combined a frequency increase with a time saving at a station only 5¾ miles from the centre, was more successful and increased peak passenger loadings by a modest 8 per cent. Both these experiments suggest that where frequency levels are already high, as they

234

will invariably be for most peak hour services in the UK for shorter distance routes to the centre, there are diminishing returns to be obtained from making such improvements; significantly they also indicate that train rather than bus frequencies when increased are more likely to stimulate demand.

While the data on shorter distance journeys are not, as we have already observed, extensive, there is evidence of some price sensitivity; for speed, frequency and comfort, demand seems less responsive than for longer distance trips.

Public transport's problem in designing services for non-central work destinations is that their locations and catchment areas are diverse. Where they are compact and provide large scale employment, the Peoria and Decatur experiment[22] offers a blue print for attracting car owners. The management resources involved are in excess of those currently available to most UK operators, or indeed to most operators in the US, but if car owners are to be attracted to public transport in situations where parking and congestion present few problems, then a similar degree of marketing sophistication is required. The operators must work closely with the personnel departments of target work destinations, identify specific household locations, determine route, timing, comfort, and fare requirements founded on consumer orientation (e.g. door-to-door travel, convenient methods of payment and guaranteed seats) and then aggressively promote the service. The result in Peoria was that some 25 per cent of passengers were previous car users for the journey-to-work. Even where the passenger does not have access to a car and has to travel more than, say, one mile to his workplace, services of this type aggressively marketed are probably required to offset the relatively strong inclination to purchase a car which may well be greater than for those with central work locations.

Shopping trips

For weekday shopping trips with much lower congestion levels, public transport has a much more difficult task in competing with the car, as is reflected in the faster rate of decline in public transport use in off-peak periods. In addition to permitting maximum flexibility in departure times, a car also provides capacity for carrying goods in bulk. The growth of super- and hyper-markets further militates against public transport in their encouragement of one-stop, car-borne shopping which might well depress the number of shopping trips per family. They will be of the greatest attraction to households having the discretionary income available to make home inventory purchases and whose purchasing motivations are economically oriented.

A number of experiments have been reported in chapters 6 and 7, mostly affecting the price and frequency dimensions, which were devised to test the sensitivity of this segment's demand. For price the indications are indeed that elasticity is greater than for the work trip, but insufficient for price reductions to increase revenue in most cases. The UK rail experiments have been among the most successful. The Liverpool-St. Helens off-peak fare reduction generated extra revenue and the reduction at Spital (experiment 5) only just failed to produce a break-even result. Bus experiments have been far less reassuring. One experiment at Boston[12] yielded sufficient incremental traffic to achieve 96 per cent of the pre-trial revenue level, whereas a second fared far worse than this. The Newcastle, Pennsylvania, test[23] only succeeded in redistributing passenger trips, while in the UK the most successful test was at Stevenage where off-peak elasticities of 0·8 have been derived in the 'Superbus' programme.[24] In our own bus tests demand was highly unresponsive in both locations for short to medium distance trips (experiments 1.2 and 1.3) and few incremental trips were created. Even in the most extreme situation at Rome 'free' fares only resulted in a modest 25 per cent gain for off-peak use.

Old age pensioners are a demand segment with distinct needs. In Los Angeles[25] this group proved responsive to price reduction; patronage levels increased by 24 per cent following a price reduction of 33 per cent. In the UK a number of operators have extended concessionary off-peak facilities to pensioners (in some cases offering free travel) and demand has been highly responsive. Many of the trips generated will probably be social and recreational in nature although shopping may provide the rationale. Such groups can be valuable sources of off-peak grant income and it is essential that management information systems are capable of accurately reflecting traffic flows so that operators may negotiate for adequate remuneration from the authorities concerned.

With respect to frequency, the number of experiments undertaken has been small, particularly for rail. The Boston and Maine programme[12] increased off-peak frequencies in the range from 44 to 143 per cent which, combined with fare reductions of between 27 and 39 per cent, increased demand in the order of 43 to 97 per cent. The same programme included bus frequency tests, and although the report on the findings concluded that carefully selected service improvements from suburban communities to the downtown core can be self-sustaining, the majority were not. Typically they caused only sufficient additional revenue to cover 20—50 per cent of the incremental costs. In the Bolton experiment (4.1) frequency increases of between 33 and 58 per cent resulted in no increases for weekday day-time off-peak traffic, but for Saturday day-time demand rose by up to 50 per cent and marginal revenue covered up to 70 per cent of the increased costs.

Other elements of the mix have not been successful in generating custom. The St. Louis 'Radials' featuring faster journeys attracted very few housewives with access to a car, and the same was the case for shoppers' express services from Peoria and Decatur and from Hale Barns.

For the reasons mentioned it is doubtful if car owners can be attracted to transport services for shopping other than for congested city centres. However, many of the experimental services reviewed, especially the longer distance rail ones, have highlighted promising ways of increasing patronage mainly by pricing action and possibly combined with frequency increases. For longer distance rail trips, while one of the objectives will be to encourage car users on to the transport system, others are aimed at attracting existing bus users and stimulating those who normally walk to their local stores to undertake longer distance shopping journeys by rail. Favourable pricing action for specific groups such as pensioners will be particularly beneficial. Within the context of Tyson's analysis,[8] which suggests that many off-peak services can show a surplus once fixed costs are equitably apportioned, such actions would have a far greater chance of achieving financial success.

To retain the loyalty of existing users, and to make an impression on the car using segments for longer, city centre-oriented journeys, operators must be more aggressive and adventurous. One possibility is the development of joint strategies with large centrally located stores or even the local chamber of commerce. Segelhorst[26] advocates such a policy for US shoppers travelling to the centre, financed by the shops themselves. He argues that large stores subsidise car shoppers by providing free or cheap parking but neglect those who travel by public transport, regarding them as captive anyway. This is not the case in the UK where fewer parking facilities and the increasing number of non-central shopping alternatives conspire to reduce the numbers of car and public transport-borne clientele. Thus it would seem to be profitable for major retailers, who seek to exploit the larger market provided by a central location, to offer promotional schemes aimed specifically at public transport passengers. Segelhorst's proposal is particularly interesting in view of the higher elasticity levels attached to daytime off-peak operations, and its appeal is bound to increase as city centre congestion and car parking conditions worsen during shopping hours.

Outer suburban trips, mainly to local shopping locations, are among the most uneconomical for public transport to serve. For journeys which cannot be conveniently undertaken on foot it invariably means that in the higher income areas concerned services are considerably under utilised, relying as they must on the relatively small minority, often teenagers and the elderly, without access to a car. The 'dial-a-bus' scheme is being regarded by some operators as a means of attracting additional custom from among the car users in these districts where telephone rental levels are normally high. Especially where an operator has an obligation to provide a service, the 'dial-a-bus' approach with its accent of consumer satisfaction should permit a larger contribution to be made towards meeting operational costs; although at the time of writing most of the services have not been available long enough for this to be validated.[27] If nothing else, by running this type of service an operator does project an image of consumer awareness which will help to offset the unsympathetic attitudes which many car users have about public transport.

Finally, attention must be brought to a paradox at the centre of the interrelationship between peak and day-time off-peak strategies. If the predominantly male car users are encouraged to use public transport for the journey-to-work, the family car becomes available to the predominantly female shopper during the day time; this will further exacerbate the problems of peak demand and off-peak surplus capacity. For the cost conscious operator, encouraging 'park-'n-ride' services would be the optimum strategy, as this would immobilise the car for shopping trips!

Leisure and social trips

Severe restrictions on the use of the car in the city centre will rarely apply because of the timing of most leisure and social trips. Two classes of journey are distinguished here by their destination objectives. Social trips are defined as visits to friends, relatives, etc., and, therefore, to highly idiosyncratic destinations; while leisure journeys are to more specific destinations selected by larger numbers of people, for example, visits to soccer matches, cinemas or theatres.

Both leisure and social trips have been shown to exhibit the greatest degree of demand responsiveness to price change. In New York[14] the result of the 33 per cent subway fare increase was a decrease in patronage between 19.00 and 23.00 hours of 14·6 per cent, giving an elasticity of 0·44 compared to 0·17 over the day as a whole. The decrease for 'low income'/inner suburb stations was even greater than this at 19·1 per cent, representing an elasticity of 0·60. Turning to experiments designed to stimulate demand by off-peak evening fare reductions, the British Rail

238

Liverpool to Rock Ferry experiment provides an example of an outstanding success, with elasticity well in excess of unity for traffic after 18.00 hours. The somewhat less successful Liverpool to West Kirby experiment was still attracting additional passengers when it was withdrawn and its withdrawal may have been misjudged.

In Rome[11] it was the evening journeys which derived the largest increase in passengers carried, 47 per cent, between 20.00 and the last service. Similarly the off-peak price reduction on the experimental Merseyside route (experiment 1.3) appears to have had the most effect during evenings and at weekends: for weekday evenings (i.e. after 18.30 hours to the last service) revenue increased 232 per cent in response to a 25 per cent fare reduction; for Saturday evenings revenue increased by 117 per cent and for Sunday traffic patronage increased, but not to the extent of increasing revenue, although elasticity approached unity. In the Bolton experiment (1.1) the fare reduction increased trips for Sunday traffic, giving an elasticity of 0·65, while for pensioners trip stimulation was even greater, with elasticity exceeding unity.

The Bolton frequency experiment (4.1) also brought the greatest response in the evening and for weekdays passengers increased on a range 23—39 per cent after 18.00 hours; by the end of the experiment the increases were self financing. At weekends the consequences of improved frequencies were highly positive; on Saturdays the extra traffic was as high as 51 per cent throughout the day and between 39 and 47 per cent of incremental costs were recovered.

Therefore, as with shopping trips, there is very strong evidence that selective improvements in frequency or price reductions will stimulate increased usage even to the extent of providing for operating surpluses. Certainly a case can be made for instituting a city-wide programme designed to improve evening off-peak transport usage featuring price reductions and/or frequency improvements. Such a programme would justify and warrant extensive promotion, using local press and radio media.

The relatively insignificant switching from the car in response to free fares in Rome[11] indicates that little car-borne leisure business can be attracted to public transport and, therefore, extra demand must come from non-car owners making more trips. The fact that there are few impediments to the use of cars during leisure time periods persuasively suggests that public transport will not make any serious incursions into the car-borne leisure market because within its present technology it can never offer the flexibility, infinite frequency, lower cost (many social and leisure trips by motorists involve passengers) and high comfort standards of the car. Thus, despite some of the encouraging results achieved, the

239

experiments must be seen within the context of increasing car ownership and the long term trend away from public transport and even when service-mixes for this segment are adjusted to optimum levels, this trend will continue. Nevertheless, the strategy can only be to optimise mixes for *specific* services as an essential prerequisite to justify subsidies and to attack aggressively those opportunities that do occur for improving patronage.

One example of this is that more recreational activities are especially well suited to public transport, particularly mass spectator sports, and most importantly in the UK, football, where the lack of parking facilities at the grounds gives the public mode the edge in terms of proximity to the destination, while the general congestion means that the car is little faster than the bus and a good deal slower than a fixed-track system. Premium priced express buses to football matches already exist in most cities but are often sadly lacking in capacity. In addition high frequency shuttle services might operate between nearby rail stations and carefully selected car parks, and the stadium. At a more general level the rigorous application of the law regarding driving and the consumption of alcohol might encourage a greater use to be made of public transport for some leisure activities and operators might well throw their weight behind the lobby for stricter enforcement.

Finally, on a more optimistic note, the increasing levels of personal discretionary income mean that society as a whole is changing from a production to a leisure economy and the fastest areas of growth in transport, including intra-urban travel, will be for leisure purposes. Although public transport can expect to obtain little leisure business from car owners and although car ownership will steadily increase, so will journeys by non-car owners, and the public mode may expect increased demand from evening users if an attractive package is offered.

No two cities are exactly alike in terms of population, population density, trip pattern, infrastructure, etc., and it is idle to transpose uncritically the findings from one urban area to another. However, many of these findings, even though they are from so many diverse backgrounds, conform to patterns which do suggest possible courses of action for the operator and the following causative relationships have been indicated:

> For longer distance work journeys to the centre there is evidence that selective improvements in the marketing-mix, e.g. speed, accessibility, frequency, price and comfort, can yield impressive increases in volume.

> There is inelasticity of demand for medium distance centre-oriented

240

journeys-to-work and a peak 'surcharge' would bring little loss in volume and of itself is likely to increase revenue considerably. However, there is little positive pricing action which can be taken to win passengers from the car.

Public transport has been demonstrated to have attracted car owners for cross-town work journeys to major employment centres while also achieving financial viability, but complete consumer orientation is demanded for this combined with aggressive promotion.

Daytime off-peak trips have shown greater than unity price elasticity in certain cases, especially for longer distance journeys to city centres and when the services have been vigorously promoted. Enhanced frequency will also generate incremental volume but has not shown elasticities close to unity, except in isolated instances. Nevertheless, in view of the low marginal cost of such operations, carefully selected frequency increases should be considered.

Leisure time journeys and particularly those conducted during the evening have exhibited the greatest elasticity of all trips in response to both price and frequency changes and a strong case can be made for operators making these more attractive and thereby improving their financial position.

Our discussion has so far concentrated upon service features and the response of specific segments to changes in these. The importance of promotion must also be stressed and indeed in the case of two peak and one off-peak tests (experiments 2, 3 and 5 respectively) its importance has been clearly demonstrated. Enhanced promotion was a feature in all the successful American programmes, with the publicity centring on significant product improvements as anchors for the campaigns. Wherever a product improvement is being implemented it must be forcefully promoted by the use of household leaflet distribution, local press and radio. Conversely, to use publicity, apart from increasing the availability of time and route information for specific services, without being able to focus on some tangible amelioration of standards will only serve to antagonise the market under present conditions. It is not anticipated that television advertising would usually be appropriate in the UK because the size of the Independent Television Authority areas is inappropriate to the PTEs and would result in too much wastage except in London and perhaps Glasgow. However, with co-operation, paired campaigns would be possible, for example, between Merseyside and Greater Manchester. Considerable opportunities for increased promotion will present themselves, and the need for it will grow more urgent, as new infrastructure is established and as it becomes necessary to impose much severer controls on the use of the car for peak hour journeys. If this type of advertising is to make a real impact, operators must expect to sponsor professionally produced campaigns scheduled for high frequency, multi-media exposure perhaps over an extended time period. In an attempt to defray the considerable costs involved special grants should be sought and all means of collaborating with other major undertakings examined. With regard to the latter it should be possible to create presentations which highlight common themes but which can be modified to accommodate more specialised local aspects.

Reference should be made to the way the industry has been forced to adapt its mix in the interests of achieving increased labour productivity mainly through the introduction of one-man bus operation. The resultant boarding time problems have been countered by the operators in a variety of ways but some of these, such as 'exact fare only' policies, have further reduced passenger convenience levels. However, where pre-purchase ticketing systems are introduced primarily for this purpose there may be opportunities for improving ridership convenience and loyalty. Both our tests (experiments 6.1 and 6.2) increased patronage of the system and one of these, the Bolton trial, which caused sufficient additional traffic to offset the cost of the discounts allowed, merits further investigation. The Merseyside 'Traveller' ticket increased demand, but at a considerable cost. The problem in evaluating this kind of scheme is in quantifying intangible benefits like the improved attitudes and loyalty of the travelling public, but as the pattern of multi-mode journeys in conurbations increases the need for these or similar methods of fare collection must grow.

A final comment must be made on the value of market research. Operators must continually research their markets, i.e. their route catchment areas, developing new routes where justified as when new residential, shopping and employment centres are built, or as the character of existing ones changes. Those routes showing the widest gap in terms of potential and patronage should be targeted for marketing action of the kind proposed. Where subsidies are sought market research is the obvious and most objective means for justifying their application and retention, and thus it provides the best tool for promoting operational efficiency.

Organisational requirements

The marketing strategies prescribed can only be successfully implemented when all levels of management have fully accepted the necessity of providing services which are more responsive to the needs of urban travellers and then only after the organisation's formal structure, its informal relationships and processes of motivation and control have been adapted to meet the essential strategic requirements involved. In chapter 5 explicit recommendations were made in these respects and thus we shall only make a brief summary of these here.

Organisationally, marketing's scope for developing a far more competitive public transport system requires that its relationship with the long term transport planners and senior operations managers be unambiguously stated. Such definition will involve the tasks of all three functions being identified and explicitly expressed, with special attention drawn to those activities which are interdependent. Chapter 5 specifies most of the principal tasks and associated functional interdependencies concerned but, as important as these recommendations are, the key to achieving an effective, harmonious interface is an unequivocal commitment from the chief executive to ensure that there exists a balance between task responsibilities and the resources and means essential for their accomplishment. Since marketing has been denied the organisational support it clearly deserves, this commitment must extend to: improving its position in the hierarchy; providing the function with many more specialist staff, especially for marketing research and promotional activities; and allocating vastly increased budgets for both areas of activity.

Enhancing its organisational status and allocating more resources to the function are obviously essential prerequisites if marketing is to set basic service standards — fares, journey times, mesh density, frequency and comfort — for the operating divisions to follow and then monitor their performance. Any department which is expected to determine standards for another to follow must have, and be seen to have, the ultimate authority and resources to establish them and control their implementation. For the marketing-operations relationship we have advised that the responsibilities for formulating and controlling service-mix standards should be largely centralised at the headquarters level. However, in the interests of securing commitment from the divisions on the need to improve customer satisfaction and to be able to draw on detailed local knowledge of the network there must be divisional involvement in the planning process: in terms of actual delegated powers this may be limited to modifying and applying headquarters' recommendations to local conditions. So as to ensure that the fullest consideration is given to all such proposals and that adaptations of these do not conflict with the essentials being prescribed, comprehensive plans should be prepared by divisional marketing managers and submitted for approval by the senior marketing executive at headquarters; plans once accepted would provide the criteria for appraising service performance, which would be done by central marketing staff.

At headquarters the aim must be to work towards the closest integration of marketing and transport planning activities. Ultimately we would wish to see marketing assuming authority for all aspects of planning related to fulfilling the urban traveller's needs, and this includes the long term development of the public transport infrastructure and network currently performed by the transport planners. Paradoxically, this might be achieved by creating a separate marketing directorate in the first instance. Especially if responsibility for gathering, analysing and interpreting all network intelligence is assigned to it, conferring directorial status should promote a more symmetrical set of relationships between marketing and transport planning (and between marketing and operations) and facilitate a better allocation of resources to the function. Once the new directorate had become established the opportunities for integrating transport planning into the marketing structure would become less difficult to realise. The marketing director should by then have acquired a sufficient appreciation of the requirements of long term transport planning to be able to guide the work of specialist planners involved and at the same time cause them to focus on market needs.

Wide ranging organisational changes are difficult to effect. This is an unmistakable conclusion which emerges from numerous studies. Chandler,[28] after making an investigation into four leading US corporations whose survival and present competitive standing owes much to their ability to make a series of major strategic and administrative adjustments, confirmed that even in these relatively responsive and thrusting organisations there had been considerable delays in effecting the necessary structural adaptations consequent upon the adoption or change of basic strategies. Among the reasons Chandler cited are, senior executives were too preoccupied with day-to-day operating activities to appreciate the long-range organisational needs of their enterprises and many executives resisted administratively desirable changes because they felt personally threatened by them. Conversely, it can be stated that where the forces for perpetuating a particular structural form are very strong then the organisation excludes itself from making any significant change in its strategic posture.

The Bains report[29] on the new local authorities makes the point that while local government management may have many lessons to learn from industry it is not possible 'to apply straight business concepts' without first making the necessary adjustments to these. Throughout we have subscribed to this opinion and we consider that all the proposals we have

244

made with a view to making urban public transport more competitive are in accord with the main objectives for the new metropolitan councils which Long and Norton[30] have interpreted as including:

(a) the exercise of wider responsibility for the development of their areas as a whole, (b) better communication with the public, (c) greater adaptivity to meet the needs of a society undergoing change at an increasing rate, and (d) greater effectiveness and efficiency.

Naturally we recognise that there are still many elected members and senior administrators and executives who have not as yet been imbued by the spirit of these objectives: our proposals have not been compromised so as to accommodate their perspectives, policies and practices.

Notes

[1] *The Royal Commission on Local Government in England, 1966—1969 Report* (Chairman, Lord Radcliffe-Maud), Cmnd. 4040, HMSO, 1969, paragraph 109.

[2] In the fifteen years preceding the establishment of the West Midland PTE in 1969 there had been four chairmen of Birmingham Corporation's Transport Committee, one of whom served five years in that capacity; during the same period there were two general managers of the city's transport department. It was customary for the chairman to have been a member of the committee for many years prior to taking the chair, often acting as deputy chairman and chairman of various subcommittees first. A very similar pattern applied in Liverpool, Manchester and Newcastle-upon-Tyne.

[3] *'The Future of London Transport: a Paper for Discussion'*, GLC, 1970.

[4] *'Public Transport Plan for the Future'*, issued by the SELNEC (now pp. 5—6.

[5] 'Public transport plan for the future', issued by the SELNEC (now styled Greater Manchester) PTE, January 1973.

[6] D. A. Quarmby, 'Choice of travel mode for the journey to work: some findings' *Journal of Transport Economics and Policy*, vol. I, no. 3, 1967, pp. 273—314.

[7] R. G. D. McGillivray, 'Demand and choice models of modal split' *Journal of Transport Economics and Policy*, vol. IV, no. 2, May 1970, pp. 192—207.

[8] W. J. Tyson, 'A study of peak cost and pricing in road passenger

transport', privately circulated paper, Department of Economics, University of Manchester, September 1970.

9 C. A. Lave, 'A behavioural approach to modal split forecasting' *Transportation Research*, vol. 3, no. 4, December 1970, pp. 463—86.

10 Charles River Associates, Inc., 'Disaggregated behavioural model of urban travel demand', US Department of Transportation, 1972.

11 See *Motor Transport*, 2 June 1972, pp. 18—19.

12 J. Maloney, 'Mass transportation in Massachusetts', Transportation Commonwealth of Massachusetts P.B. 174 422, July 1964.

13 'Commuter rail/road service improvement for a metropolitan area,' SEPACT I and II, PA-MTD-1, 1966.

14 M. A. Kemp, 'Some evidence of transit demand elasticities' *Transportation*, vol. 2, 1973, pp. 25—52.

15 T. Buck, 'Skokie Swift — the commuter's friend', Chicago Transit Authority PB 175 734, Chicago 1968.

16 'The radial express and suburban cross town bus rider', final report, Department of Housing and Urban Development INT MTD 8, 1965.

17 L. M. Schneider, *Marketing Urban Mass Transit*, Harvard University Graduate School of Business Administration, Boston, 1965.

18 'Park-'n-ride rail service: final report', PB 174 740, Tri-state Transportation Commission, New York, May 1967.

19 Peat, Marwick, Mitchell and Company, 'Public transport interchanges on Merseyside', November 1973.

20 Washington Metropolitan Area Transit Commission, 'The minibus in Washington DC — final report, DC — TD — 2, May 1965.

21 R. C. Van Tassel, 'Economics of the pricing of urban bus transportation', Brown University Ph.D.thesis. Ann Arbor: University Microfilms, 1956.

22 See 'The Decatur and Peoria premium special services' *Passenger Transport*, May 1967, pp. 183—87.

23 John Blackman Associates, 'Mass transportation in a small city', Newcastle Transit Authority, Autumn 1968.

24 M. G. Smith and P. T. McIntosh, 'Public response to change in fare levels: proceedings of a symposium on public transport fare structures,' Transport and Road Research Laboratory, November 1973.

25 L. M. Schneider, op. cit.

26 S. W. Segelhorst, 'Transit validation for city centres' *Journal of Transport Economics and Policy*, vol. 5, no. 1, January 1971, pp. 28—39.

27 In the UK a variety of 'dial-a-bus' schemes have recently commenced operation at Maidstone, Harrogate, Eastbourne, Carterton, Harlow New Town, Hampstead Garden Suburb (Greater London) and Sale (Greater

Manchester). Further schemes are planned for Milton Keynes, Yeovil, and possibly on Merseyside. All the services introduced claim highly favourable passenger response, but as with the US 'dial-a-bus' schemes, none is so far breaking even financially, although in most it is far too early to make any final assessment. The Hampstead Garden Suburb service provides an interesting example of a 'many origins to many destinations' type service operated throughout the day in a middle class residential suburb where the residents had objected to a full bus service because of the narrowness of the streets and the character of the area. The service may be called by telephone to pick up passengers at their houses, will stop at fixed stops which it must pass on its route, and may be hailed like a taxi at any point in the suburb. Pre-booking facilities are also available. The fare for the service is 15p and a reduced 5p fare is available to pensioners. The operation of the service is obviously helped by the exceptionally high telephone rental level of 81 per cent. It has also been strongly promoted, has had considerable co-operation from the local Residents' Association, and at the time of writing, a month after its introduction in October 1974, the service is already carrying 650—700 passengers per week, well in excess of the forecast level. As a service it is particularly useful to shoppers and serves the Golders Green and two smaller local shopping centres. For a review of US projects see D. Roos, 'Operational experience with demand responsive transportation systems', Highway Research Record No. 397, prepared for the 51st meeting on 'New transportation systems and technology,' 1972. For a review of UK projects see 'The proceedings of the symposium on 'dial-a-bus' services', Cranfield Centre for Transport Studies, September 1974.

[28] A. D. Chandler, Jnr. *Strategy and Structure,* MIT, 1962.

[29] *'The New Local Authorities: Management and Structure',* Report of the Working Group of Local Authority Associations (under the chairmanship of M. A. Bains), HMSO, 1972, p. 5.

[30] J. Long and A. Norton, *Setting up the New Authorities,* Charles Knight, London 1972, p. 1.

Bibliography

Books

Burns, T. and Stalker, G. M., *The Management of Innovation*, Tavistock Publications, 1961.

Cameron, G. C. and Johnson, K. M., 'Comprehensive Urban Renewal and Industrial Relocation in the Glasgow Area' in S. C. Orr and J. B. Cullingworth (eds) *Regional Economic Studies*, Geo. Allen and Unwin, 1969.

Chandler, A. D., Jnr., *Strategy and Structure*, Massachusetts Institute of Technology, 1962.

Christeller, W., *Central Places in Southern Germany*, Prentice Hall, 1966.

Cowan, P., *Developing Patterns of Urbanization*, Oliver and Boyd, 1970.

Cyert, R. M. and March, J. G., *A Behavioural Theory of the Firm*, Prentice Hall, 1963.

Dalton, M., *Men Who Manage*, Wiley, 1959.

Denning, B. W., *Corporate Planning: Selected Concepts*, McGraw-Hill, 1972.

Festinger, L., *A Theory of Cognitive Dissonance*, Stanford University Press, 1957.

Fishbein, M., 'Attitude and the Predicion of Behaviour' in M. Fishbein (ed.), *Readings in Attitude Theory and Measurement*, Wiley, 1967.

Ginzberg, E. and Reilly, E. W., *Effective Change in Large Organisations*, Columbia University Press, 1966.

Koontz, H. and O'Donnell, C., *Principles of Management: an Analysis of Managerial Functions*, 5th edition, McGraw-Hill, 1972.

Kotler, P., *Marketing Management: Analysis, Planning and Control*, 1st and 2nd editions, Prentice Hall, 1967 and 1972.

Lambden, W., *Bus and Coach Operation: Principles and Practice for the Transport Student*, 4th edition, Iliffe, 1969.

Lawrence, P. R. and Lorsch, J. W., *Organisations and Environment*, Irwin, 1967.

Long, J. and Norton, A., *Setting up the New Authorities*, Charles Knight, 1972.

Meyer, J. R., Kain, J. F. and Wohl, M., *The Urban Transportation Problem*, Harvard University Press, 1965.

Newman, J. W., *Motivational Research and Marketing Management,* Harvard University Press, 1957.

Oi, W. Y. and Schuldiner, P., *An Analysis of Urban Travel Demand,* Northwestern University, Chicago, 1962.

Perrow, C., 'Departmental Power and Perspective in Industrial Firms' in M. N. Zald (ed.), *Power in Organisations,* Vanderbilt University Press, 1970.

Pryke, R., *Public Enterprise in Practice,* McGibbon & Kee, 1971.

Schneider, L. M., *Marketing Urban Mass Transit,* Harvard University Press, 1965.

Thompson, J. D., *Organisations in Action,* McGraw-Hill, 1967.

Wilson, F. R., *Journey to Work,* Maclaren and Sons, 1967.

Woodward, J., *Industrial Organisation, Theory and Practice,* Oxford University Press, 1965.

Journal articles

Beacham, A., 'The Position of the Coal Industry in Great Britain' *The Economic Journal,* March 1950, pp. 8—18.

Beesley, M. E., 'Value of time spent travelling: some new evidence' *Economica,* May 1965, pp. 174—85.

Bennett, R. F., 'Road Transport in a Rapid Transit System' *Institute of Transport Journal,* March 1968, pp. 333—44.

Bennett, R. F. and McCorquodale, D., 'Public Transport's Role in Urban Areas' *Traffic Engineering and Control,* April 1968, pp. 596—601.

Cameron, G. C. and Evans, A. W., 'The British Conurbation Centres' *Regional Studies,* vol. 7, 1973, pp. 47—55.

Denning, B. W. and Lehr, M. E., 'The Extent and Nature of Corporate Long Range Planning in the United Kingdom—I' *Journal of Management Studies,* May 1971, pp. 145—61.

Denning, B. W. and Lehr, M. E., 'The Extent and Nature of Corporate Long Range Planning in the United Kingdom—II' *Journal of Management Studies,* February 1972, pp. 1—18.

Fishwick, F., 'One Man Operation in Municipal Transport' *Institute of Transport Journal,* no. 33, March 1970, pp. 413—25.

Foster, C. D. and Beesley, M. E., 'Estimating the Social Benefit of Constructing an Underground Railway in London' *Journal of the Royal Statistical Society,* vol. 126, 1963, pp. 46—58.

Golob, T. F., Canty, E. T. and Gustafson, R. L., 'An Analysis of Consumer Preferences for a Public Transportation System' *Transportation Research,* vol. 6, no. 1, March 1972, pp. 81—102.

Greiner, L. R., 'Patterns of Organisational Change' *Harvard Business Review,* May/June 1967, pp. 119—30.

Hovell, P. J., 'Applying the Marketing Concept to Urban Passenger Transport' *British Journal of Marketing,* no. 3, Summer 1969, pp. 152—63.

Insko, C. A., and Schopler, J., 'Triadic consistency: a statement of effective cognitive—conative consistency' *Psychological Review,* vol. 74, 1967, pp. 361—76.

Kemp, M. A., 'Some Evidence of Transit Demand Elasticities' *Transportation,* vol. 2, 1973, pp. 25—52.

Landsberger, H. A., 'The Horizontal Dimension in a Bureaucracy' *Administrative Science Quarterly,* vol. 6, 1961, pp. 298—333.

Lave, C. A., 'A Behavioural Approach to Modal Split Forecasting' *Transportation Research,* vol. 3, no. 4, December 1970, pp. 463—86.

McGillivray, R. G. D., 'Demand and Choice Models of Modal Split' *Journal of Transport Economics and Policy,* vol. IV, no. 2, May 1970, pp. 192—207.

Pettigrew, A. M., 'Information Control as a Power Resource' *Sociology,* vol. 6, 1972, pp. 187—204.

Prest, A. and Turvey, R., 'Cost-Benefit Analysis' *Economic Journal,* vol. 7, pp. 683—735.

Quarmby, D. A., 'Choice of Travel Mode for the Journey-to-Work: Some Findings' *Journal of Transport Economics and Policy,* September 1967, vol. I, no. 3, pp. 273—314.

Quinby, H. D., 'Major Urban Corridor Facilities: a New Concept' *Traffic Quarterly,* April 1962, pp. 242—59.

Schiller, R. K., 'Location Trends of Specialist Services' *Regional Studies,* vol. 5, 1971, pp. 1—10.

Schnore, L. E., 'Use of Public Transport in Urban Areas' *Traffic Quarterly,* October 1962, pp. 488—99.

Segelhorst, S. W., 'Transit Validation for City Centres' *Journal of Transport Economics and Policy,* vol. 5, no. 1, January 1971, pp. 28—39.

Seiller, J., 'Diagnosing Interdepartmental Conflict' *Harvard Business Review,* September/October 1967, pp. 121—32.

Shipman, W. D., 'Rail Passenger Subsidies and Benefit-Cost Considerations' *Journal of Transport Economics and Policy,* January 1971, pp. 4—37.

Sleeman, J., 'The Rise and Decline of Municipal Transport' *Scottish Journal of Political Economy,* vol. 9, 1962, pp. 46—64.

Smeed, R. J., 'The Road Space Required for Traffic in Towns' *Town Planning Review,* no. XXXIII, January 1963, pp. 279—92.

Smeed, R. J. and Wardrop, J. G., 'An Exploratory Comparison of the Advantages of Cars and Buses for Urban Areas' *Journal of the Institute of Transport,* vol. 30, no. 9, March 1964.

Strauss, G., 'Tactics of lateral relationship: the purchasing agent' *Administrative Science Quarterly,* vol. 7, 1962, pp. 161—86.

Thompson, J. M., 'An Evaluation of Two Proposals for Traffic Restraint in Central London' *Journal of the Royal Statistical Society,* Series A, vol. 130, part 3, 1967, pp. 327—77.

Tipping, D. G., 'Time Savings in Transport Studies' *Economic Journal,* December 1968, pp. 843—54.

Tyson, W. J., 'Financing of Public Transport' *Local Government Finance,* July 1972, pp. 273—76.

Uhl, K. P., 'Better Management of Market Information' *Business Horizons,* Spring 1966, vol. 9, pp. 75—81.

Walton, R. E. and Dalton, J. M., 'The Management of Interdepartmental Conflict: a Model and a Review' *Administrative Science Quarterly,* vol. 14, 1969, pp. 73—84.

Williams, P. M., 'Low Fares and the Urban Transport Problem'. *Urban Studies,* vol. 6, no. 1, February 1969, pp. 83—92.

Wright, M., 'Provincial Office Development' *Urban Studies,* vol. 4, 1967, pp. 218—57.

Also

Motor Transport, 3 March and 2 June 1972.
'The Decatur and Peoria Premium Special Services' *Passenger Transport,* May 1967, pp. 183—87.

Reports and papers

Alonso, W., 'A Theory of Urban Land Market', Papers and Proceedings of the Regional Science Association, vol. 6 (6th Annual Meeting).

Bennett, R. F., 'Increasing the Attractiveness of Public transport', U.I.T.P. Conference Paper, Rome 1971.

Blackman, John Associates, 'Mass Transportation in a Small City', Newcastle Transit Authority, Newcastle, Penn. 1968.

Brown, A. C. N., 'The Development and Marketing of Public Transport Services', Proceedings of the Symposium on Promoting Public Transport, University of Newcastle-upon-Tyne, April 1973.

Buck, T., 'Skokie Swift—the commuter's friend', Chicago Transit Authority, PB 175 734, Chicago 1968.

Burt, E. J., 'Plant Relocation and the Core City Worker', US Department of Housing and Urban Development, Washington 1967.

'Bus Demonstration Project: Summary Report No. 6, Formby, Bus Feeder Service to the Local Railway Station', Department of the Environment, HMSO, 1974.

'Bus Priority: Proceedings of a Symposium Held at TRRL, 1972', Transport and Road Research Laboratory Report LR 570, 1973.

Carstens, J. P., *et al.* 'Literature Survey of Passenger Comfort Limitations of High-Speed Ground Transportation', Department of Commerce, FCSTI:PB 168, July 1965.

Charles River Associates, Inc., 'Disaggregated Behavioural Model of Urban Travel Demand', US Department of Transportation, 1972.

City of Atlanta Department of Planning and Eric Hill and Associates, 'Town-Flyer: Atlanta's City Centre Shuttle Bus', SA-MTD-1, 2, 1972.

Collier, J. C., 'Transport Policies and Programmes Associated with Transport Grant', a paper read to a seminar organised by the Planning and Transport Research and Computation Company Ltd. at the University of Sussex, 25—29 June 1973.

'Commuter Rail/Road Service Improvement for a Metropolitan Area', SEPACT I and II, PA-MTD-1, 1966.

Cooper, J. B., 'Transport Policies and Programmes — a Local Authority View', a paper read to a seminar organised by the Planning and Transport Research and Computation Company Ltd. at the University of Sussex, 25—29 June 1973.

Cundill, M. A. and Watts, P. F., 'Bus Boarding and Alighting Times', Transport and Road Research Laboratory Report LR 521, 1973.

Curtin, J. F., 'Effect of Fares on Transit Riding', Highway Research Record 213, Highways Research Board, Washington DC 1968.

Davis, E. W., 'Comparison of Noise and Vibration Levels in Rapid Transit Vehicle Systems', Operations Research Inc. for the National Capital Transportation Agency, NCTA TR 216, April 1964.

Ellen, E. R., 'Ways of Helping Buses in Urban Areas', Papers and Proceedings of 9th International Study Week in Traffic and Safety Engineering, Munich, September 1968.

The Expenditure Committee's Second Report on Urban Transport Planning, HMSO, December 1972.

'Financial and Economic Obligations of the Nationalised Industries', Cmnd. 1337, HMSO 1961.

Frebault, J., 'Assessment of the Effects of Introducing Reserved Bus Lanes, Conference of Ministers of Transport, Paris 1969.

'The Future of Development Plans', HMSO 1965.

'The Future of London Transport', Greater London Council Department of Highways and Transportation Green Paper, 1970.

Hillman, M., Henderson, I. and Whalley, A., 'Personal Mobility and Transport Policy', PEP Broadsheet 542, June 1973.

Hirschfeld, C. F., 'Disturbing Effects of Horizontal Acceleration', Electric Railway President's Conference Committee Bulletin no. 3, September 1932.

Hoinville, G. and Johnson, E., 'Commuter Preferences: Summary Report', Social and Community Planning Research, July 1972.

Hovell, P. J. and Jones, W. H., 'The Formby Bus-Rail Demonstration Project: A Pre-Service Feasibility Study', University of Liverpool, August 1970.

Hovell, P. J. and Jones, W. H., 'The Formby Bus-Rail Demonstration Project: A Study of its Effect on Modal Split for the Journey to Work', University of Liverpool, July 1971.

Hyde, D. L., 'Multi-Journey Discount Ticket Systems', Report to the Municipal Passenger Transport Association, 1970.

Institut d'Amenagement et d'Urbanisme de la Region Parisienne, *Choix du Moyen de Transports par les Usagers,* October 1963.

Jones, W. H., 'The Formby Bus-Rail Demonstration Project: A Survey Analysis of the Changed Demand Pattern', University of Liverpool, July 1972.

Kanwit, E. L. and Eckartt, A. F., 'Transportation Implications of Employment Trends in Central Cities and Suburbs', Highway Research Record no. 187, 1967.

Kemp, M. A., 'Some Evidence of Transit Demand Elasticities', Working Paper, Urban Institute, November 1971.

Lansing, J. B. and Hendricks, G., 'Automobile Ownership and Residential Density', Survey Research Centre, University of Michigan, 1965.

Lansing, J. B. *et al.,* 'Residential Location and Urban Mobility', Survey Research Centre, University of Michigan, June 1964.

Latscha, W., 'Economic Viability in Public Transport Undertakings', UITP Conference, London 1968.

Lever, W. F., 'The Intra-urban Movement of Manufacturing Firms: A Markov Approach', privately circulated paper, University of Glasgow, 1971.

Lichfield, Nathaniel and Partners, 'Stevenage Public Transport: Cost-Benefit Analysis', 1967.

Maloney, J. F. and Associates, 'Mass Transportation in Massachusetts', Transportation Commonwealth of Massachusetts, PB 174 422, July 1964.

'Maxi-Cab Commuter Club', Flint Transportation Authority and the

American Academy of Transportation Project Technical Managers, MICH-MTD-2, 1970.

'The Metro Flyer: A Suburban Express Bus Service to Downtown Area, Baltimore County-Baltimore City', Maryland Metropolitan Transit Authority, PB 177 030, 1967.

National Analysts Inc., 'A Survey of Commuter Attitudes Towards Rapid Transit Systems', vol. 2, for the National Capital Transportation Agency (now the Washington Metropolitan Area Transit Authority), March 1963.

National Economic Development Office (NEDO), Distributive Trades, 'The Future Pattern of Shopping', 1971.

Newman, D. K., in United States Bureau of Labour Statistics, Division of Economic Studies, 1966.

'The New Local Authorities: Management and Structure', report of the working group of Local Authority Associations (under the chairmanship of M. A. Bains), 1972.

Paine, F. T., Nash, A. N., Hille, S. J. and Brunner, G. S., 'Consumer Conceived Attributes of Transportation', Department of Business Administration, University of Maryland, 1967.

'A Passenger Transport Development Plan for the West Midlands', West Midlands PTE, November 1972.

Peat, Marwick, Mitchell and Company, 'Public Transport Interchanges on Merseyside', November 1973.

Port Authority of Allegheny County and Transport Research Institute of Carnegie-Mellor University, 'Advertising and Promotion Demonstration Programme', PA MTD-7, Pittsburgh 1970.

'The Proceedings of the Symposium on "Dial-a-Bus" Services', Cranfield Centre for Transport Studies, September 1974.

'Public Transport and Traffic', Cmnd. 3481, HMSO, 1967.

'Public Transport Plan for the Future', Greater Manchester PTE, January 1973.

'The Radial Express and Suburban Cross Town Bus Rider', Final Report, Department of Housing and Urban Development, INT MTD 8, 1965.

Research Projects Ltd., 'The Importance of Service Features to Passengers and the Effects on Traffic', London Transport Board, October 1966.

Report of the Planning Advisory Group to the Ministry of Housing and Local Government, HMSO, 1965.

Roos, D. 'Operational Experience with Demand Responsive Transportation Systems', Highway Research Record no. 397, prepared for the 51st meeting on 'New Transportation Systems and Technology', 1972.

Royal Commission on Local Government in England, 1966—1969 Report

(Chairman Lord Radcliffe-Maud), Cmnd. 4040, HMSO, 1969.

The Select Committee on Nationalised Industries, report on 'Ministerial Control of the Nationalised Industries', HMSO, 1968.

Sheehan, J. K., 'A Discussion of Transit Car Features', Operations Research Inc. for the National Capital Transportation Agency, CFSTI:PB 176, 901, June 1964.

Smith, M. G. and McIntosh, P. T., 'Public Response to Change in Fare Levels', proceedings of a symposium on public transport fare structures, Transport and Road Research Laboratory, November 1973.

Smith, Wilbur and Associates, 'Chesapeake Mass Transportation Demonstration Project', Department of Housing and Urban Development, VA-MTD-1, 1969.

Soloman, K. M., Soloman, R. J. and Silien, J. S., 'Passenger Psychological Dynamics', H804, US Department of Transportation, Urban Mass Transportation Administration, June 1968.

Stopher, P. R., 'A Probability Model of Travel Mode Choice for the Work Journey', Highway Research Record No. 283, 1969.

Stopher, P. R., 'Report on the Journey to Work Survey', Greater London Council Department of Highways and Transportation Research Memorandum 48, 1966.

'Traffic and the Environment', Greater London Council Department of Highways and Transportation Green Paper, 1972.

'Traffic in Towns', Steering Group of Buchanan Report, HMSO, 1963.

'Transit Information Aids', Washington Metropolitan Area Transit Commission and Sidney Hollander and Associates, INT-MTD-10, 1969.

Transport Act, 1968, HMSO, 1970.

'A Transport Plan for Merseyside', Merseyside PTE, March 1972.

TriState Transportation Commission, 'Park-n-Ride Rail Service: Final Report', PB 174 740, New York, May 1967.

Tyson, W. J., 'A Study of Peak Cost and Pricing in Road Passenger Transport', privately circulated paper, University of Manchester, Department of Economics, September 1970.

'Urban Transport Planning', Second Report of the Expenditure Committee, HMSO, December 1972.

'Urban Transport Planning', Cmnd. 5366, HMSO, July 1973.

Wasey, Erwin, 'Report of a Study into the Motivation and Attitudes of Passengers and Potential Passengers of London Transport Buses', London Transport Executive, 1968.

Washington Metropolitan Area Transit Commission, 'The Minibus in Washington DC—Final Report', DC-MTD-2, May 1965.

Working Group on Bus Demonstration Projects: Report to the Minister,

Department of the Environment, HMSO, 1970.

Yates, L. B., 'Vauxhall Bridge Bus Lane 12 Months After Study', Research Memorandum 178, Greater London Council Department of Highways and Transportation, July 1969.

Index

TV scanning system 174; *see also* Television viewing, effect of public's increased
Twelve-journey tickets 183
Tyson, W. J. 38, 78-9, 84, 231, 237

Uhl, K.P.
Under-privileged groups, safeguarding the 29-30
Urban public transport: demand for 35-62; decline of 35-40; statistical evidence 35-7; factors relating to impairment of efficiency 37-40; competition to 40-58: consumer needs, nature of 40-2; modal choice 42-58; service attributes 43-7; promotion 47; competitive travel modes 47-58; future of 58-62: technological environment 58-9; political environment 59-62; marketing in 95-116: nature 95-6; need for 96-9; evidence of, in PTEs 99-104; organisational acceptance of: executives and status of 104-8; factors inimical to 109-15; marketing — transport planning relationship 109-11; marketing—operations relationships 111-12; nature of process 112-15; reasons why marketing personnel should be given a strong organisational role 115-16; planning of 67-91: planning and marketing, interrelationships of 67-8; corporate planning, need for 68-70; constraints on strategy formulation 70-9; strategic 70-2;

product—market scope 70-1; managerial discretion 71; objectives 72; constraints and nationalised industries 72-9; public service and profit 72-3; constraints and PTEs 75-9; purpose of PTEs 75; external relation of PTEs 75-9; planning undertaken by PTEs 79-84; objectives 80-1; long-term 81-4; project planning 84-5; operational planning 85; strategies for management of *see* Management, strategies of, for urban passenger transport; *see also* Cars; Public transport; Transport planning
Urban—rural balance, preserving the 30-2

Van Tassel, R. C. 160, 234
Vehicles, classes of, in use 37; *see also* Cars
Vending machines 184
Vibration, annoyance of 175

Walton and Datton 124
Wasey, Erwin 100, 175
Way, Sir Richard 39-40
Wholesaling processes, changes in 14-15
Williams, P. M. 50
Wilson, F. R. 54-6, 151
Woodward, J. 15
Work, journey-to- 231-5
Wright, M. 24

Yates, L. B. 161

The Authors

Peter Hovell, a graduate of Cambridge University, was a manager in the telecommunications industry before taking up research and lecturing posts at the Universities of Salford and Liverpool. He has been consultant to the Transport and Road Research Laboratory, Department of the Environment and what is now the Greater Manchester Passenger Transport Executive, and is currently Assistant Director of Business Studies, Liverpool University.

William Jones, a graduate of Newcastle University, has held research and lecturing posts with Salford, Liverpool and Aston Universities. He has been consultant to the Transport and Road Research Laboratory, Department of the Environment and what is now the Greater Manchester Passenger Transport Executive, and is currently lecturer in marketing, Aston University.

Alan Moran graduated from London University and holds a doctorate from Liverpool University where he was also on the research staff. Before taking up his present post as Senior Economic Analyst with the Australian Government he held executive positions in the UK commercial vehicle industry, including one with the truck and bus division of British Leyland.